Signs in situations

Photographs for a smile

Copyright © 2010 Bob Bovin,
Publisher: Bovin Design Hb, Kåkbrinken 3, Stockholm, Sweden
Print and distribution: CreateSpace, an Amazon.com company

ISBN 978-91-978005-3-2

No part of this book may be reproduced in any form without
written permission from the publisher.
None of the pictures in this book have been digitally
manipulated to change its content.

Homepage: www.bovin.nu/bob
E-mail: bob@bovin.nu

Signs in situations

Photographs for a smile

Bob Bovin

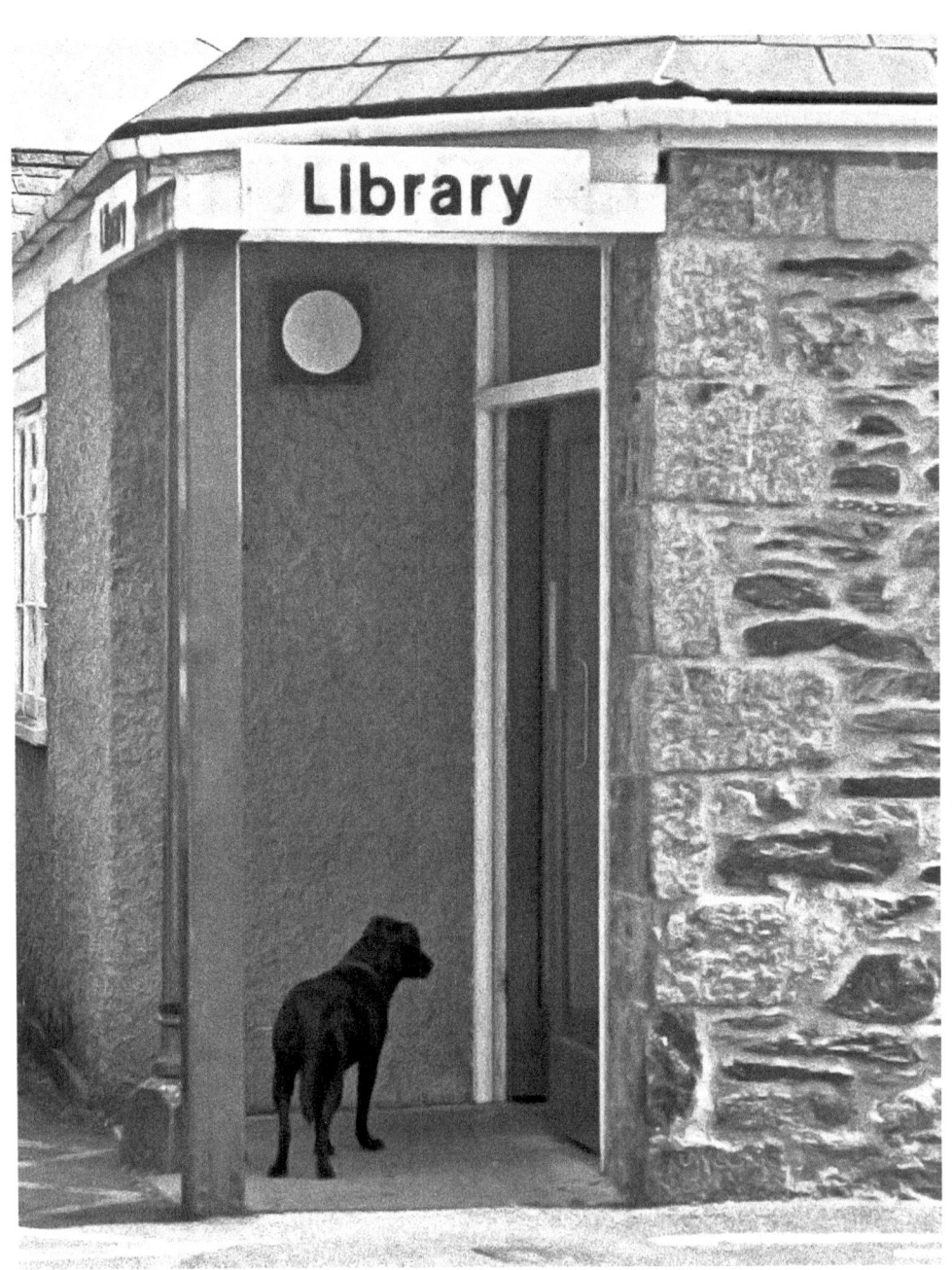

I was 16 years old when I became freelance press photographer.

Funny situations of modern ways of living are my favorite theme.

I want my pictures to be two dimensional sources of inspiration to a multi dimensional world, where the viewer can get the smile of the day.

Bob Bovin

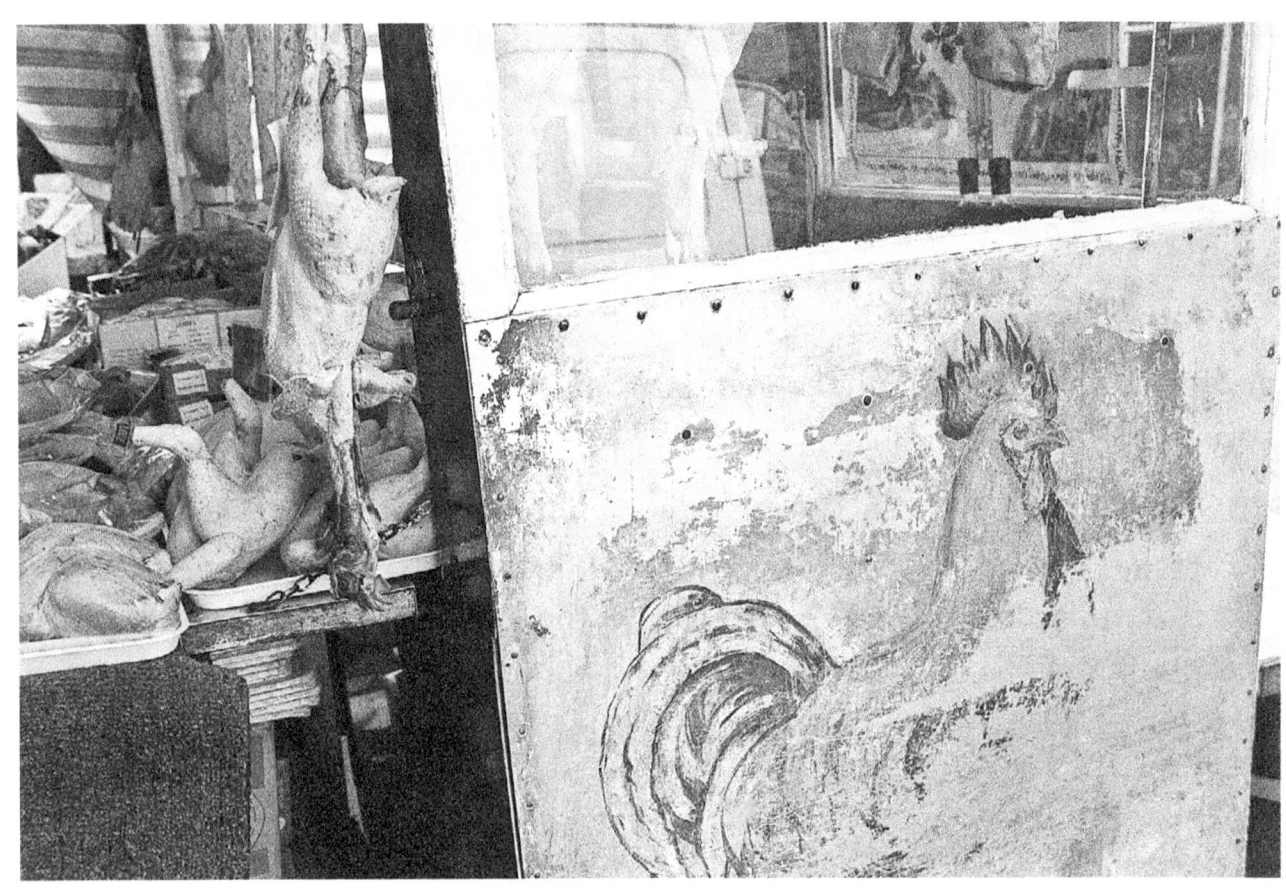

London, 2001

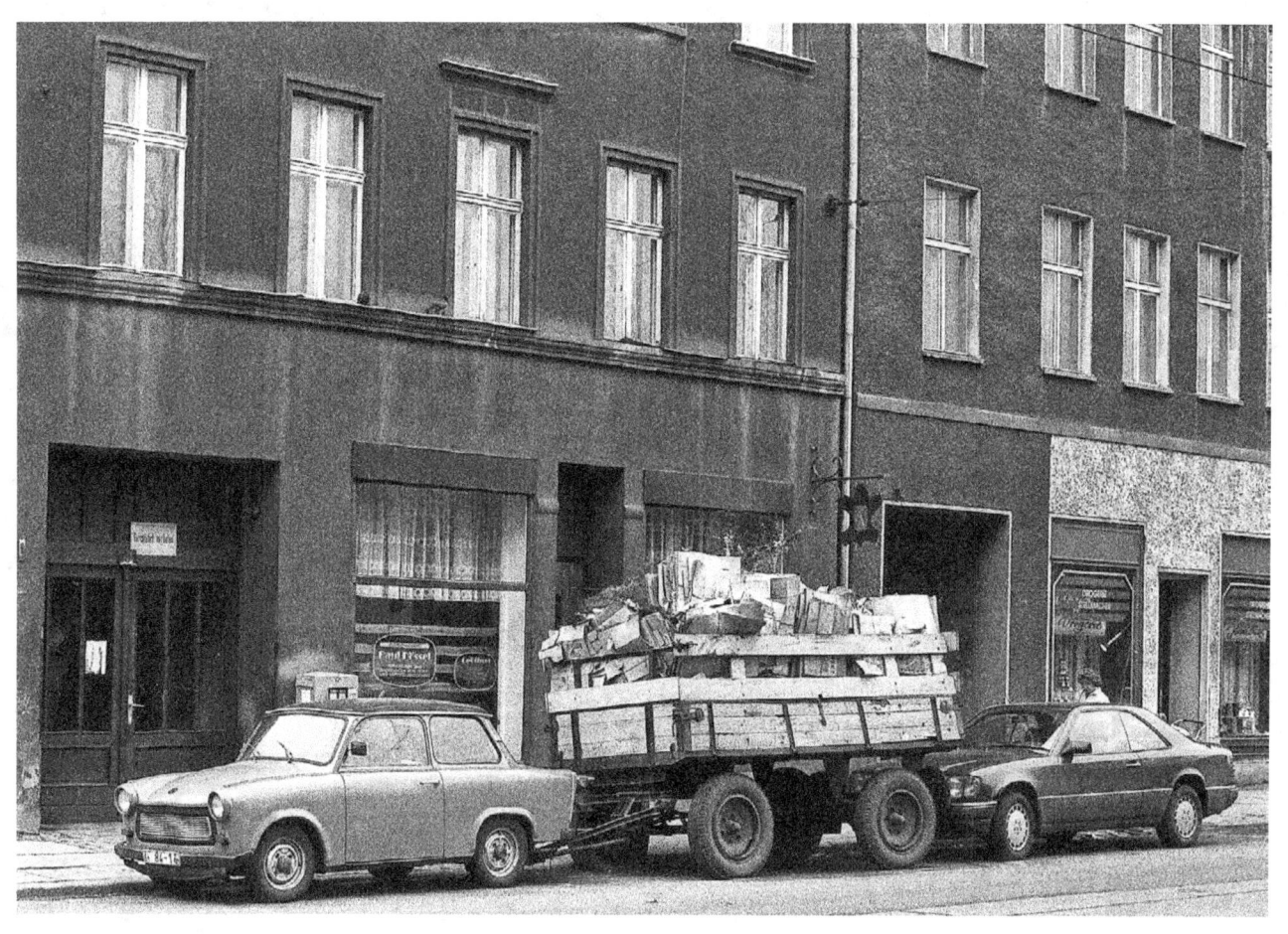

New York, 2007

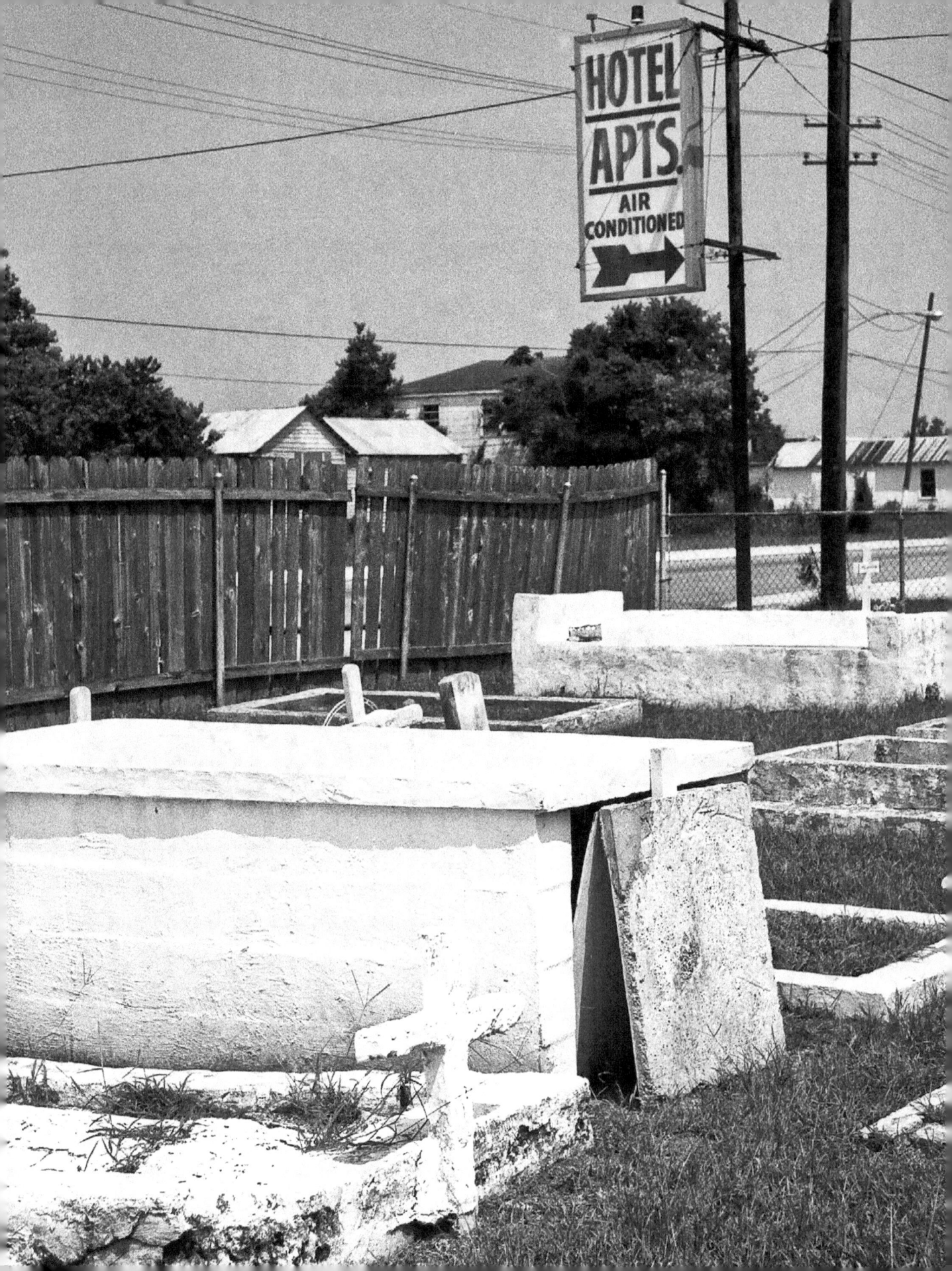

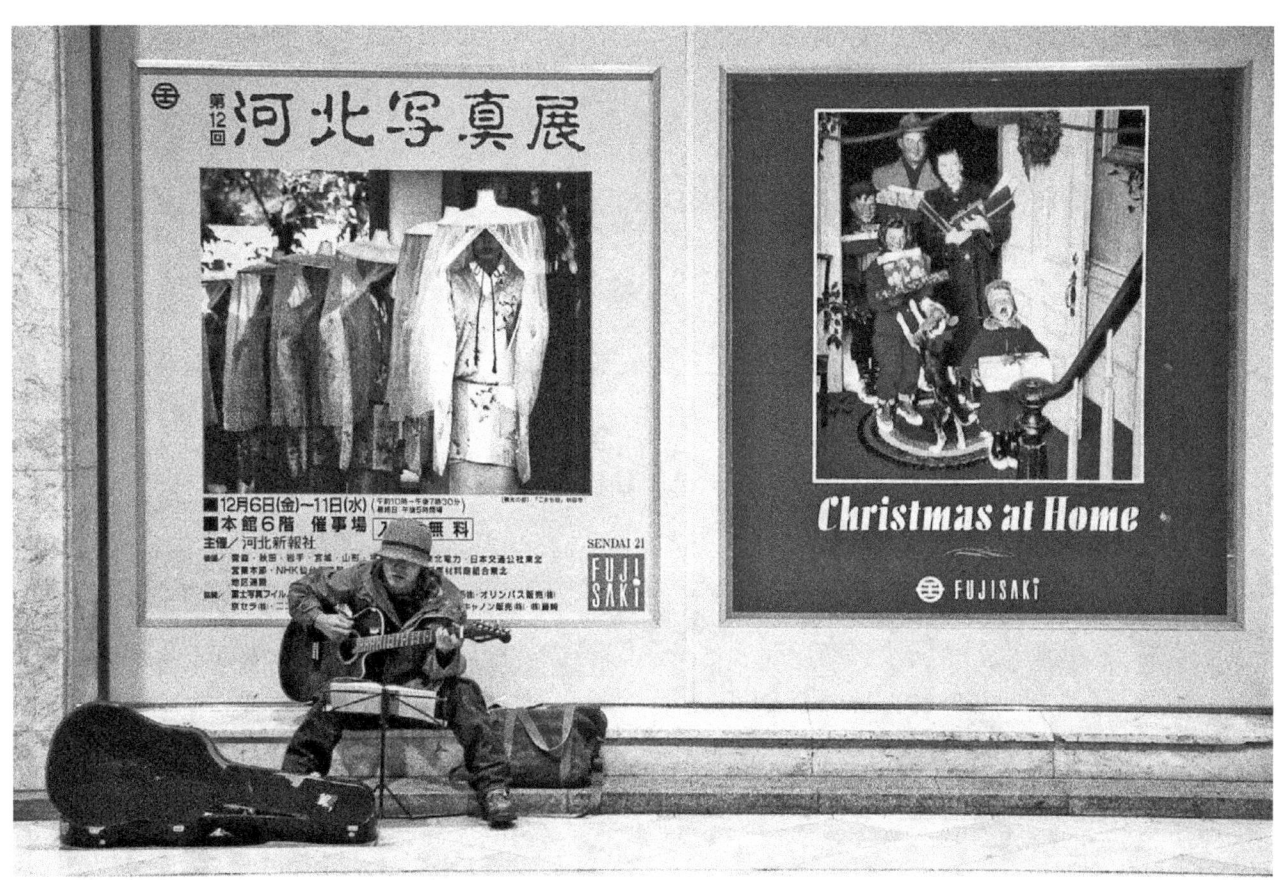

Sendai, Japan, 1996

New Orleans, 1994

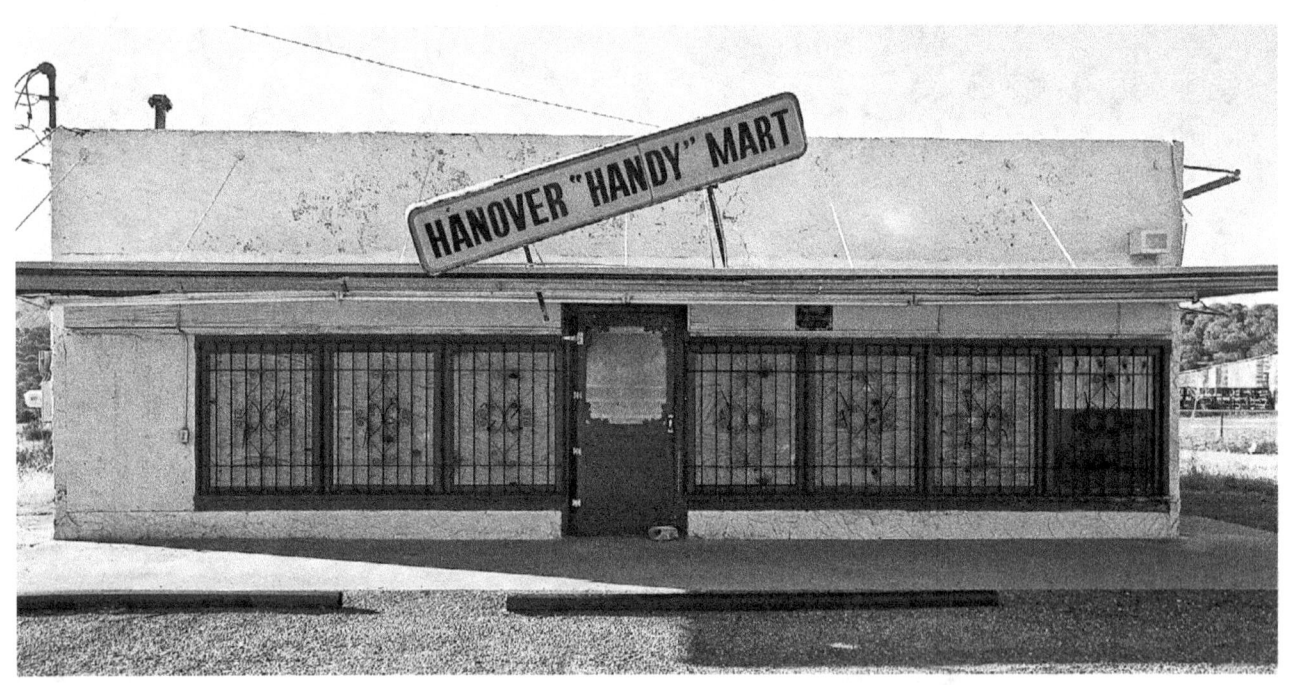

Hanover, New Mexico, 2003

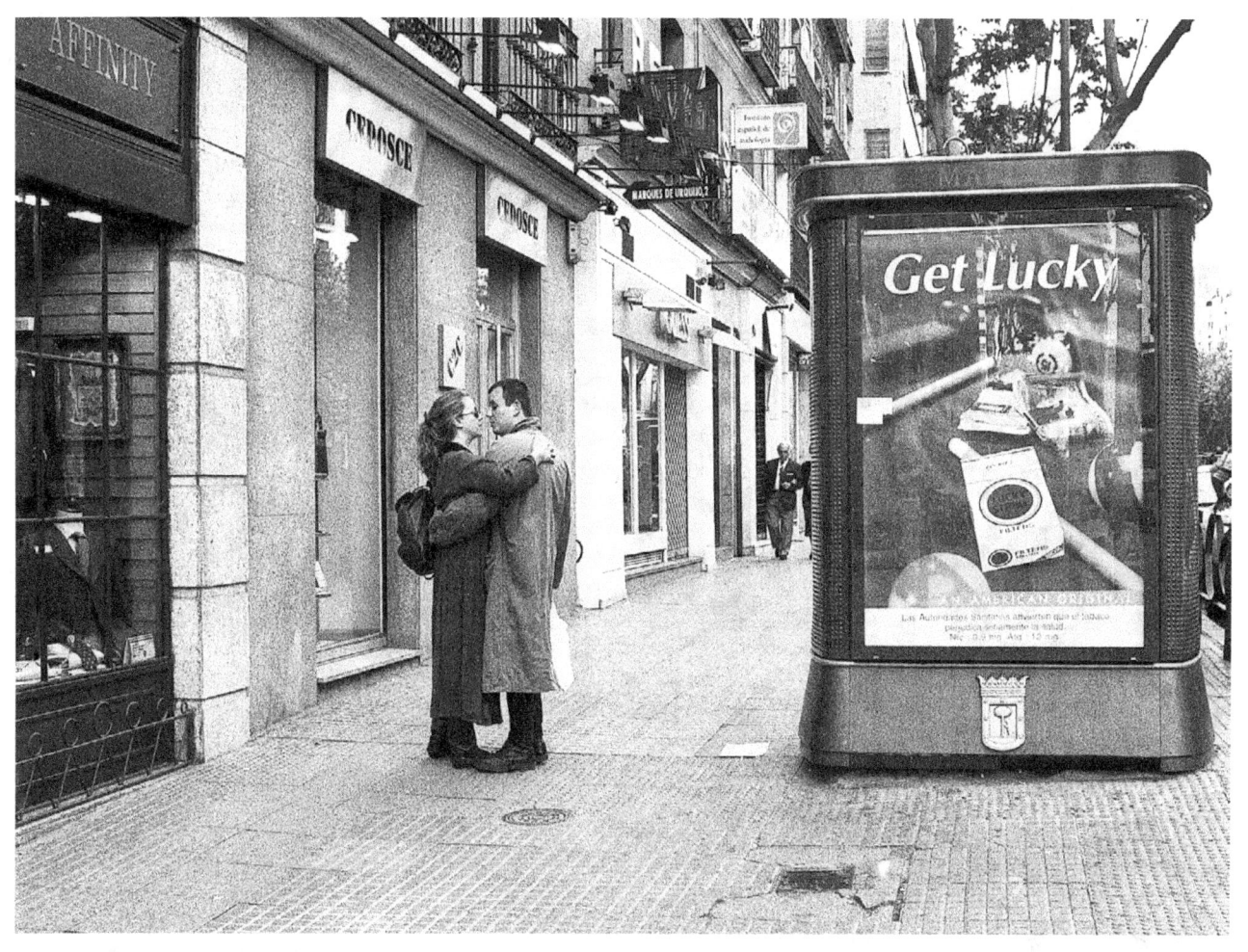

Madrid, Spain, 1999

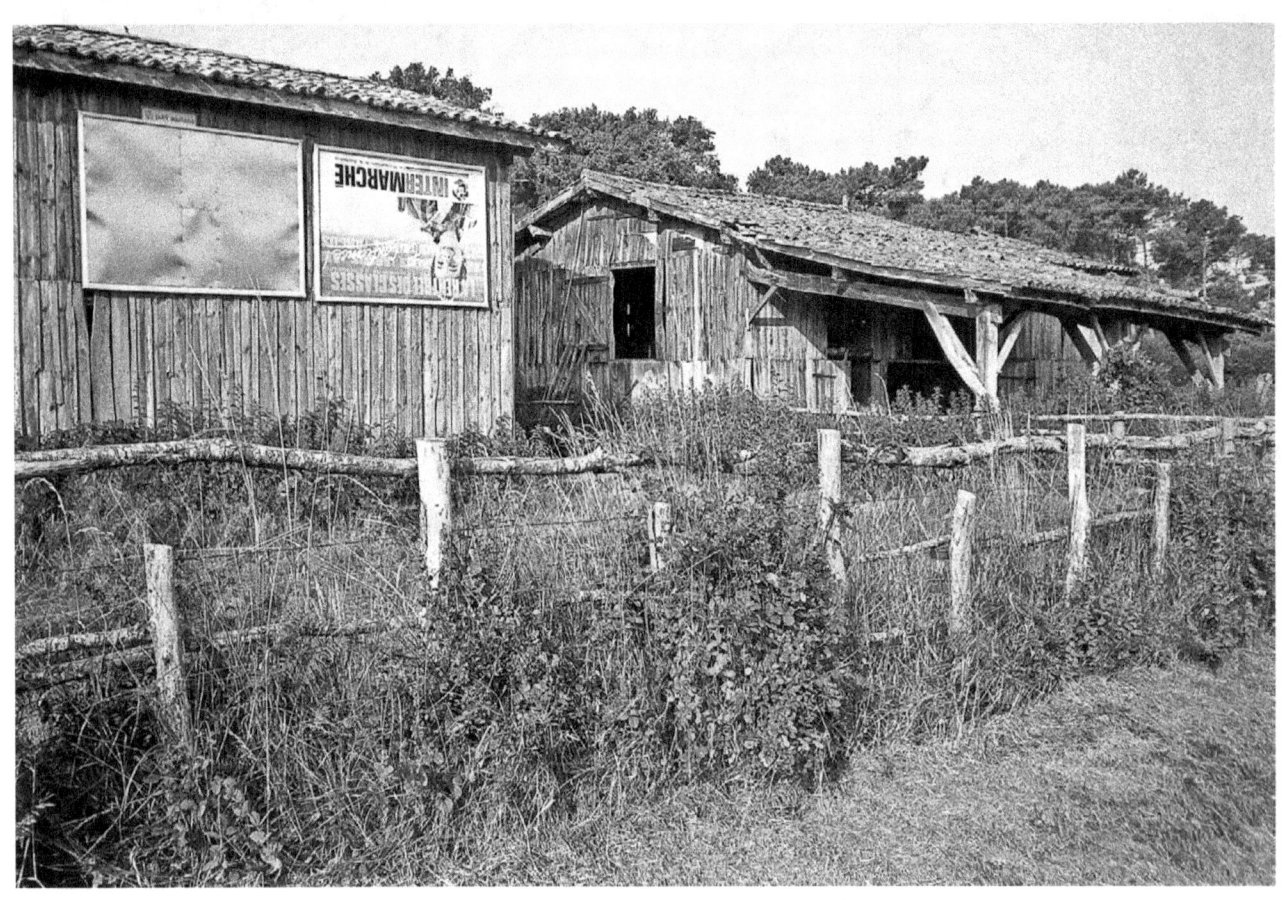

Salles, France, 1989

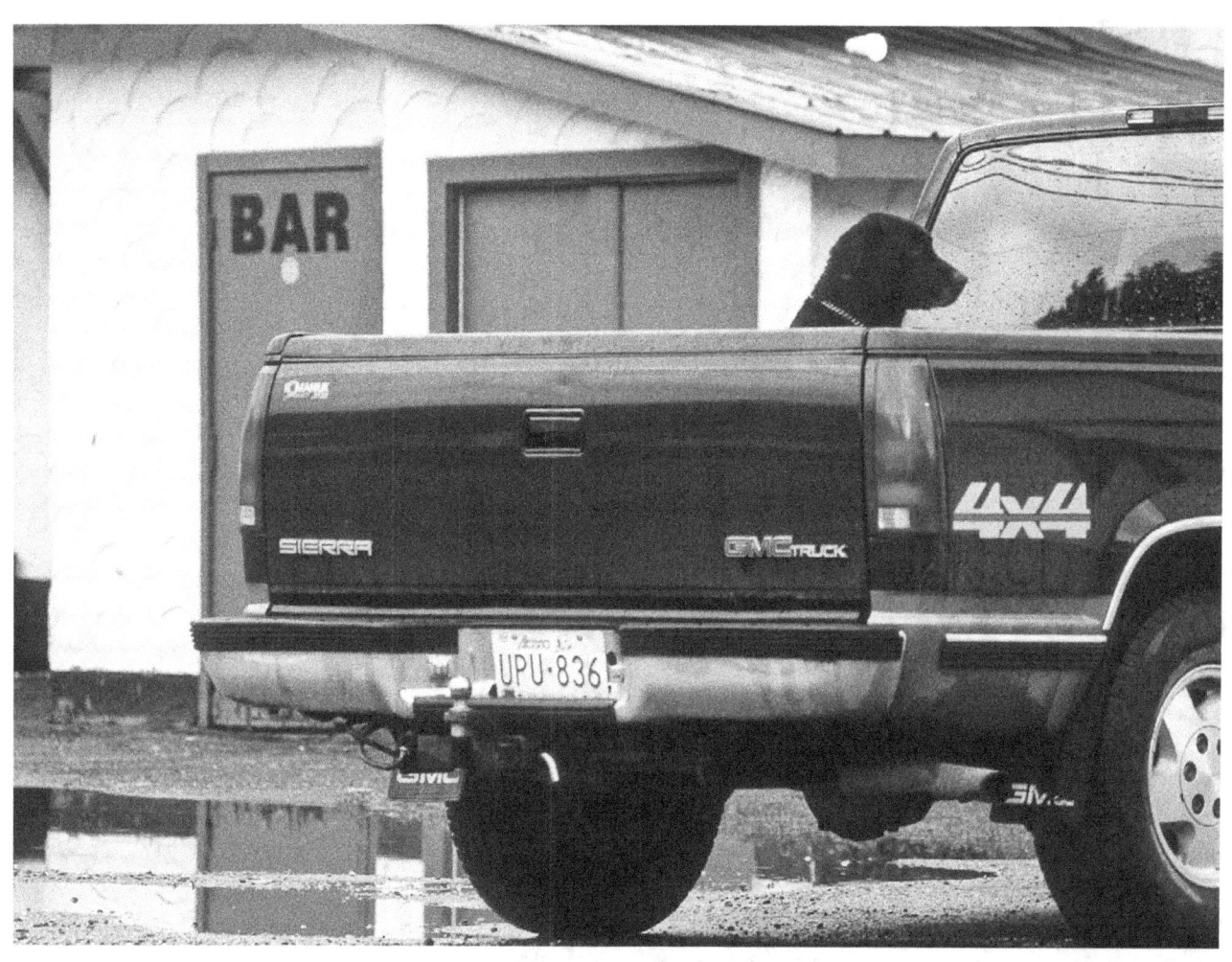

Valemount, Canada, 2001

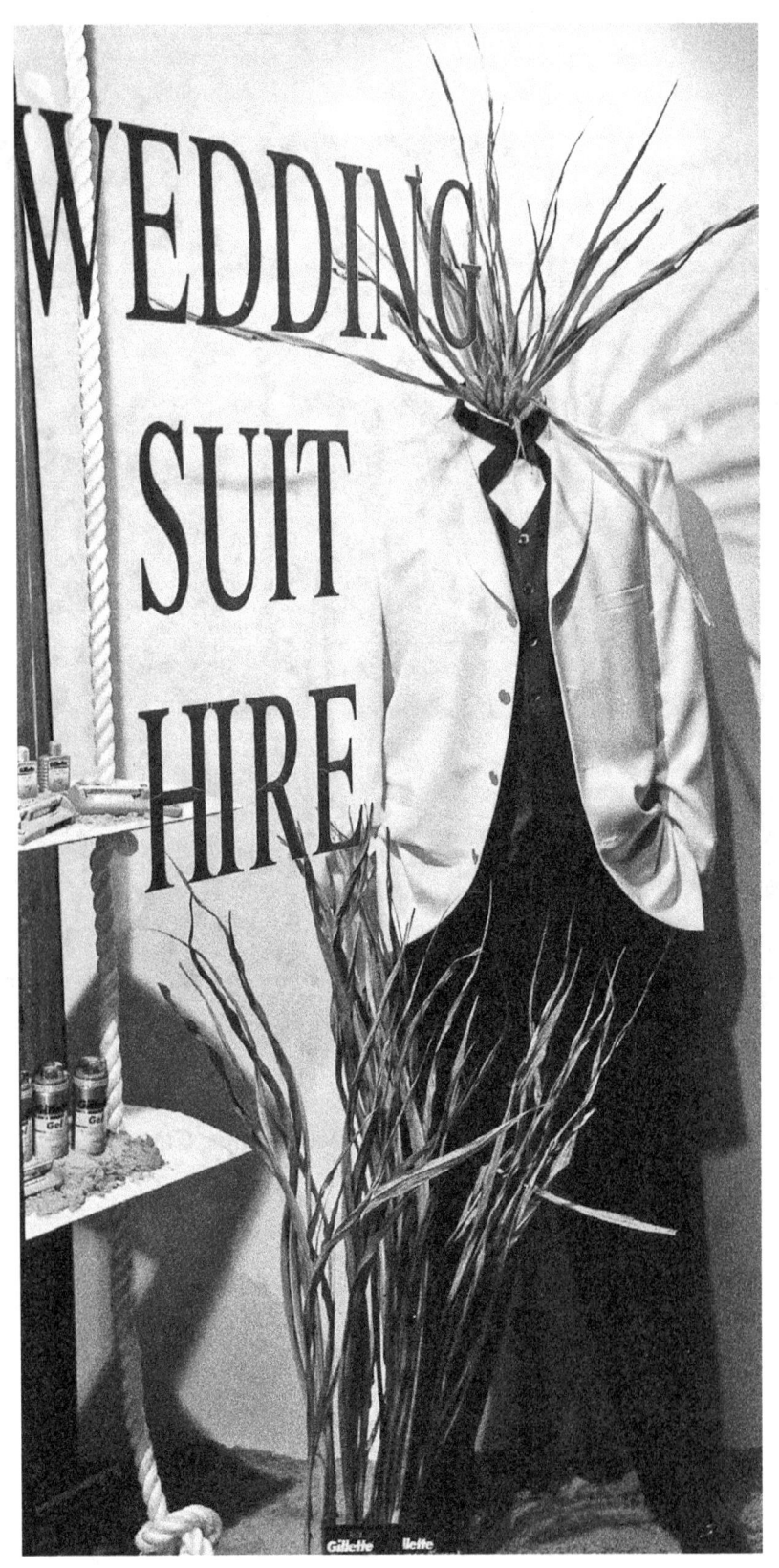

Dublin, Irland, 1996

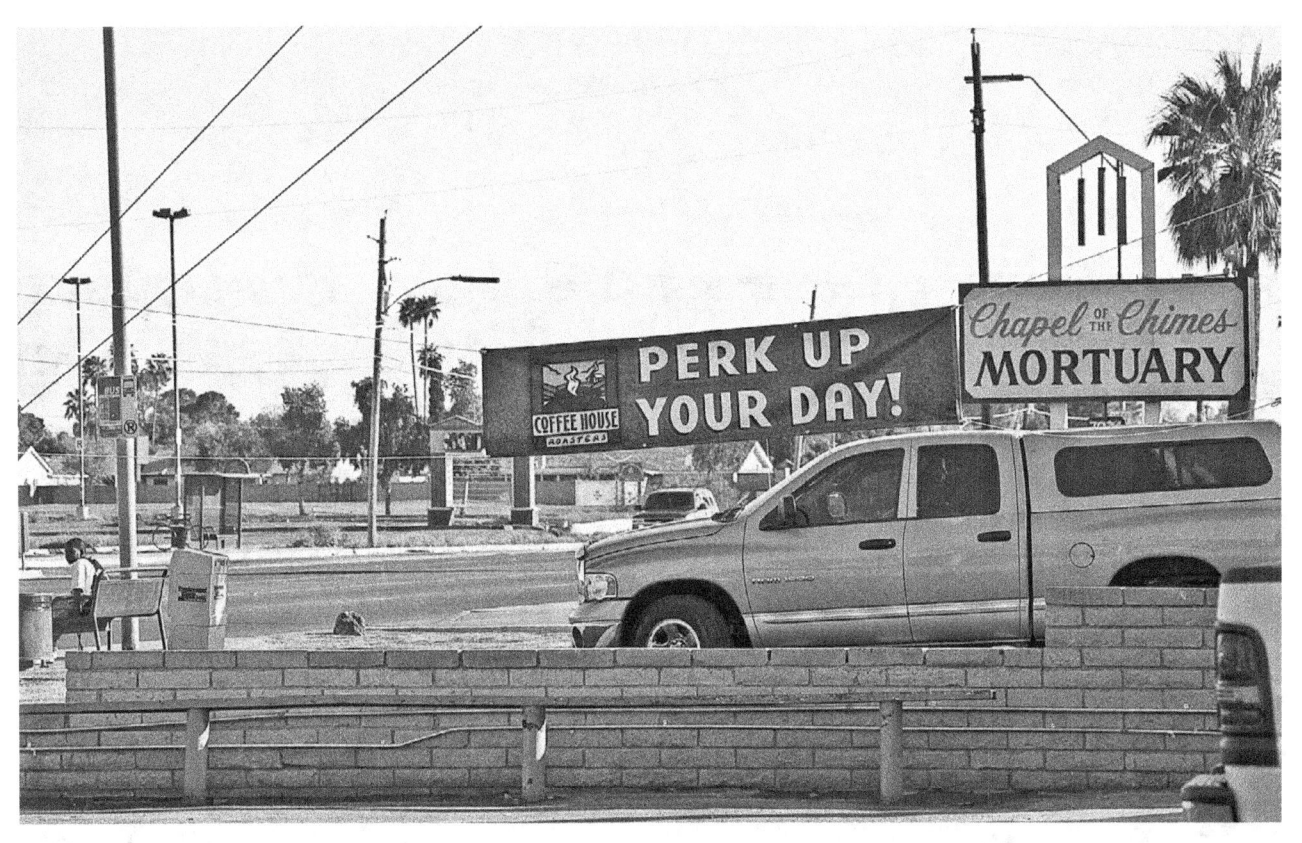

Phoenix, Arizona, 2003

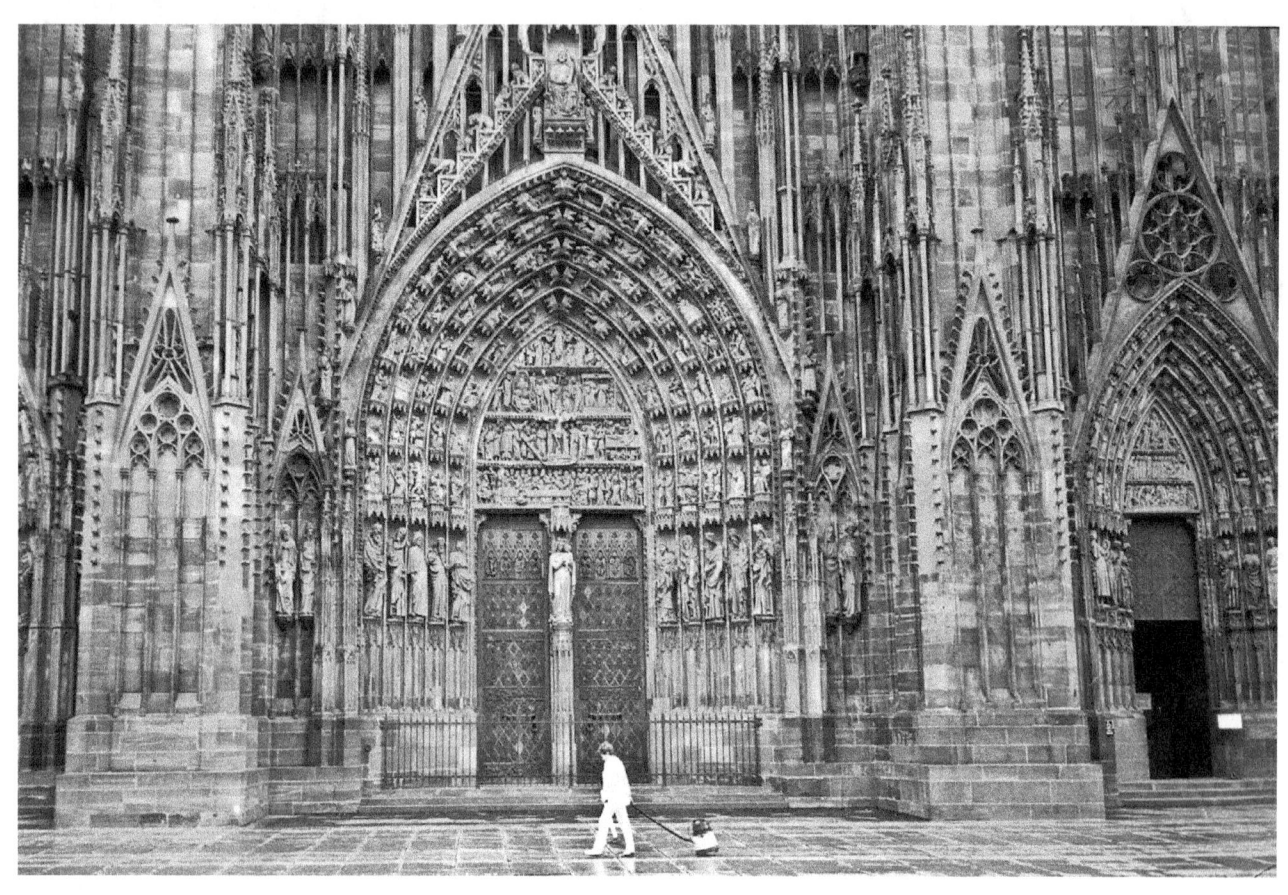

Strasbourg, France, 1991

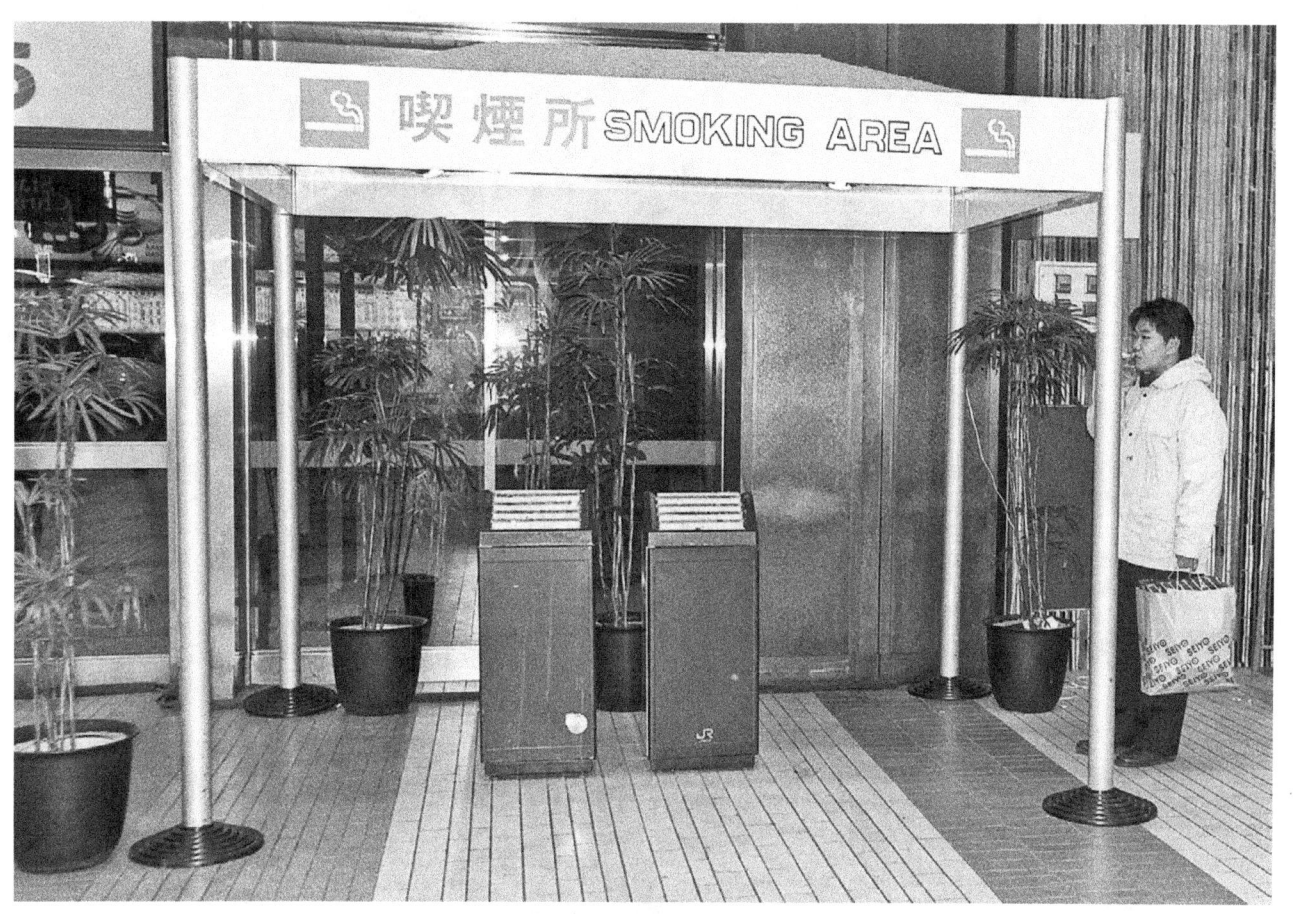

Sendai, Japan, 1996

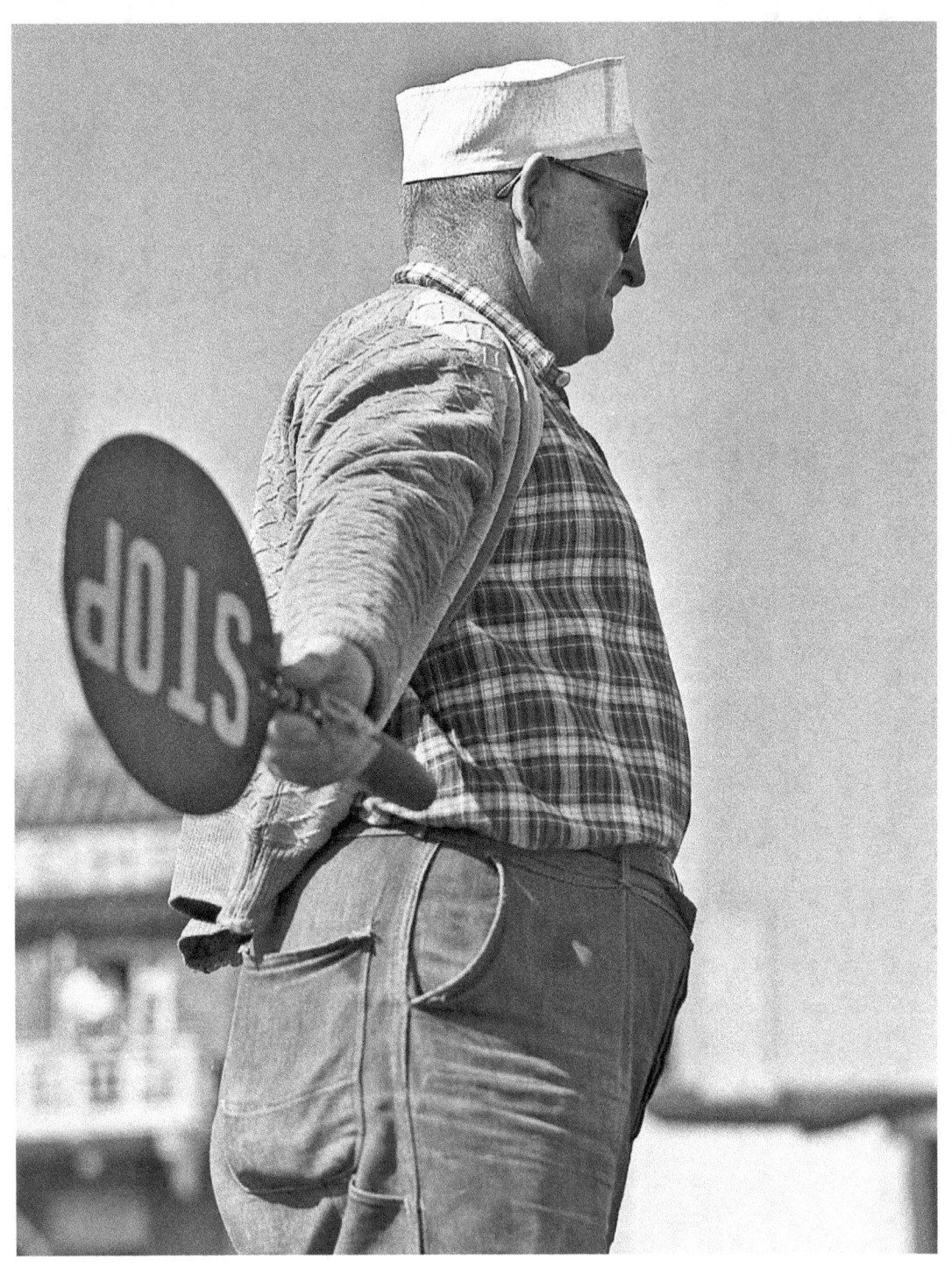

Allinge, Denmark, 1960

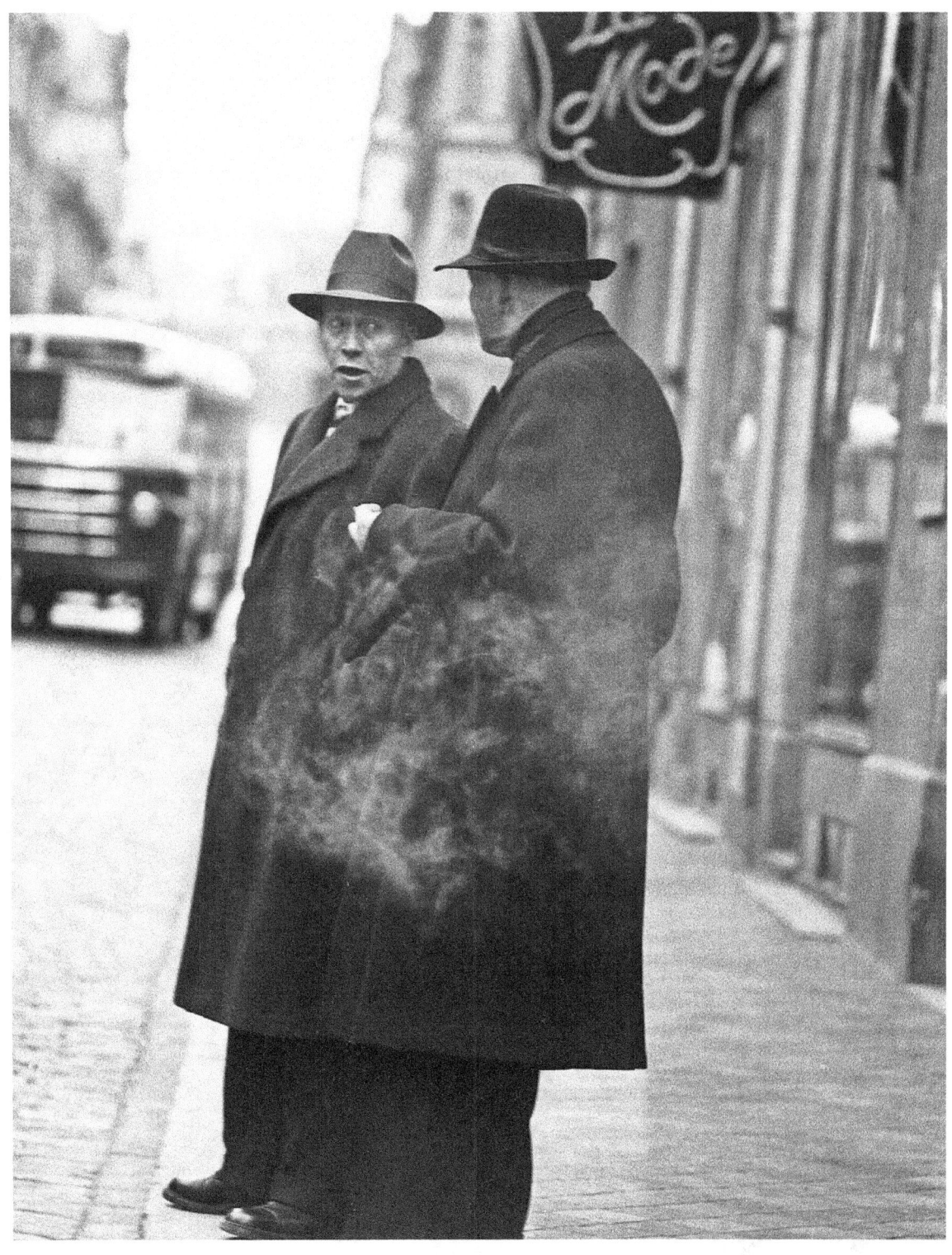

Linköping, Sweden, 1959

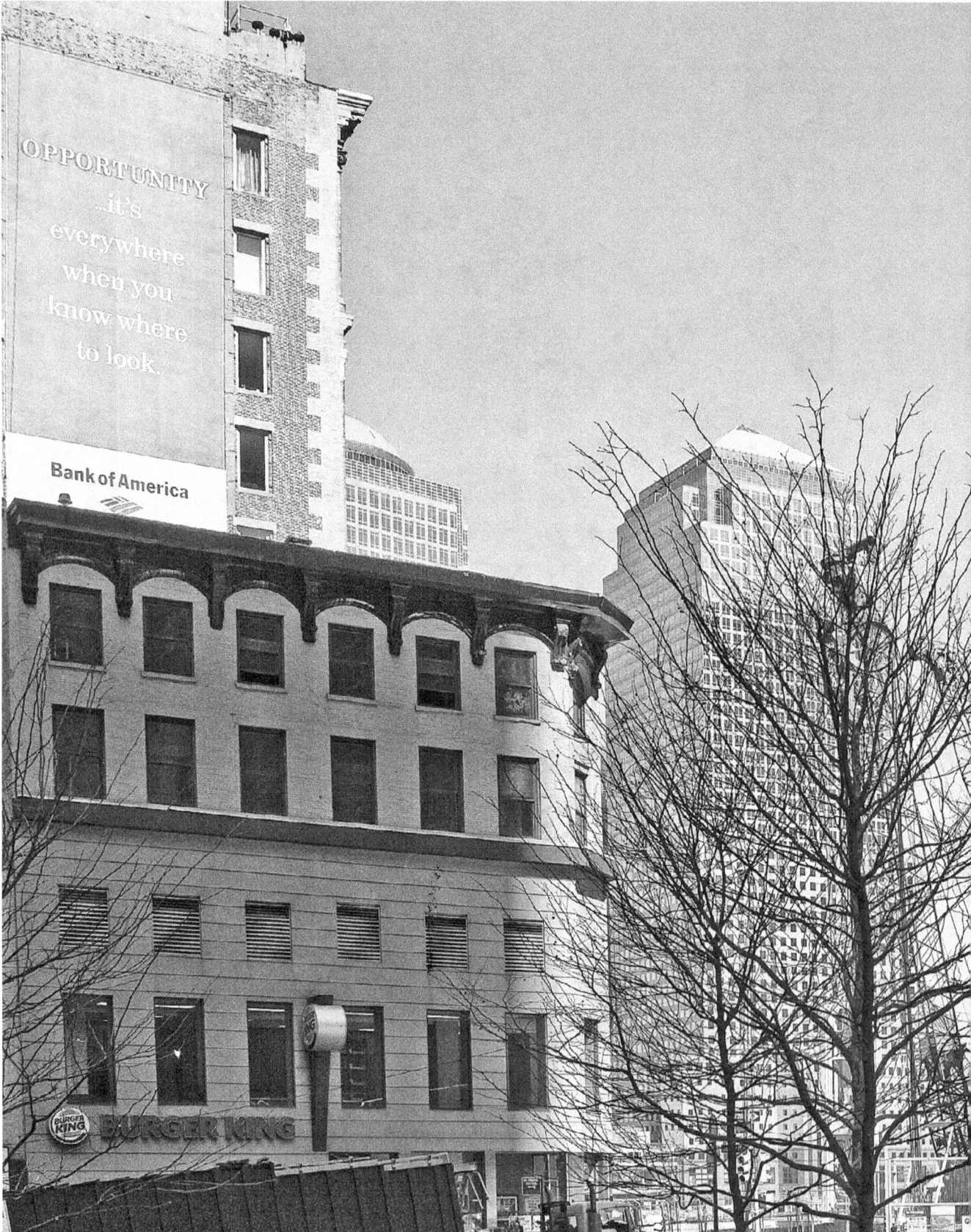

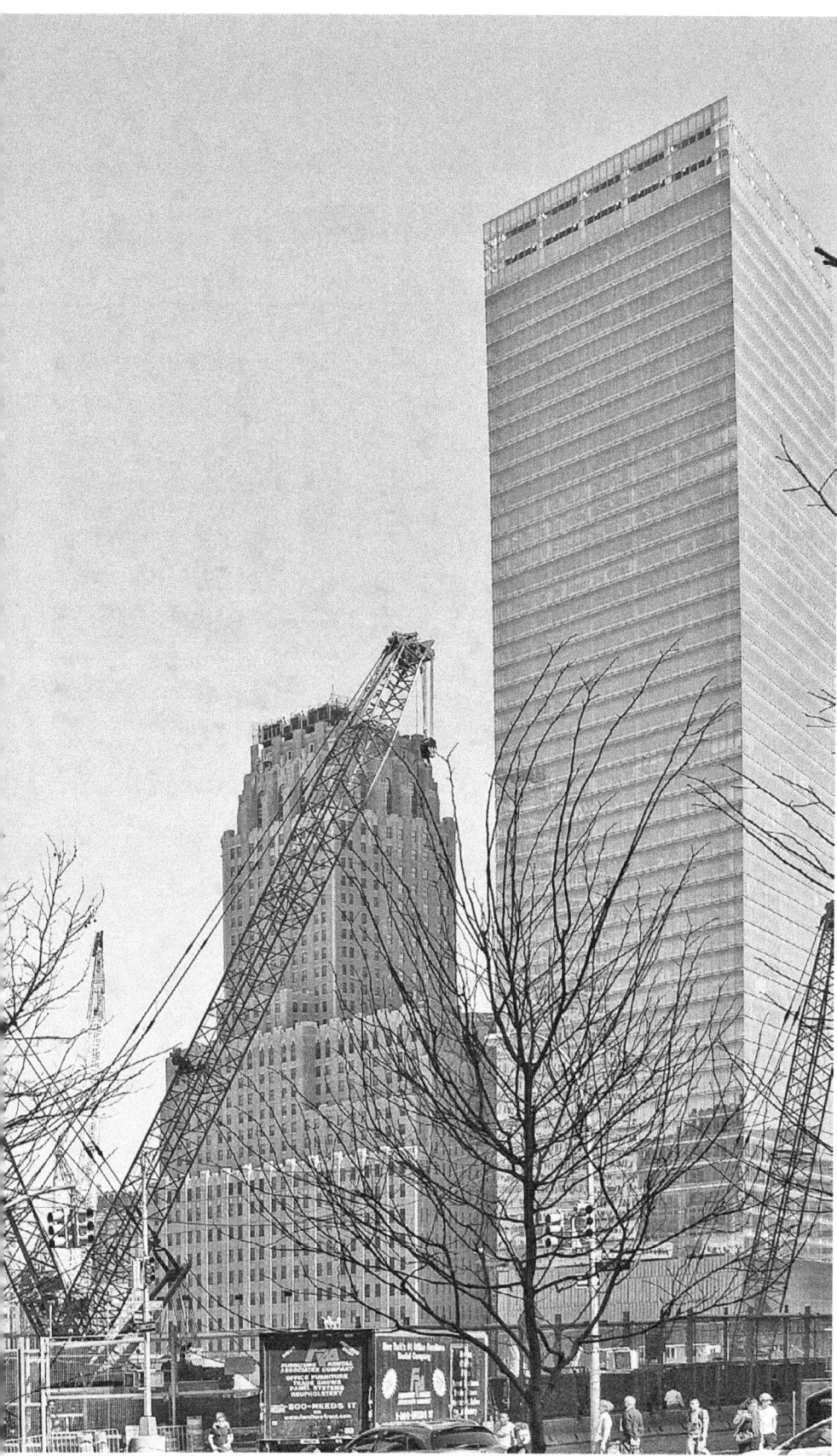

New York, 2007

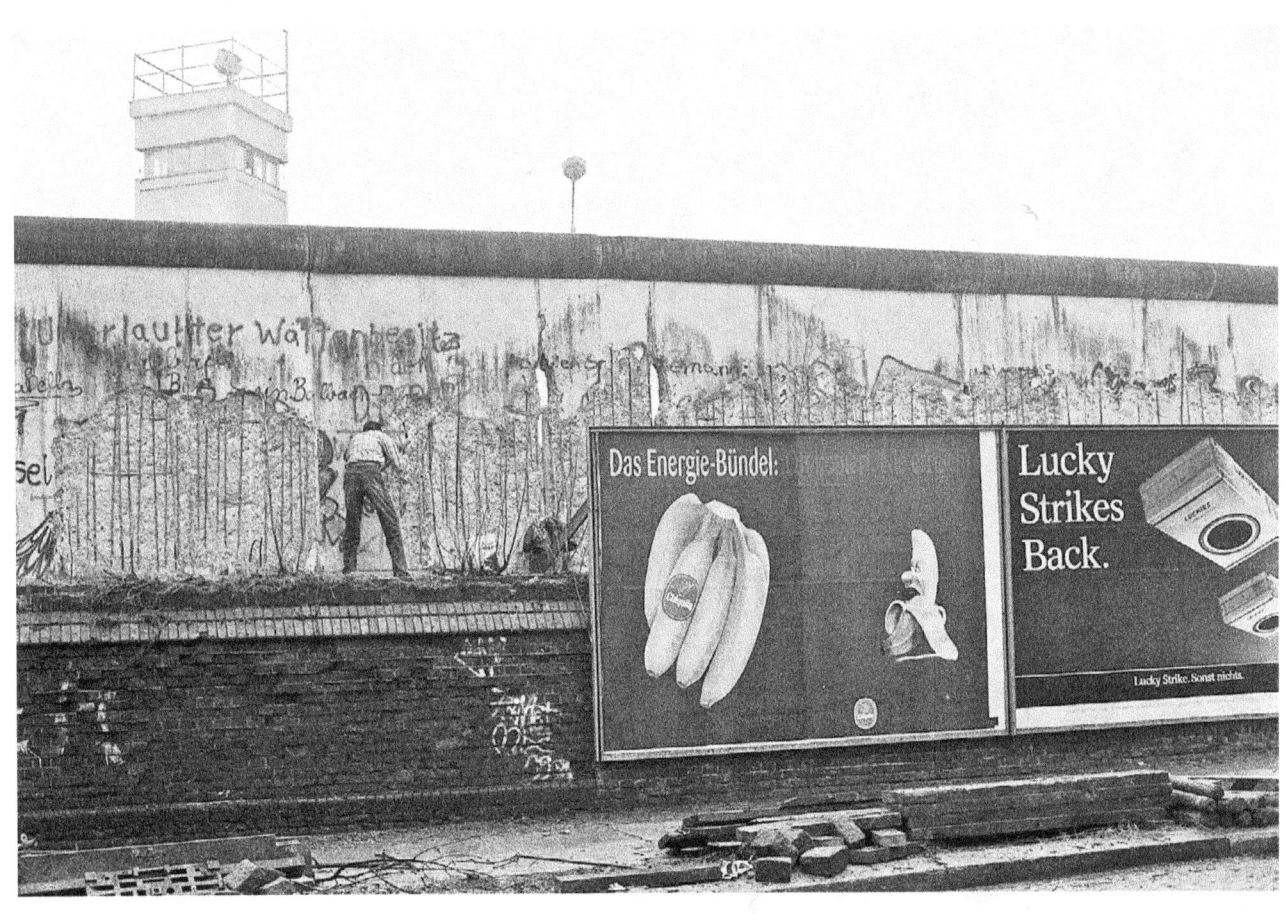

Berlin, 1990

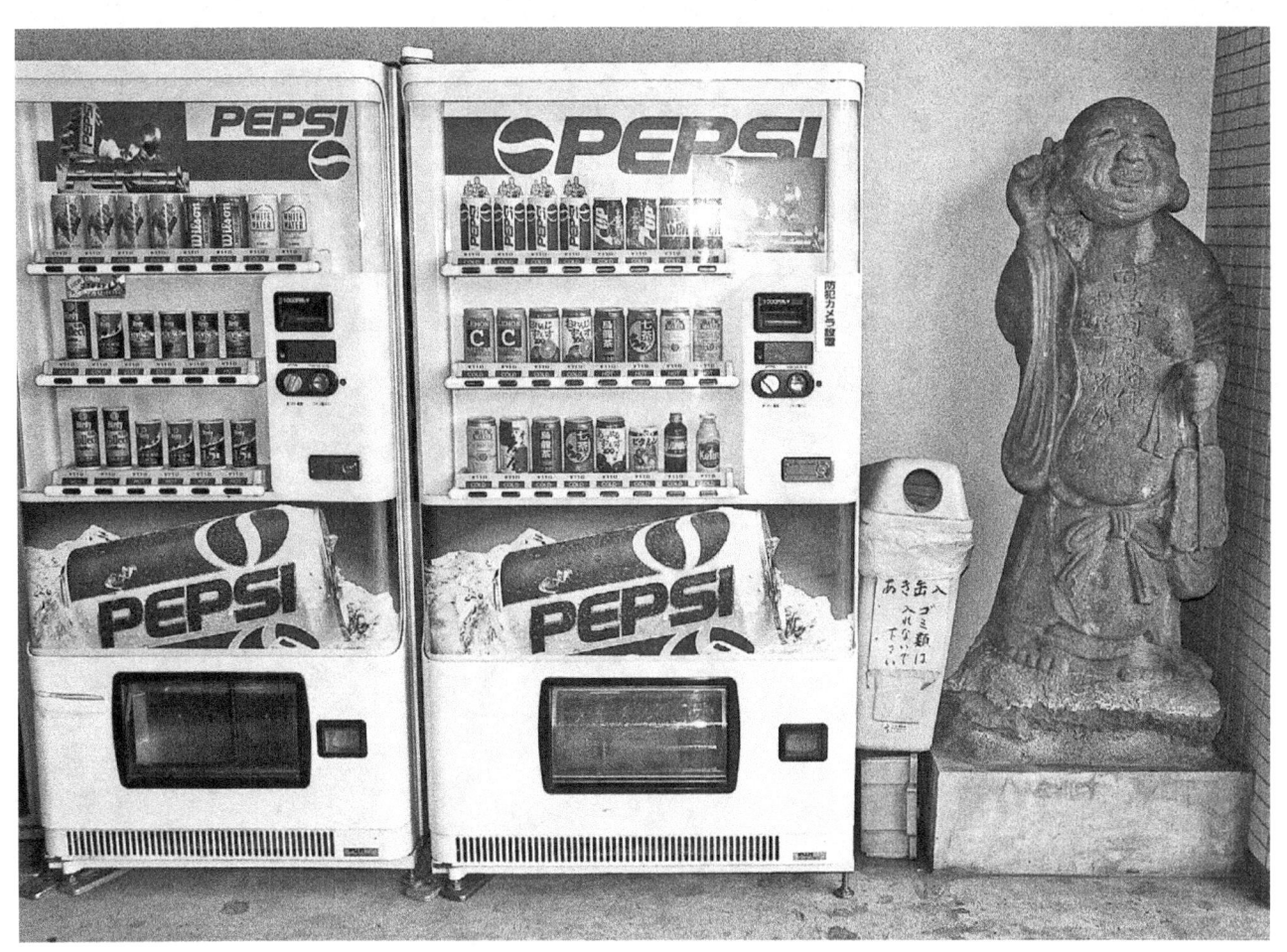

Sendai, Japan, 1996

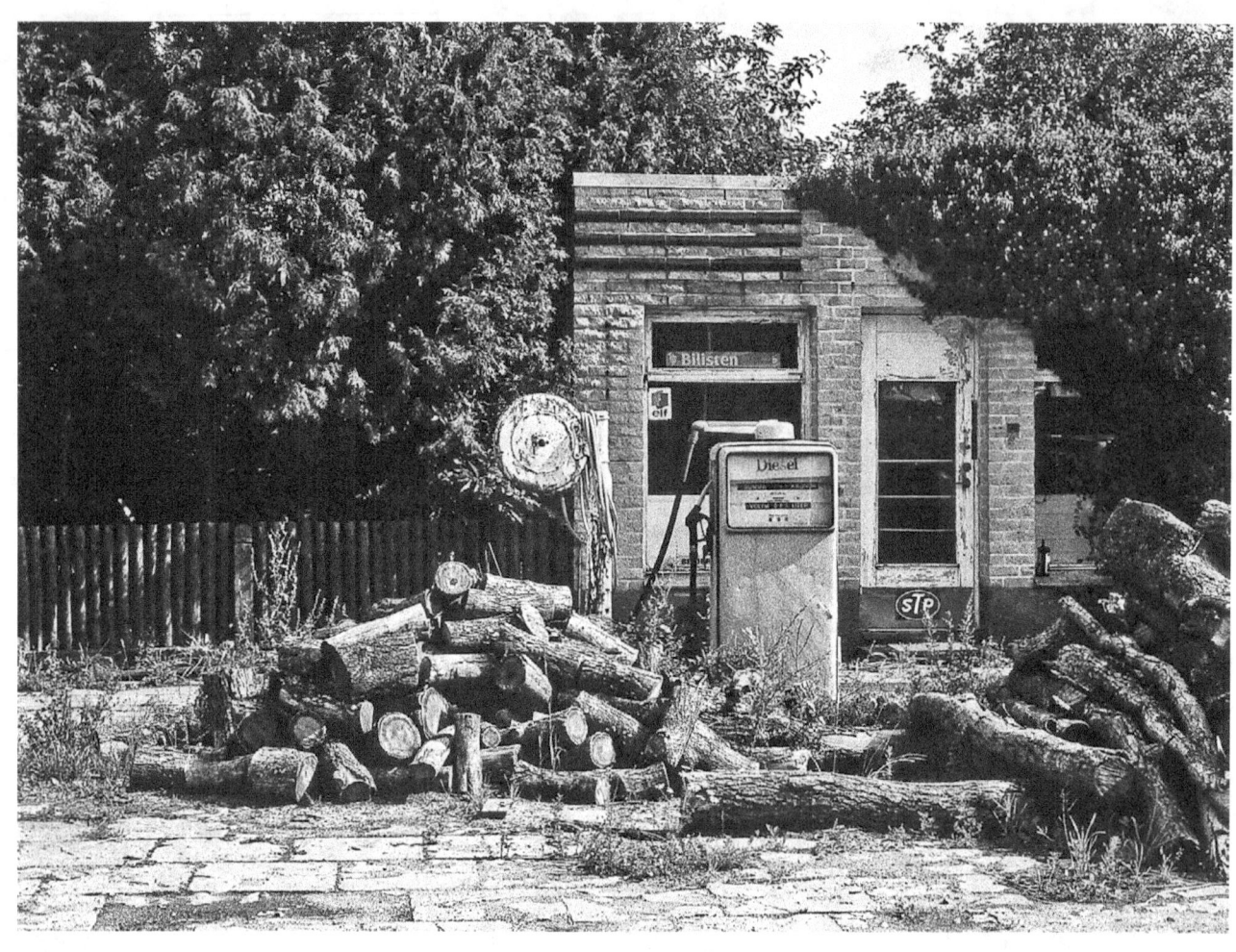

Norra Rörom, Sweden, 1995

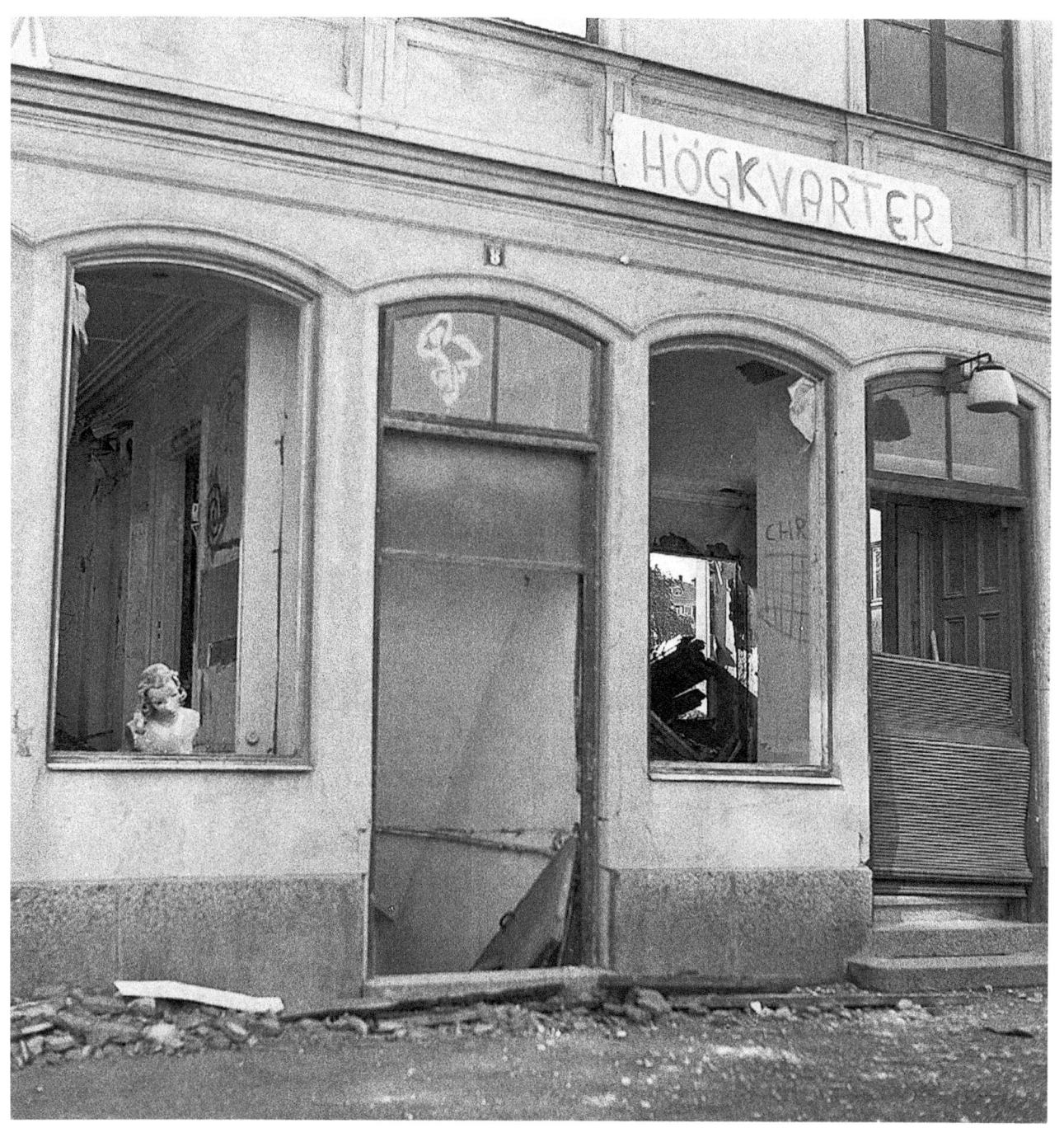

Linköping, Sweden, 1959

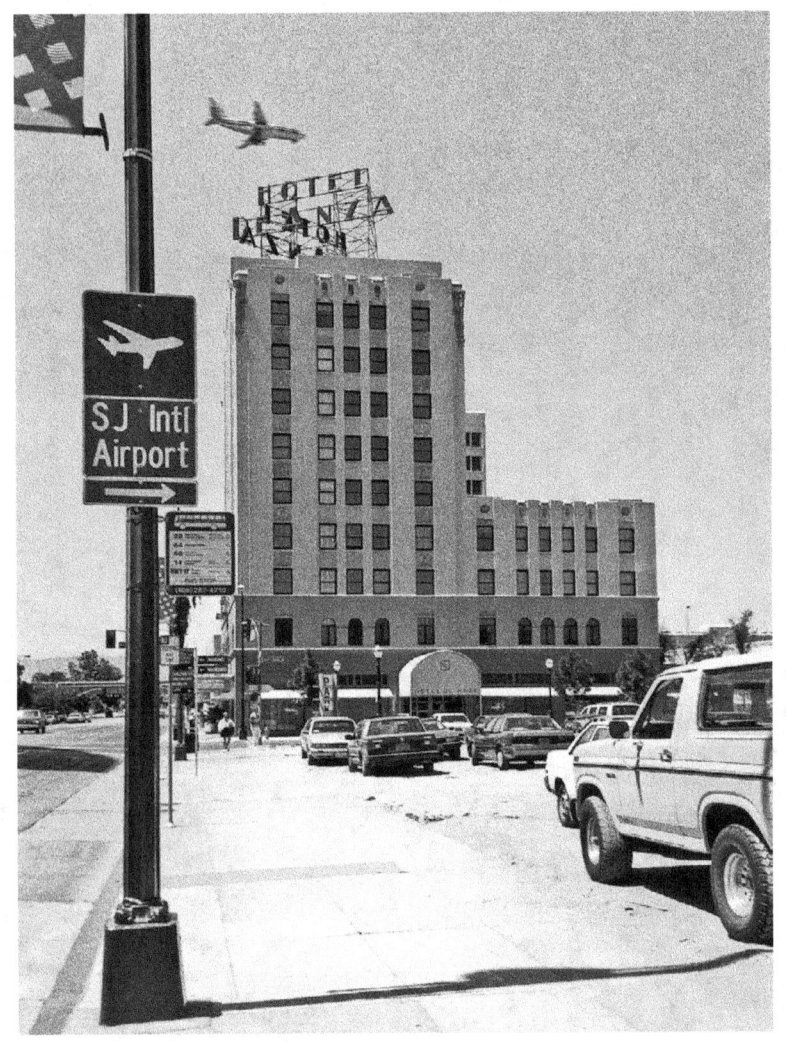

San Jose, California, 1990

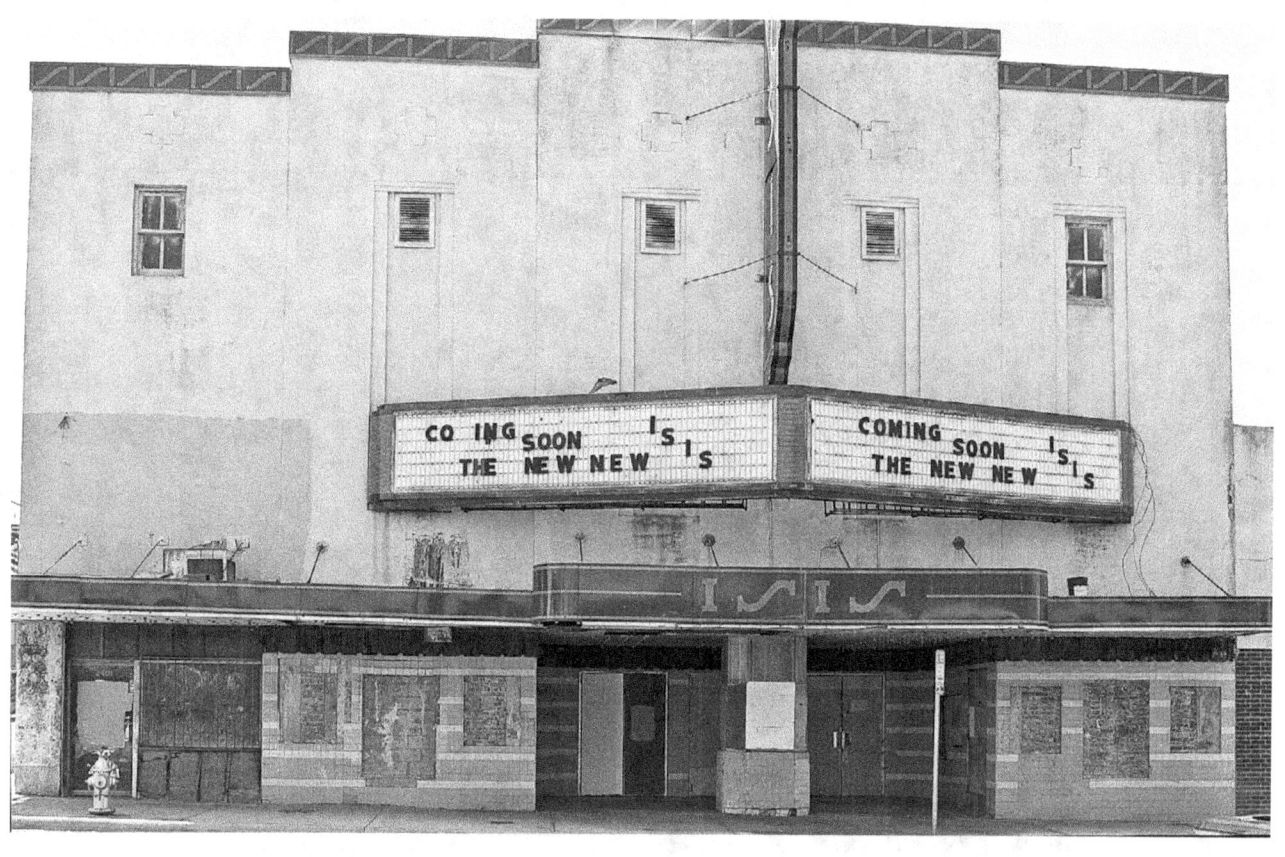

FortWorth, Texas, 2007

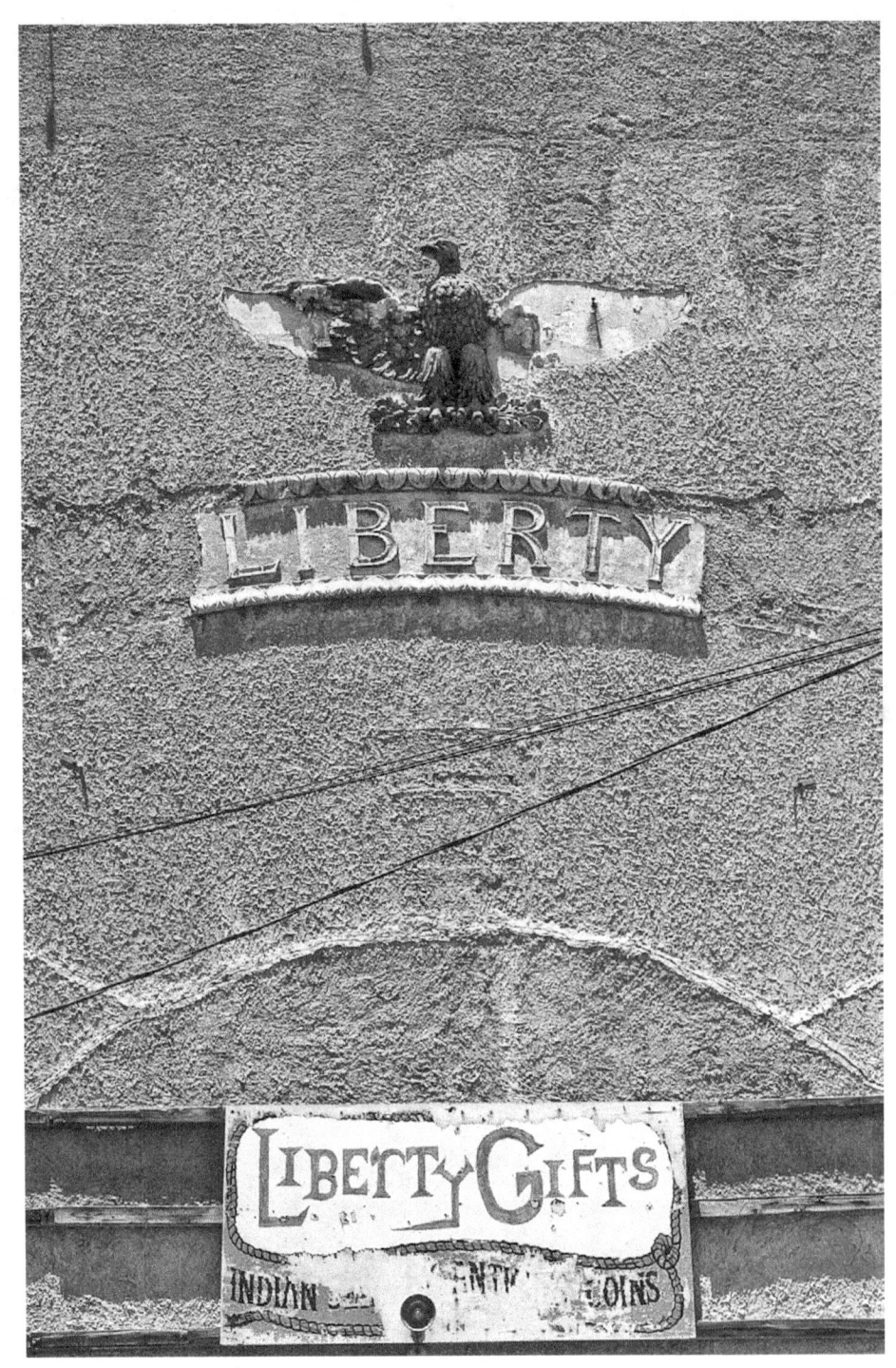

Jerome, Arizona, 1978

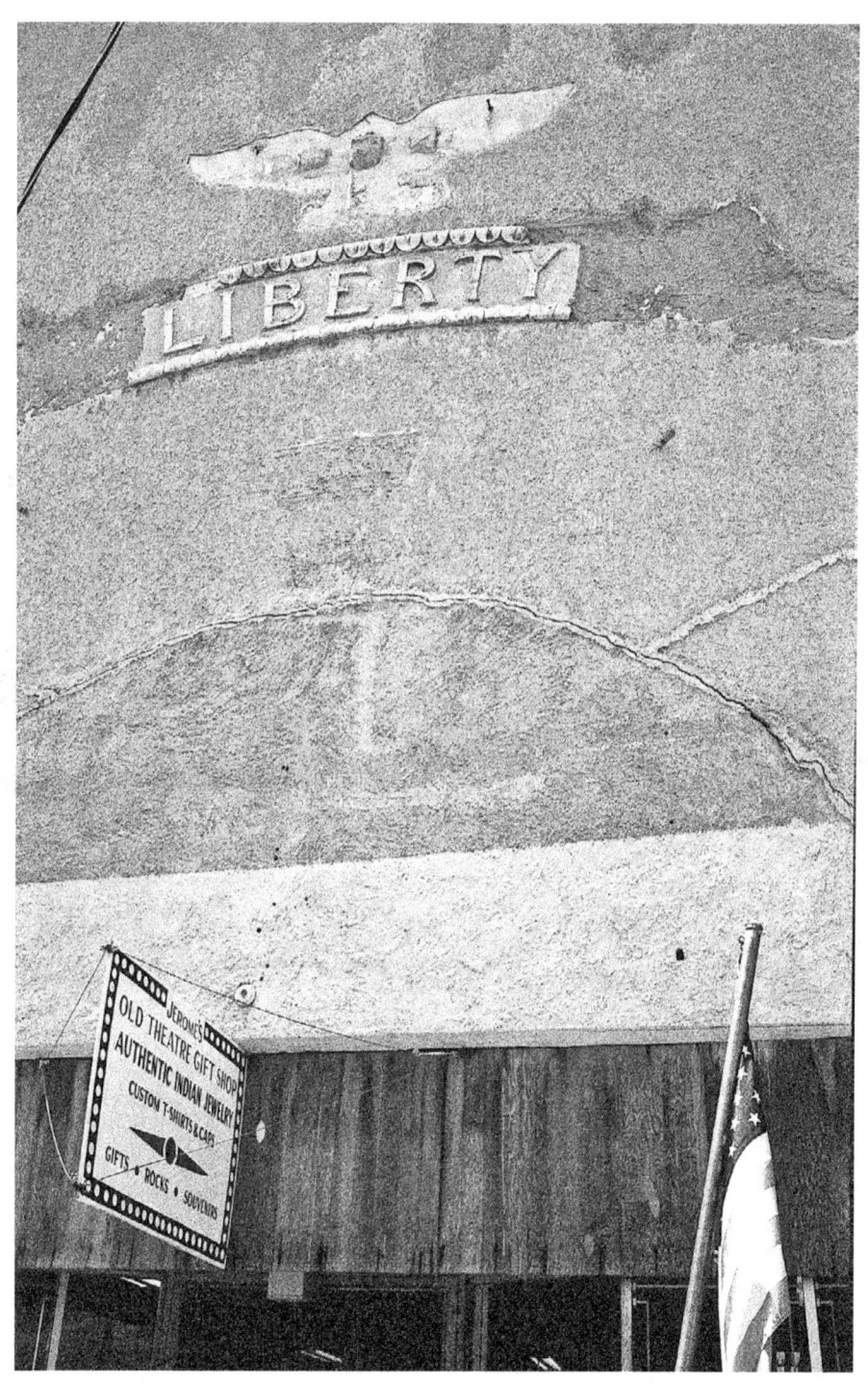

Jerome, Arizona, 1986

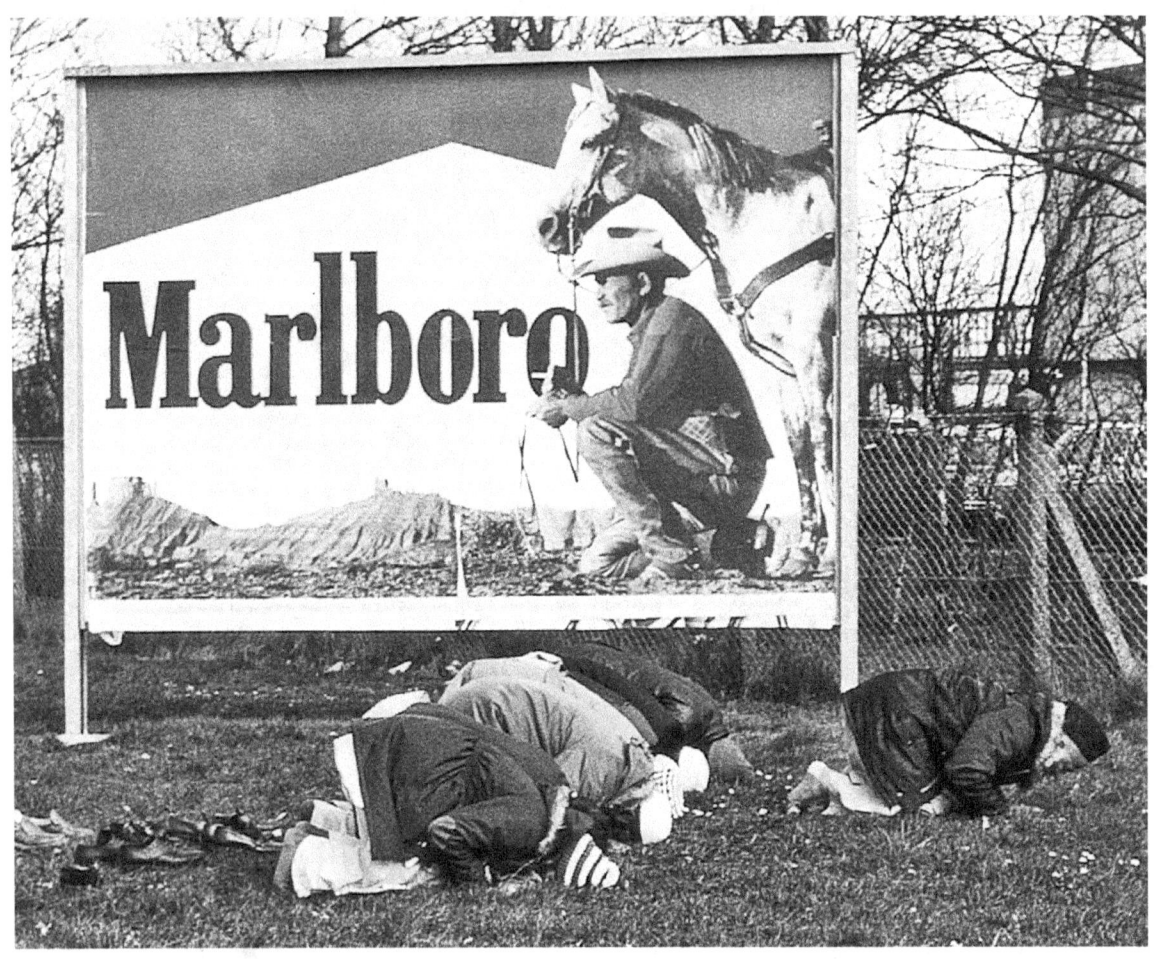

Puttgarten, Germany, 1982

Lidingö, Sweden, 1998

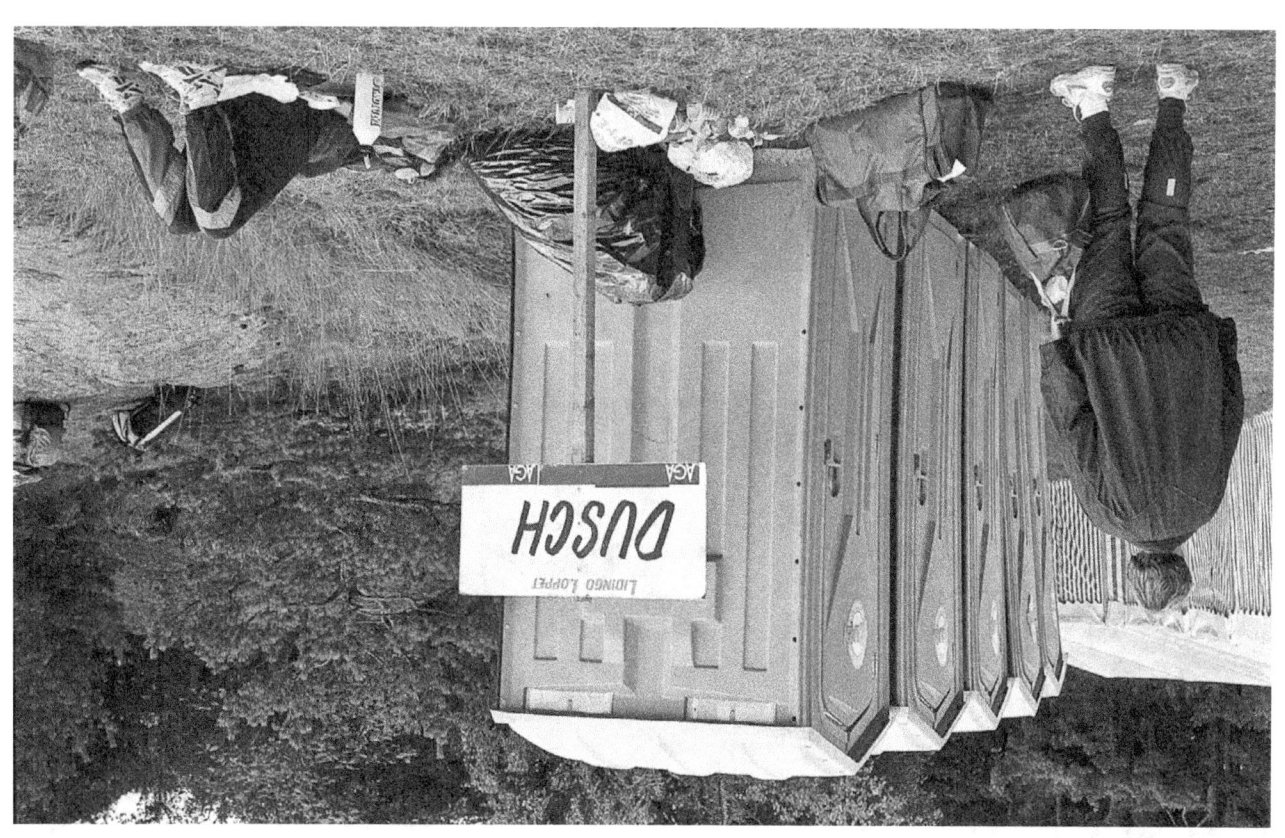

Maui, Hawaii, 1998

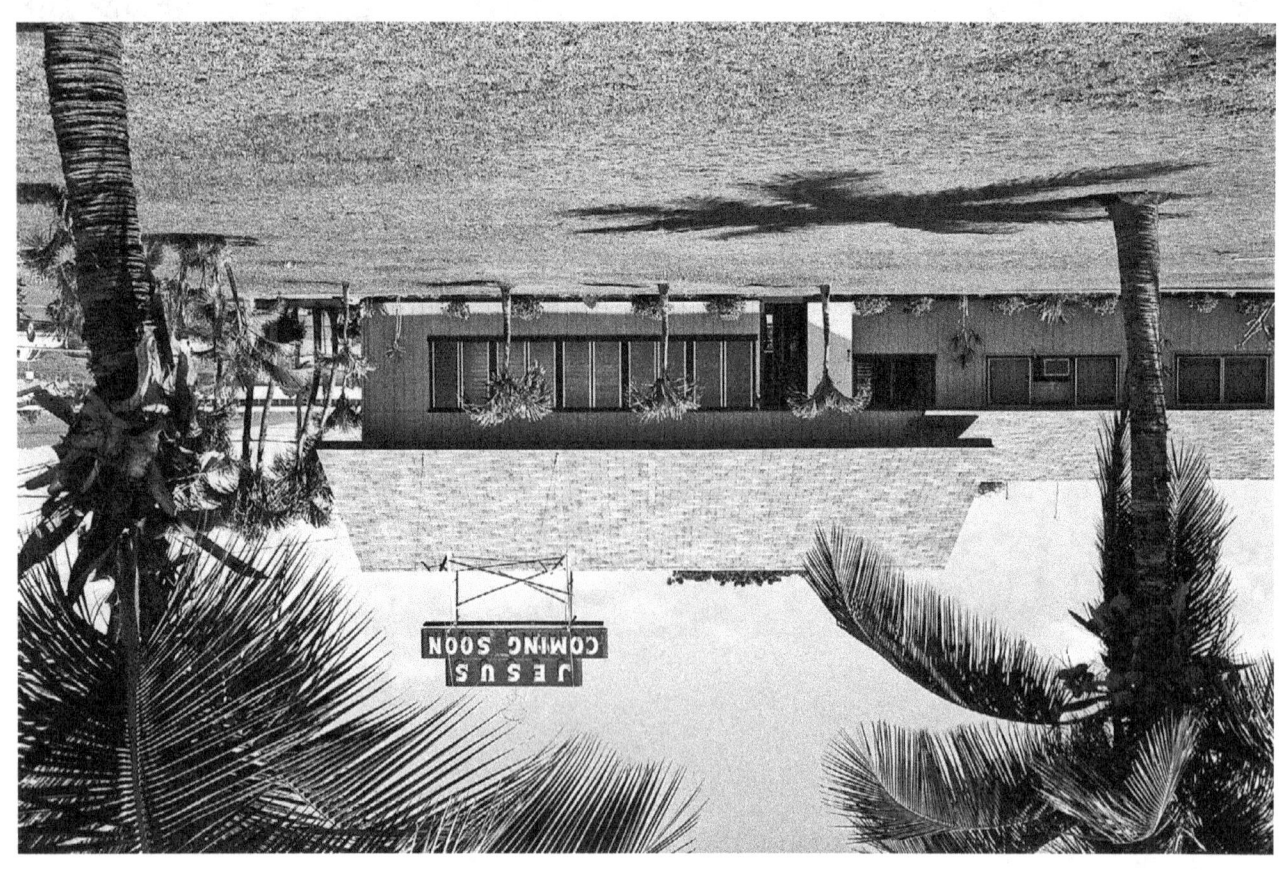

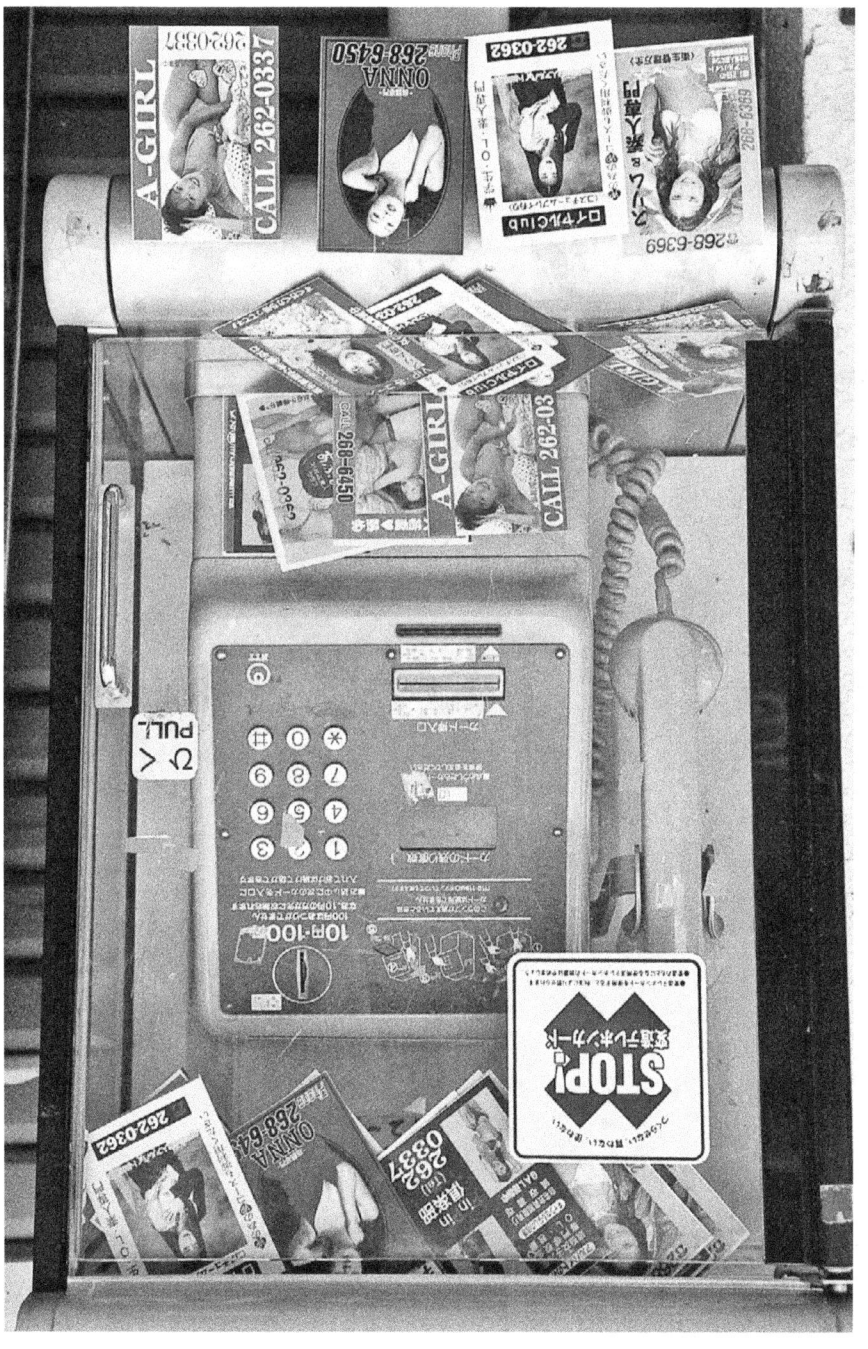

Sendai, Japan, 1996

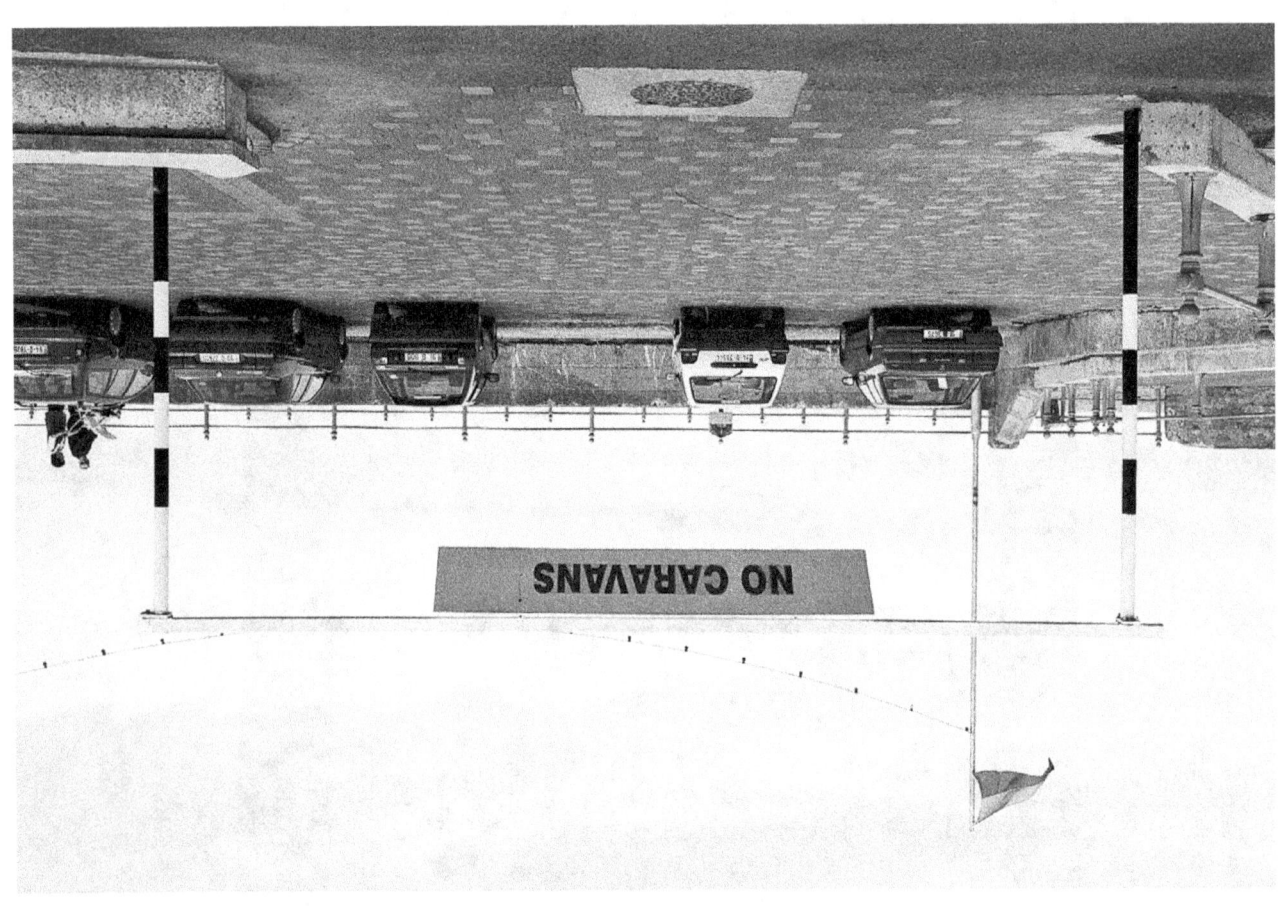

Bray, Ireland, 1996

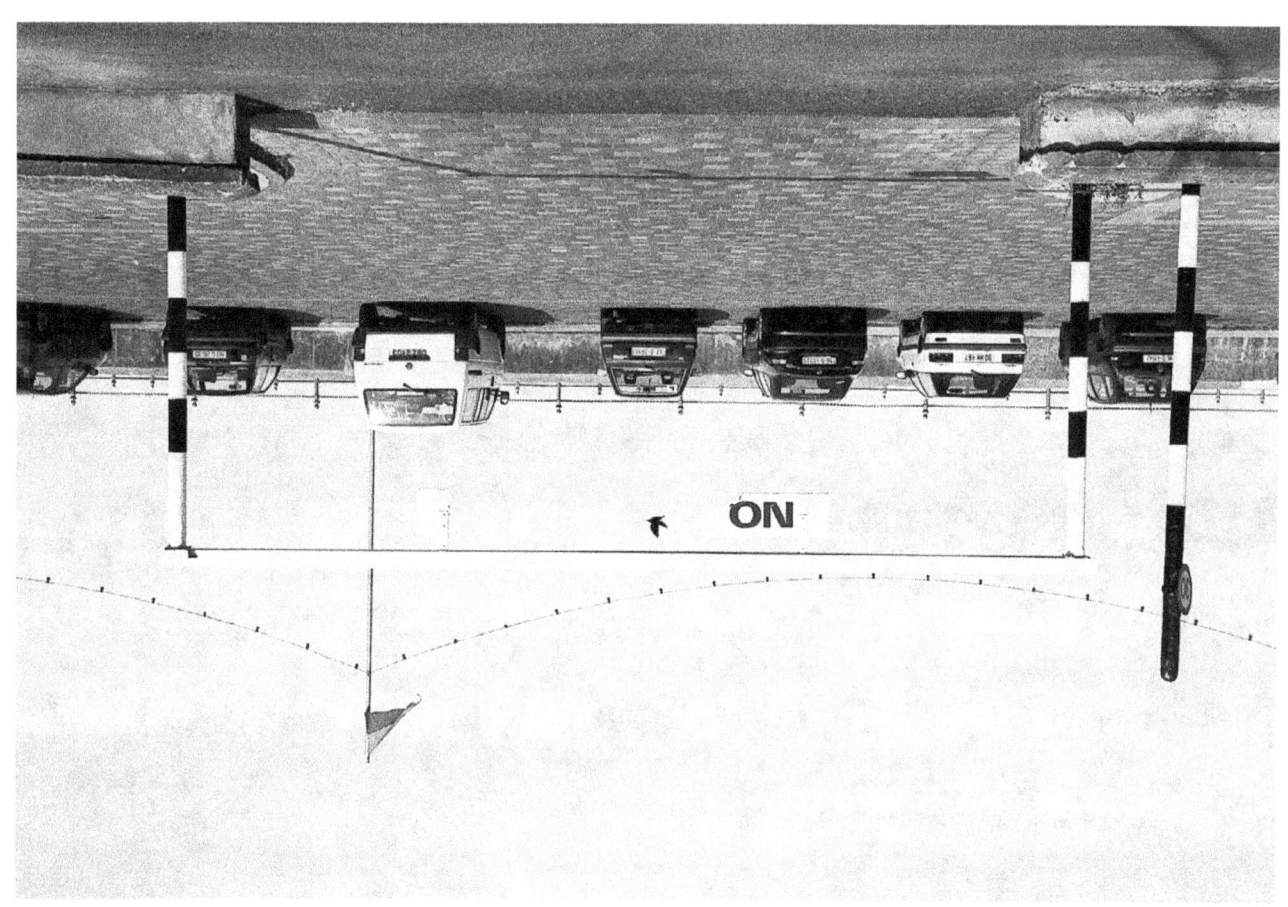

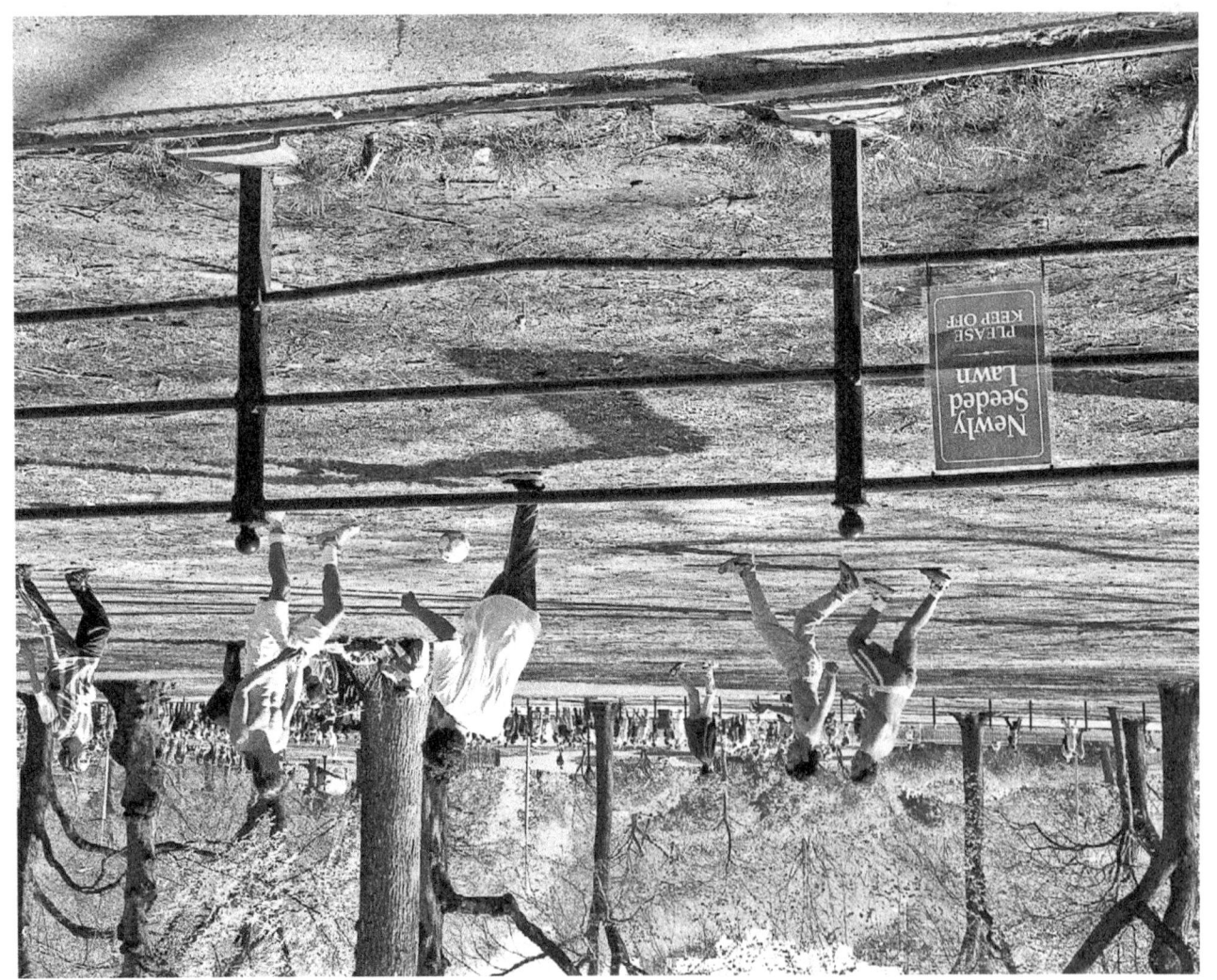

New York, 1998

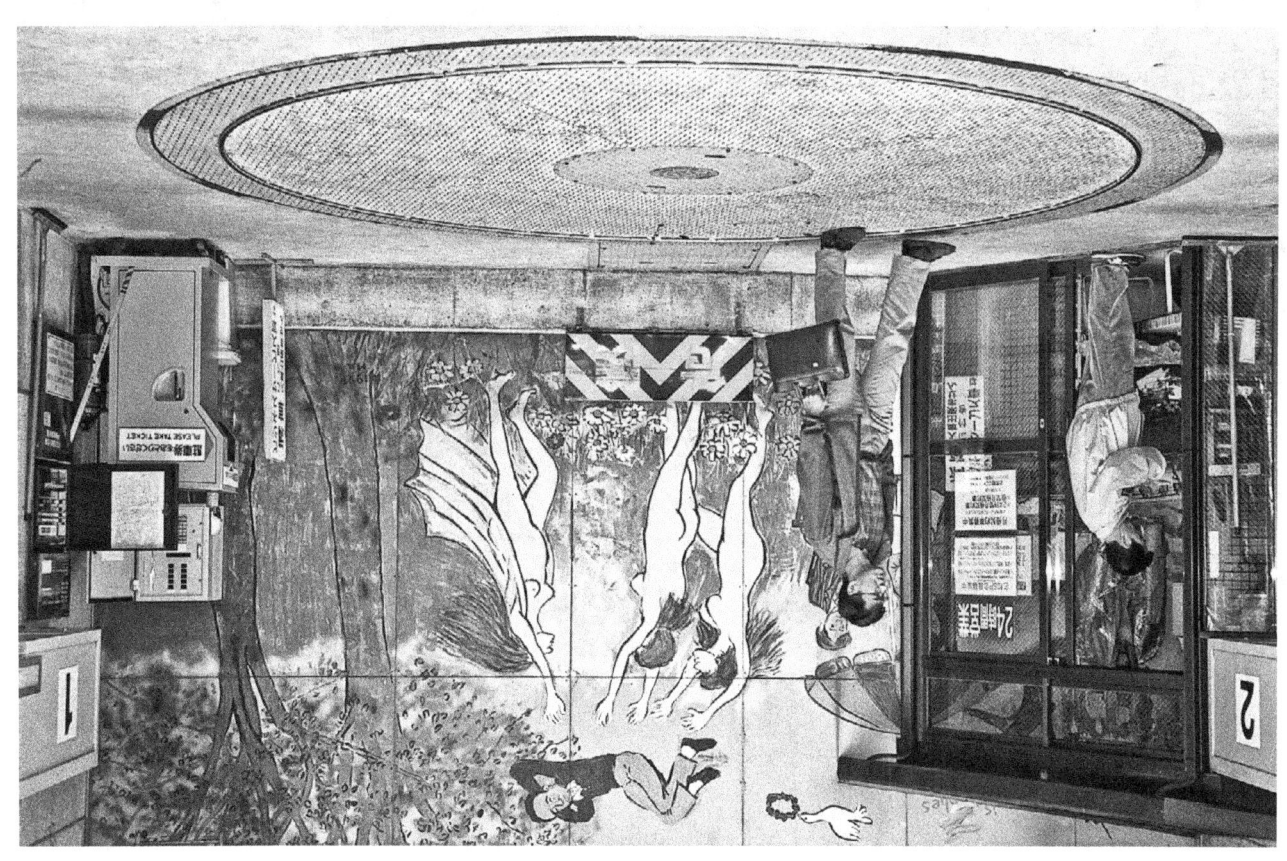

Sendai, Japan, 1996

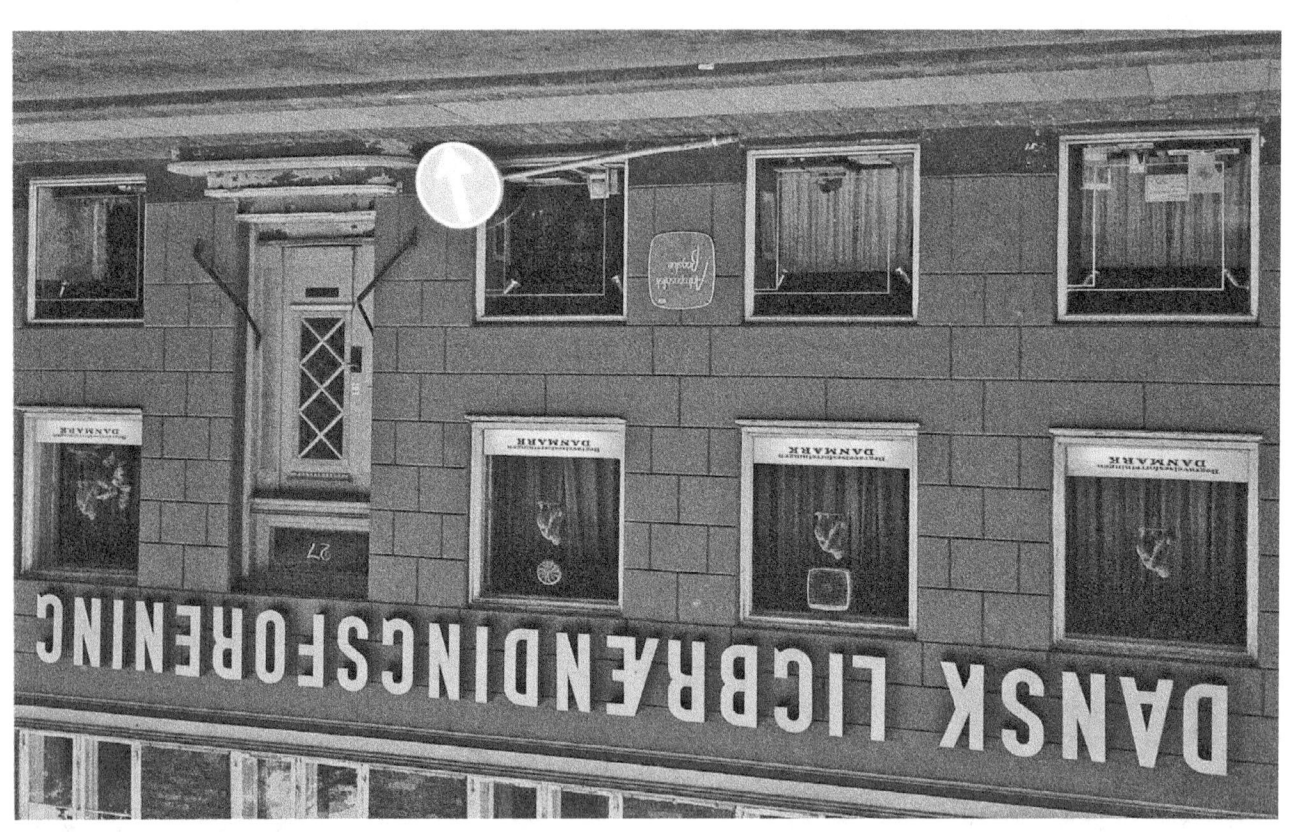

Copenhagen, 1993

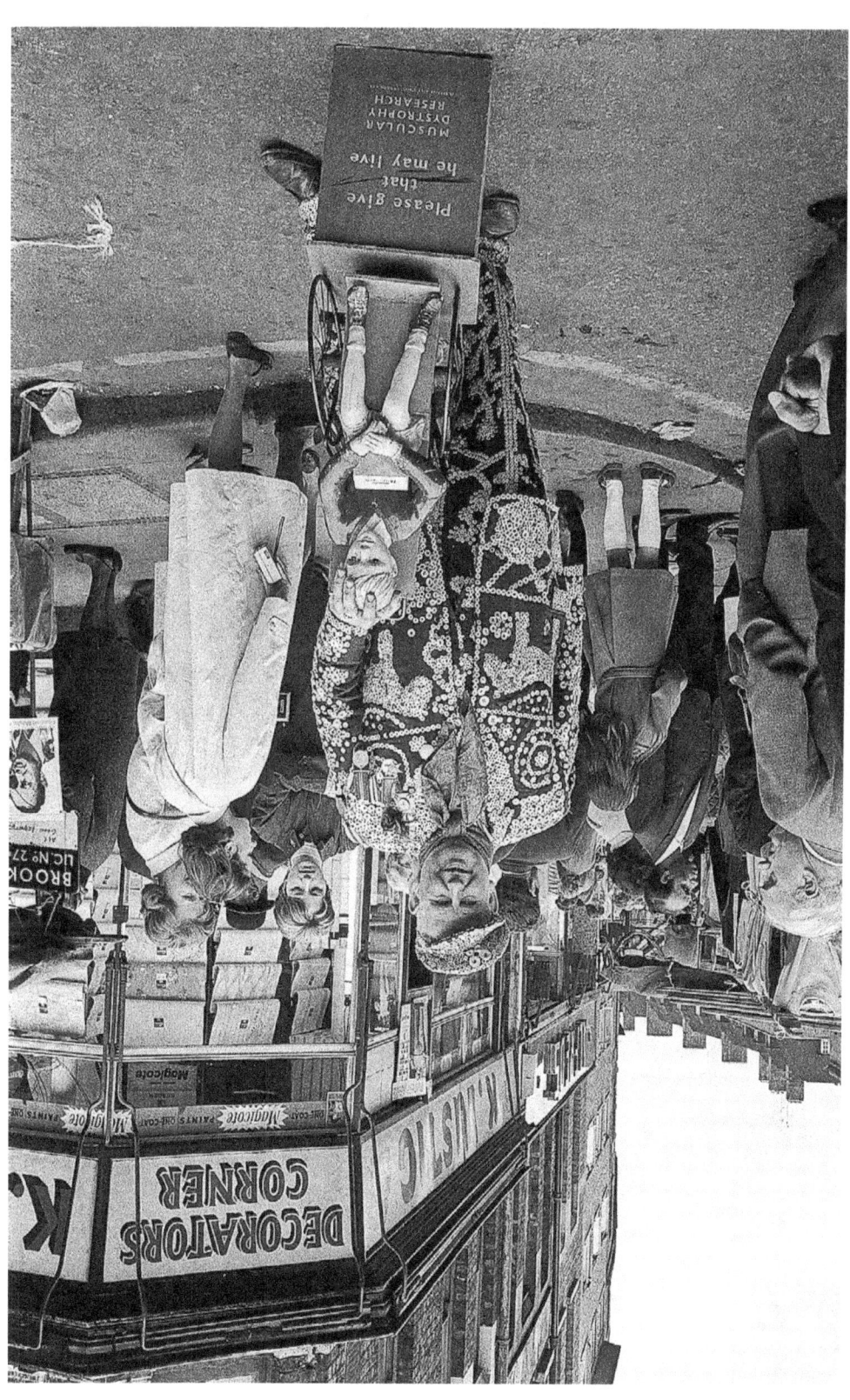

London, 1967

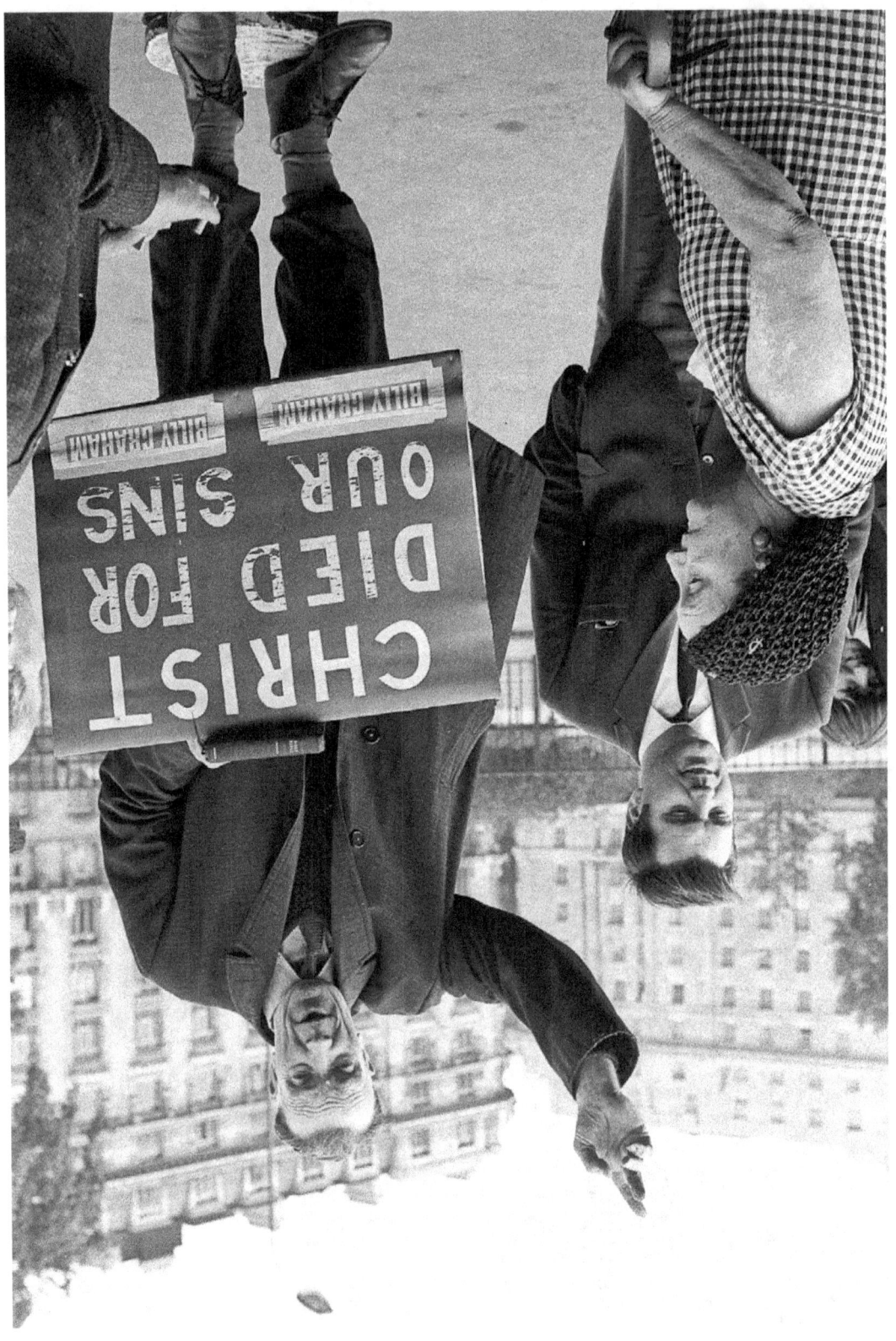

London, 1967

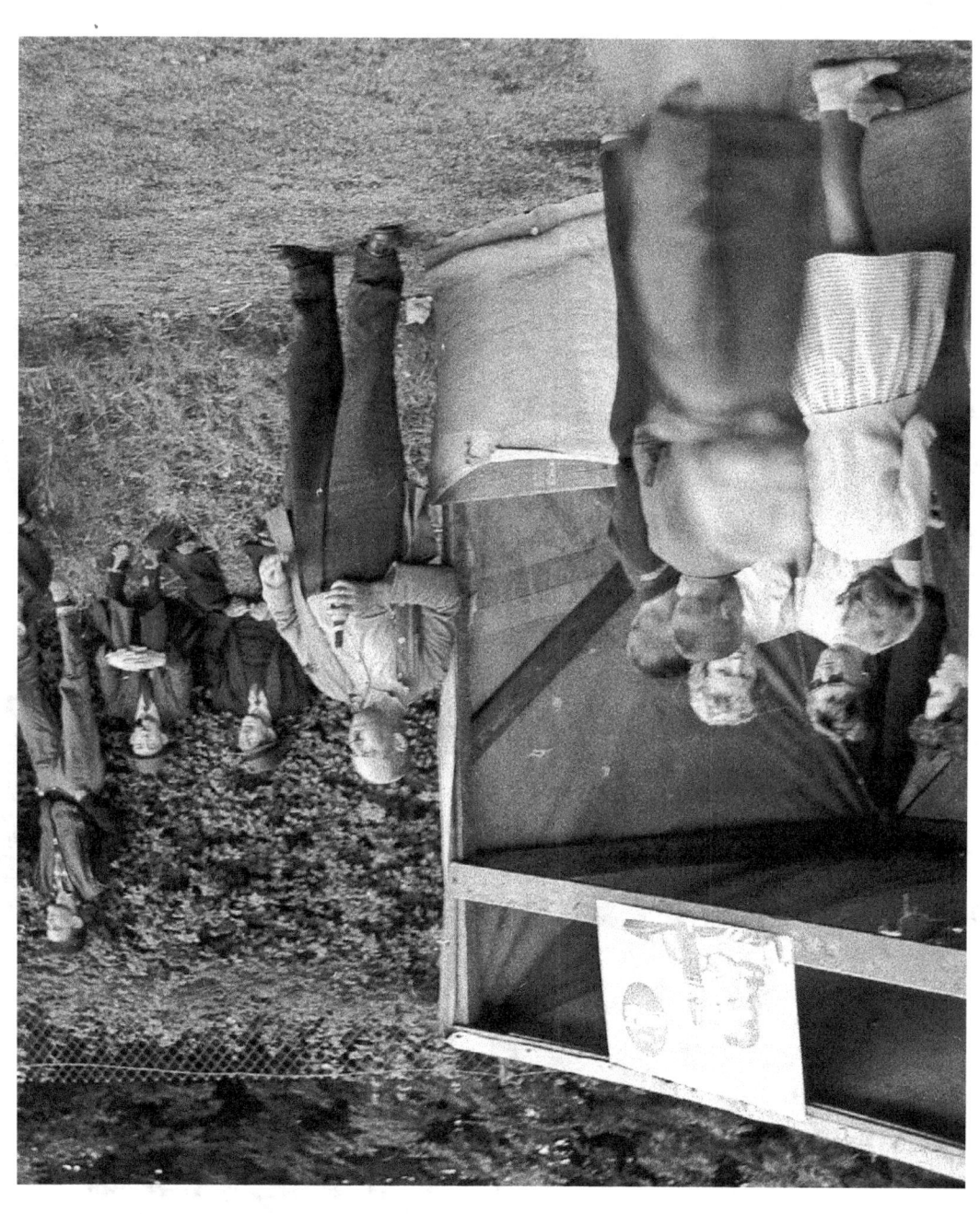

Bornholm, Denmark, 1960

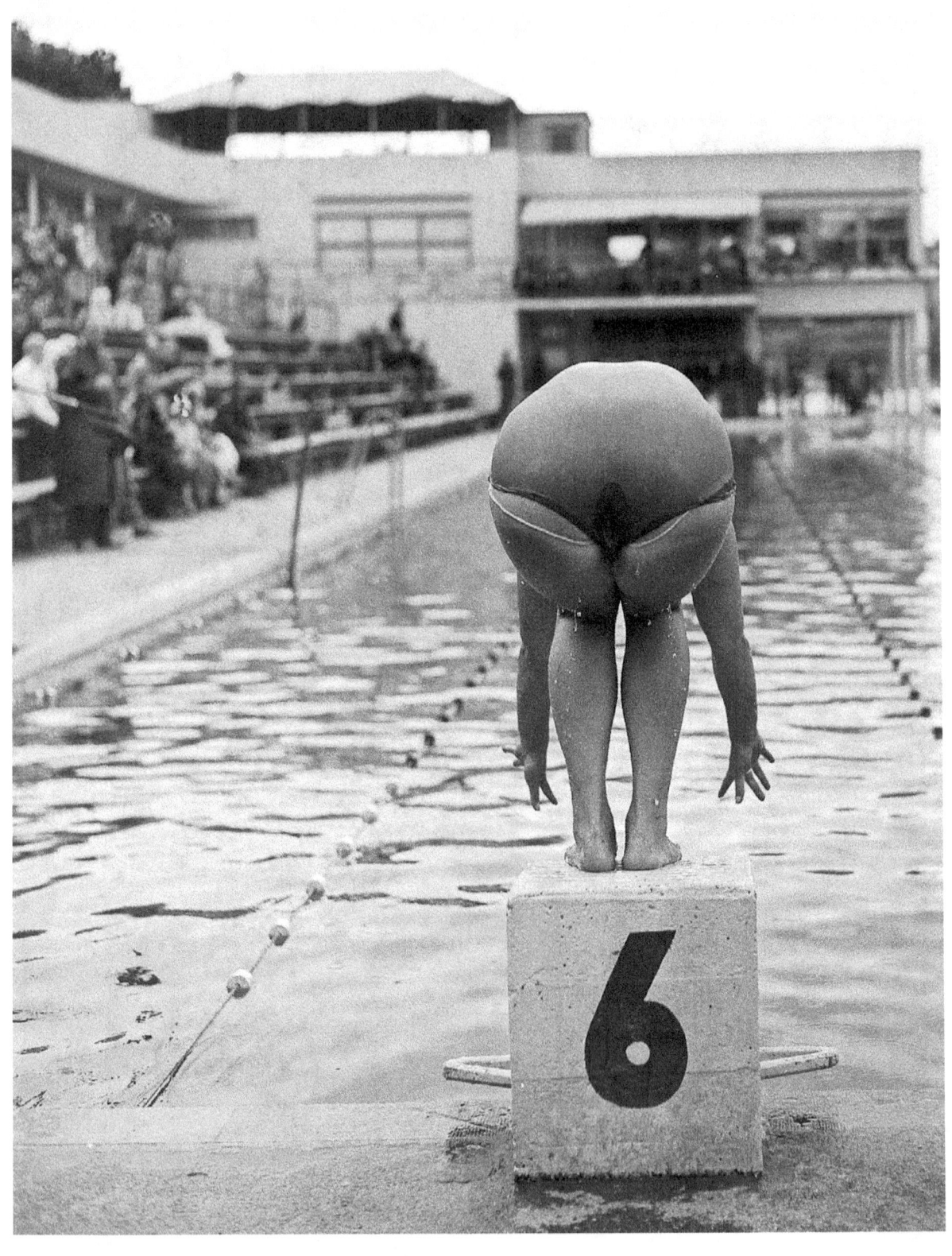

Linköping, Sweden, 1960   Phoenix, Arizona, 2003

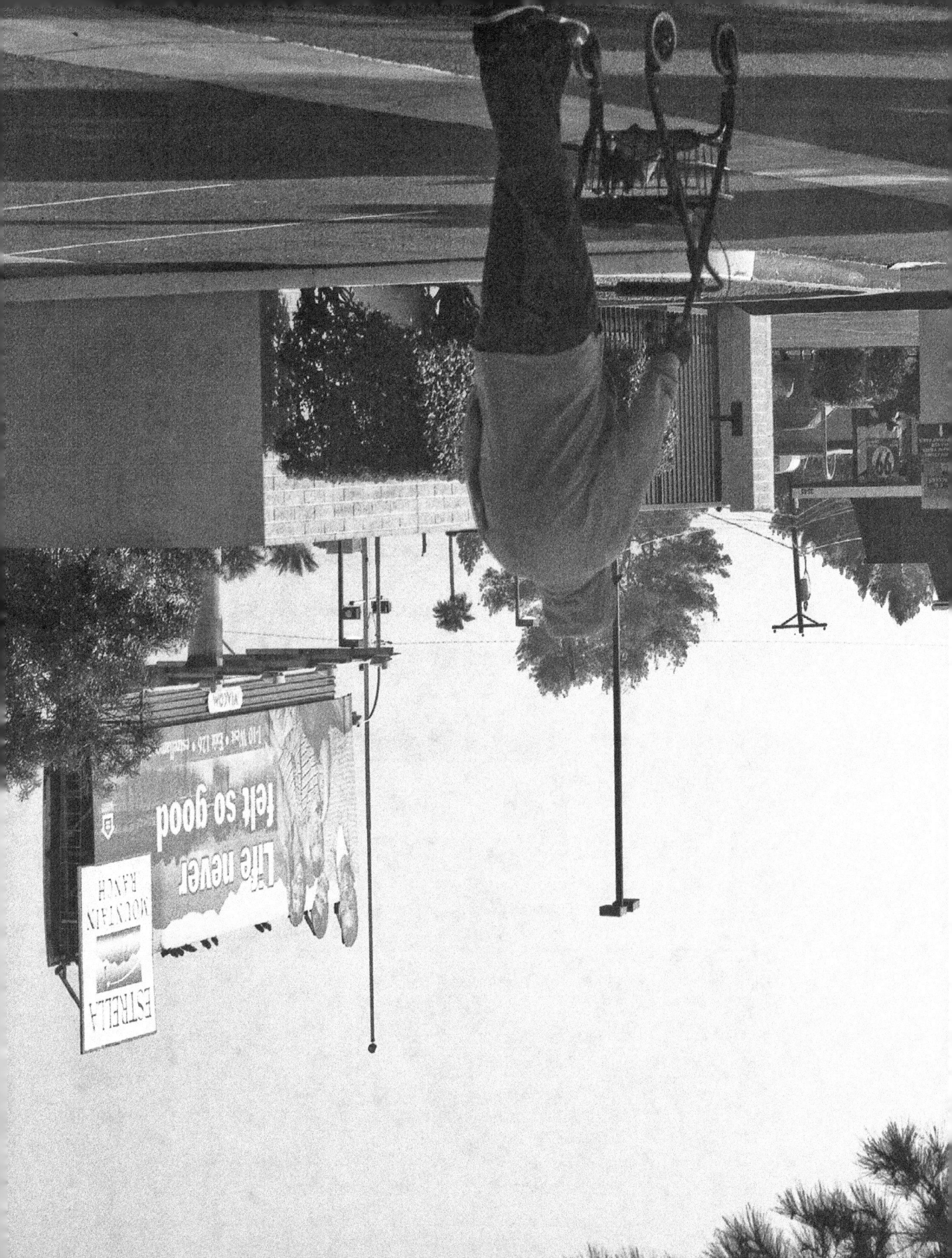

Stuttgart, Germany, 1987 — London, 1967

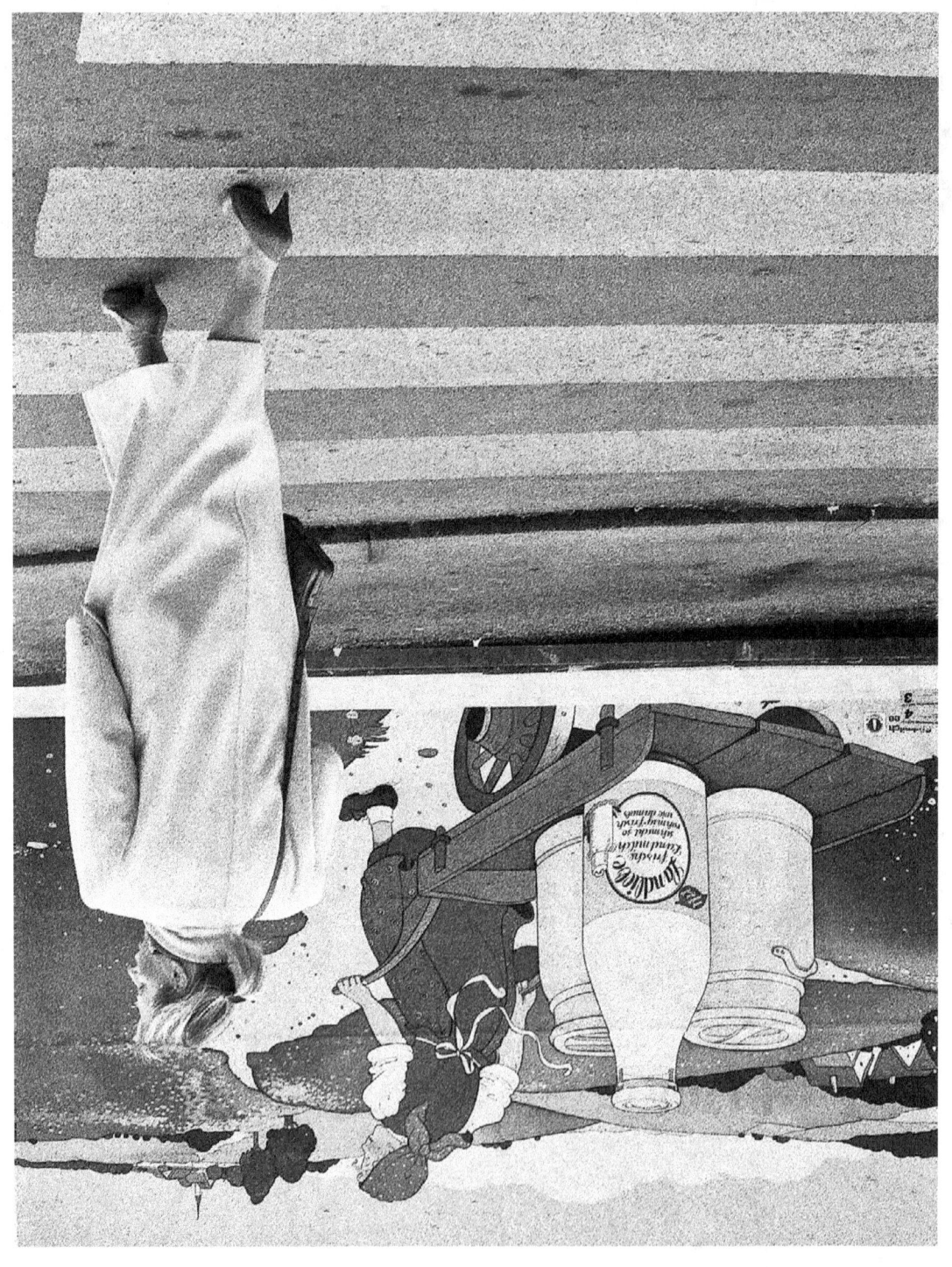

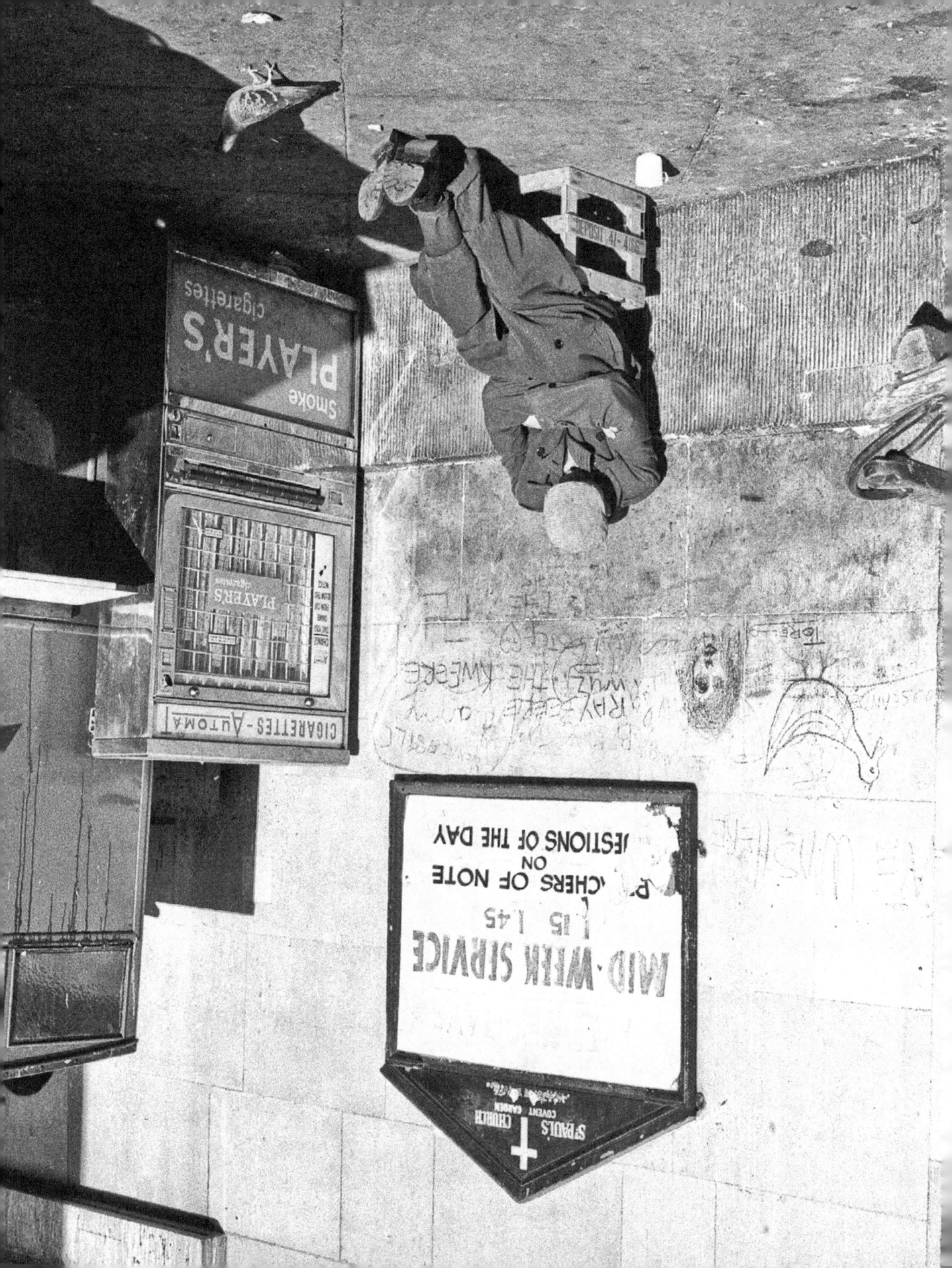

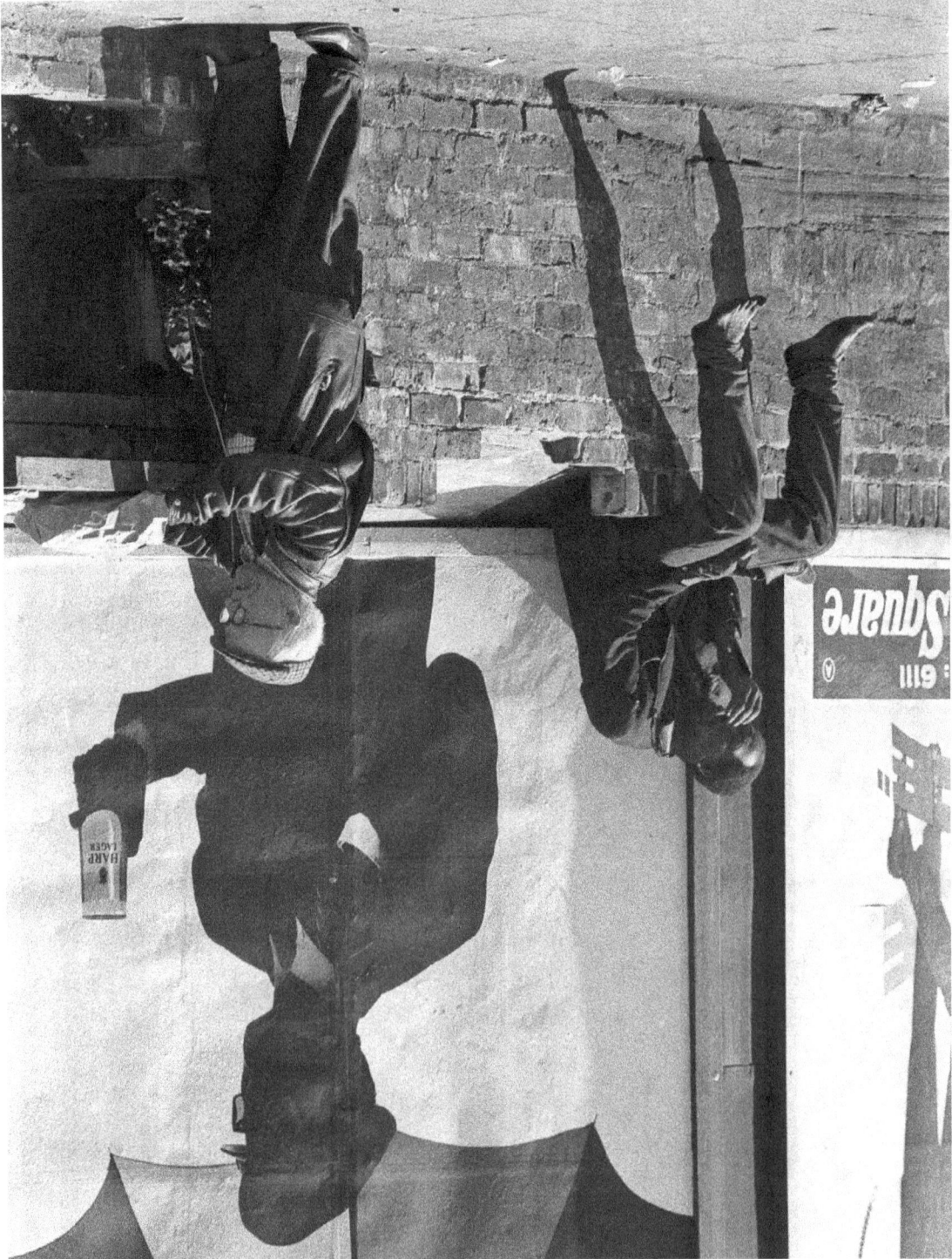

London, 1967

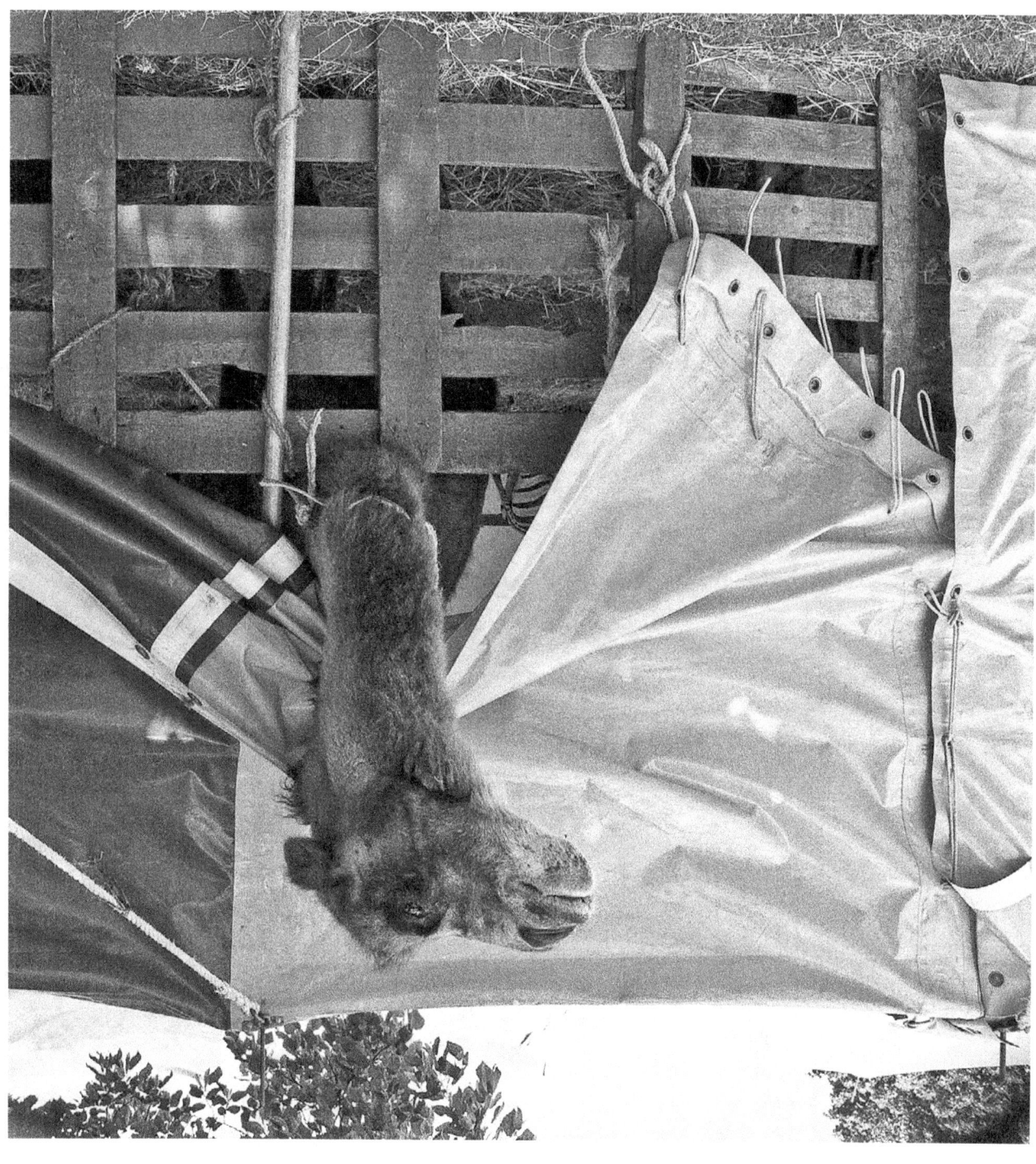

Lund, Sweden, 1996

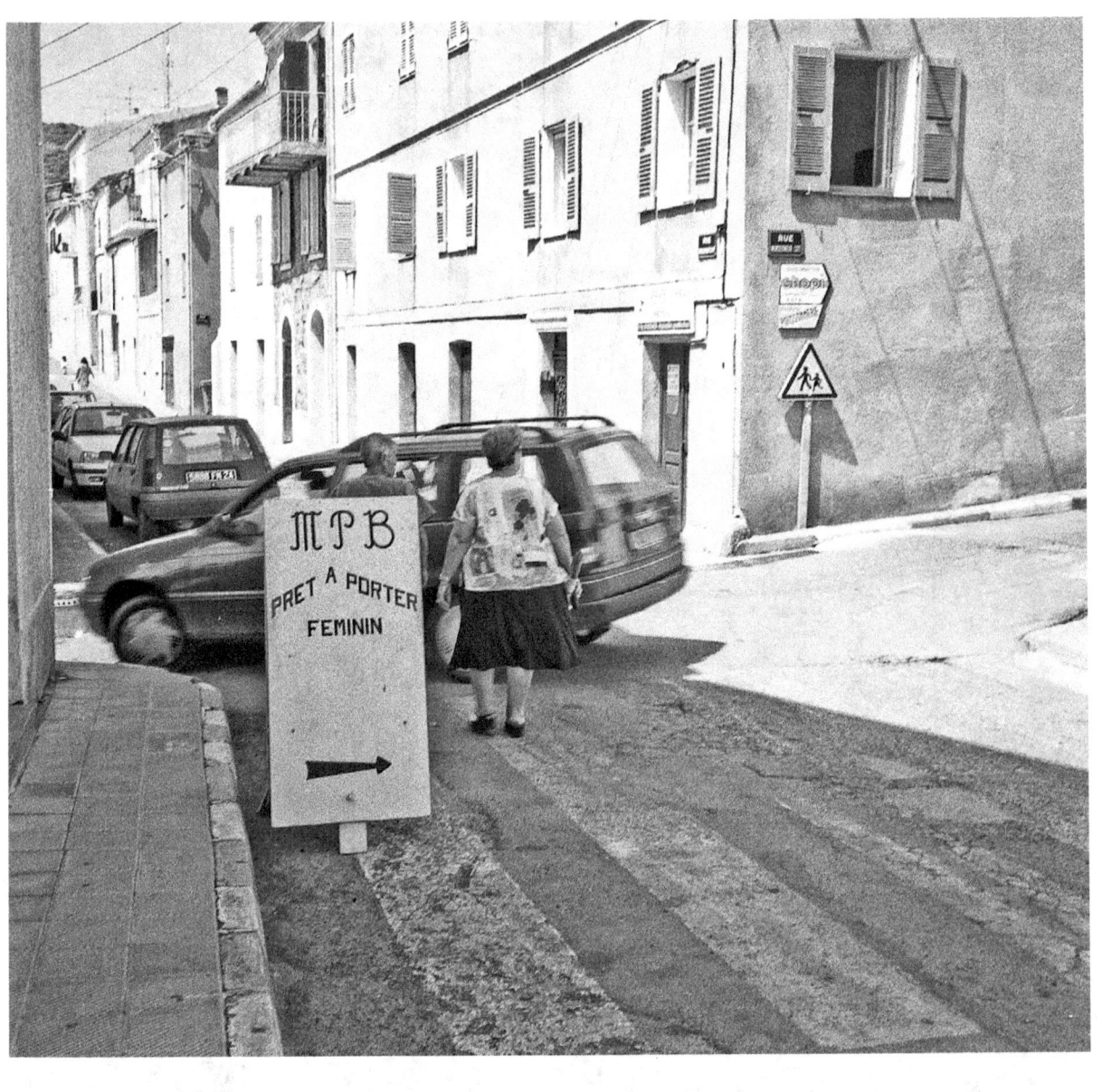

Cargése, Corsica, 2000

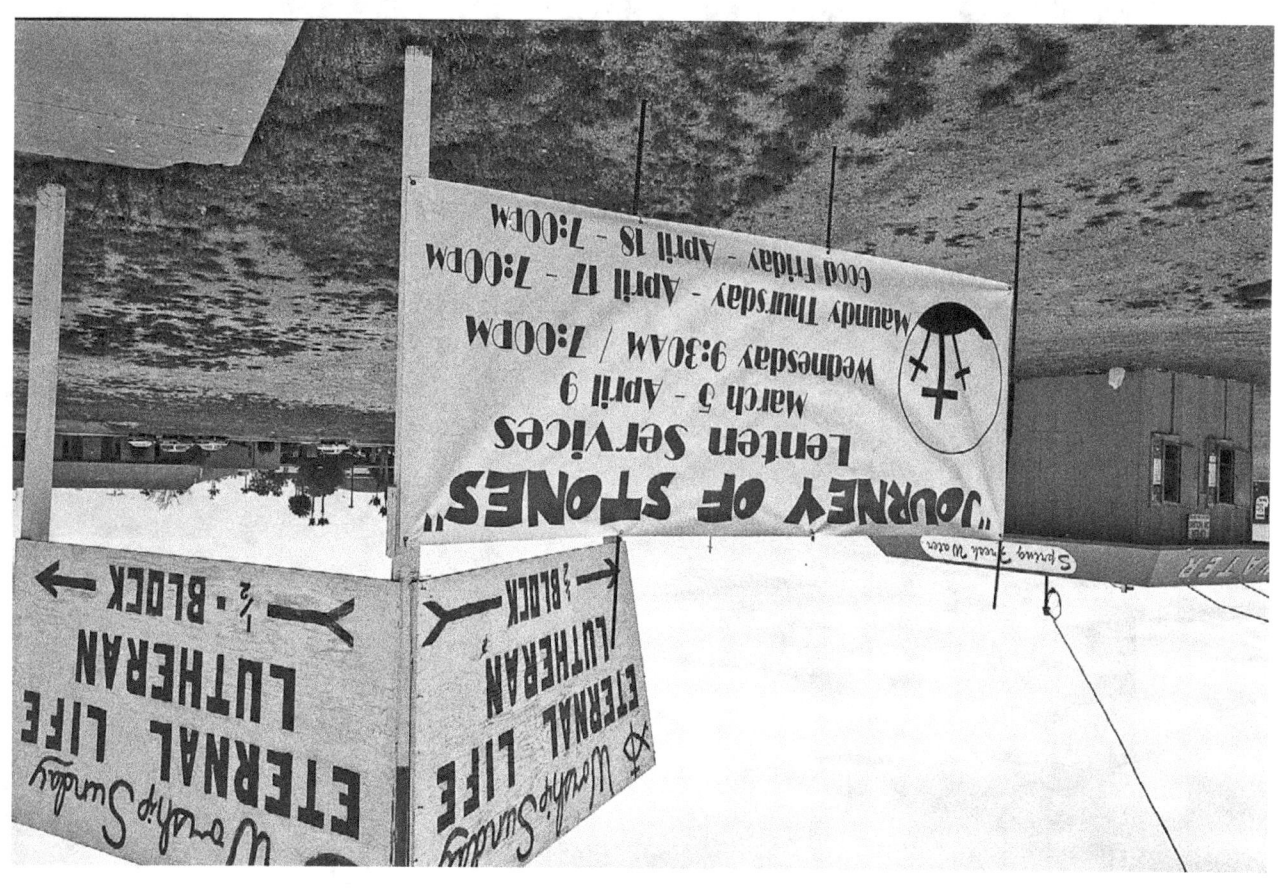

Phoenix, Arizona, 2003

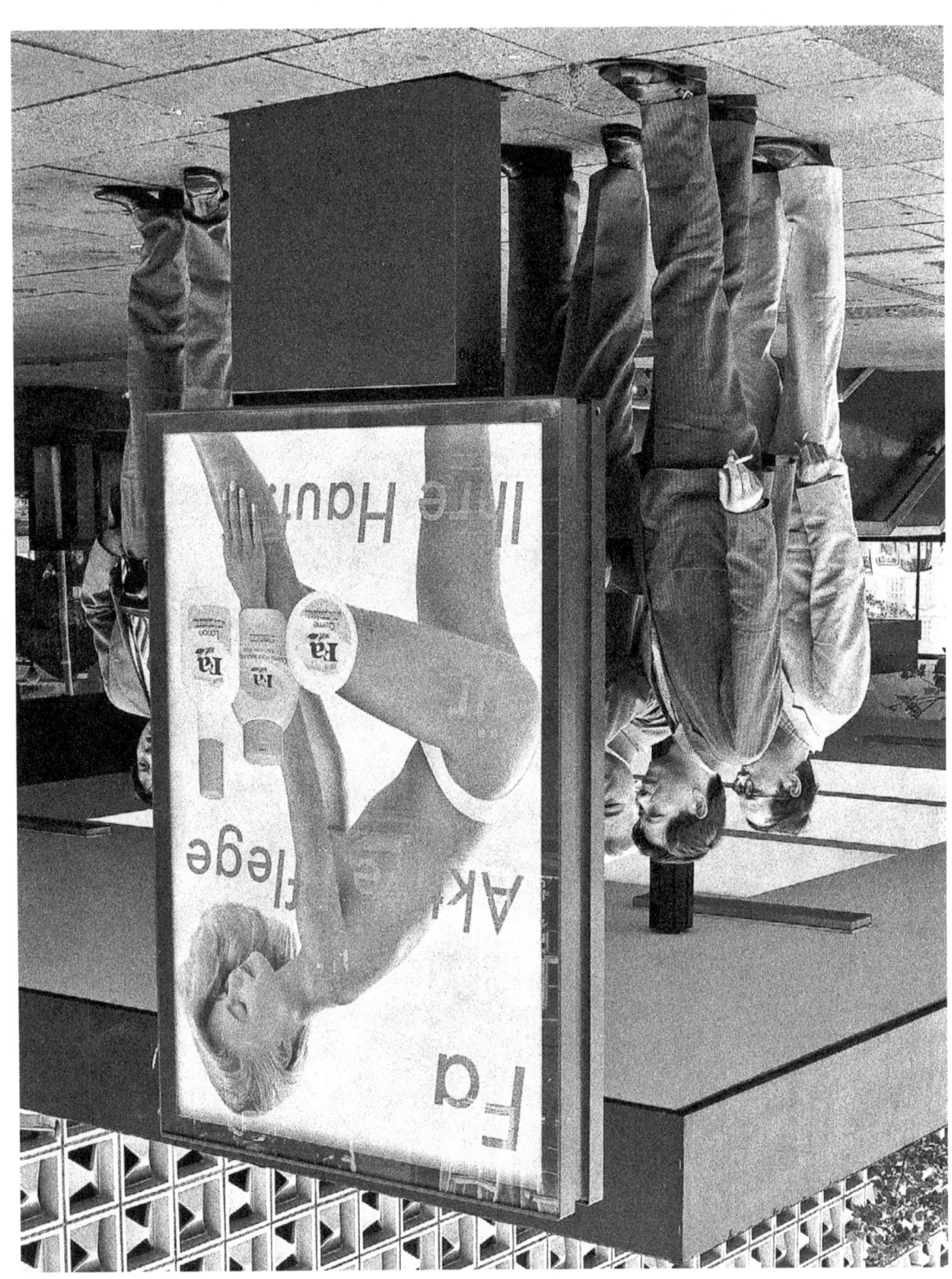

Hamburg, Germany, 1987

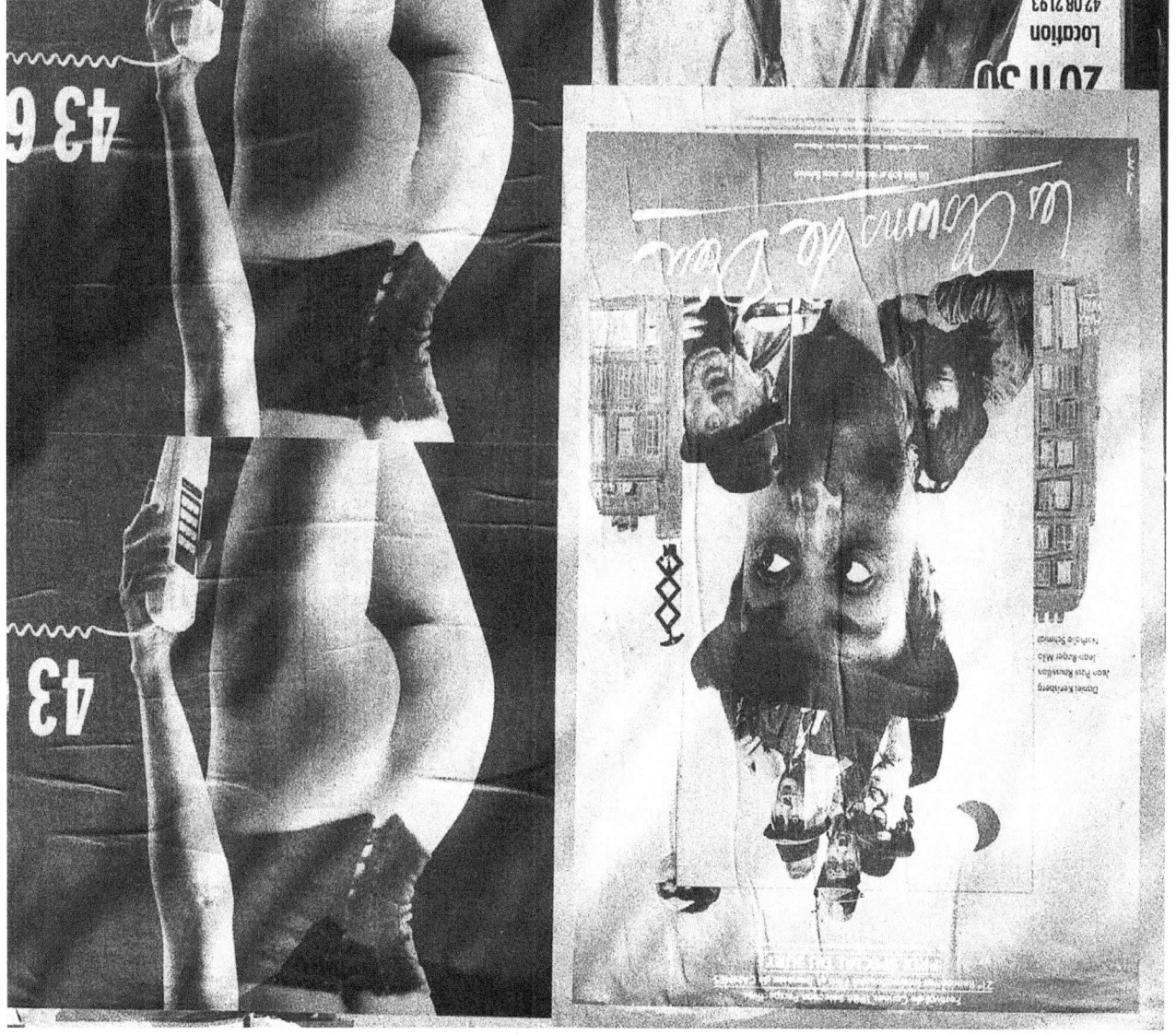

Paris, 1987

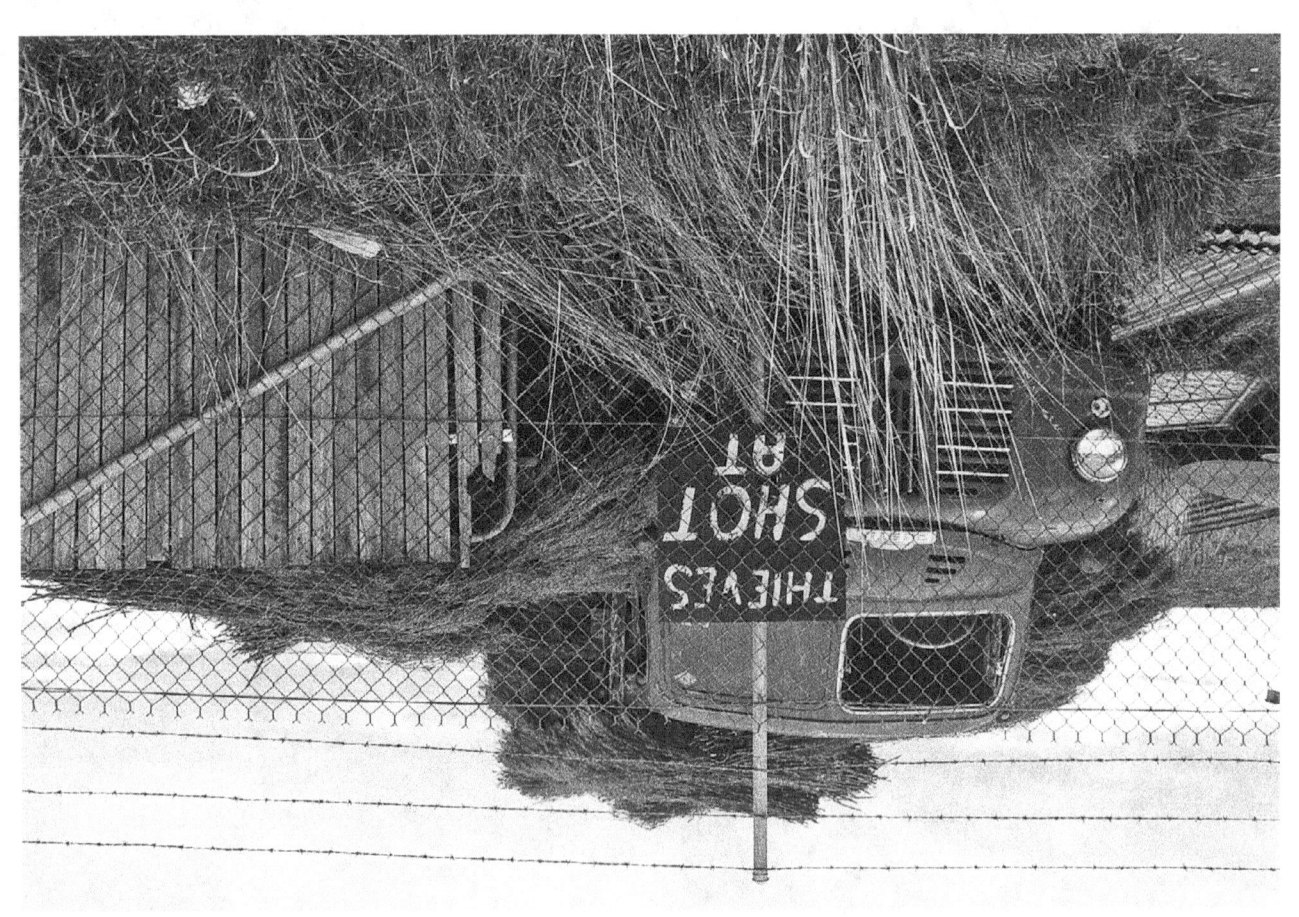

Canberra, Australia, 1987

New York, 2007

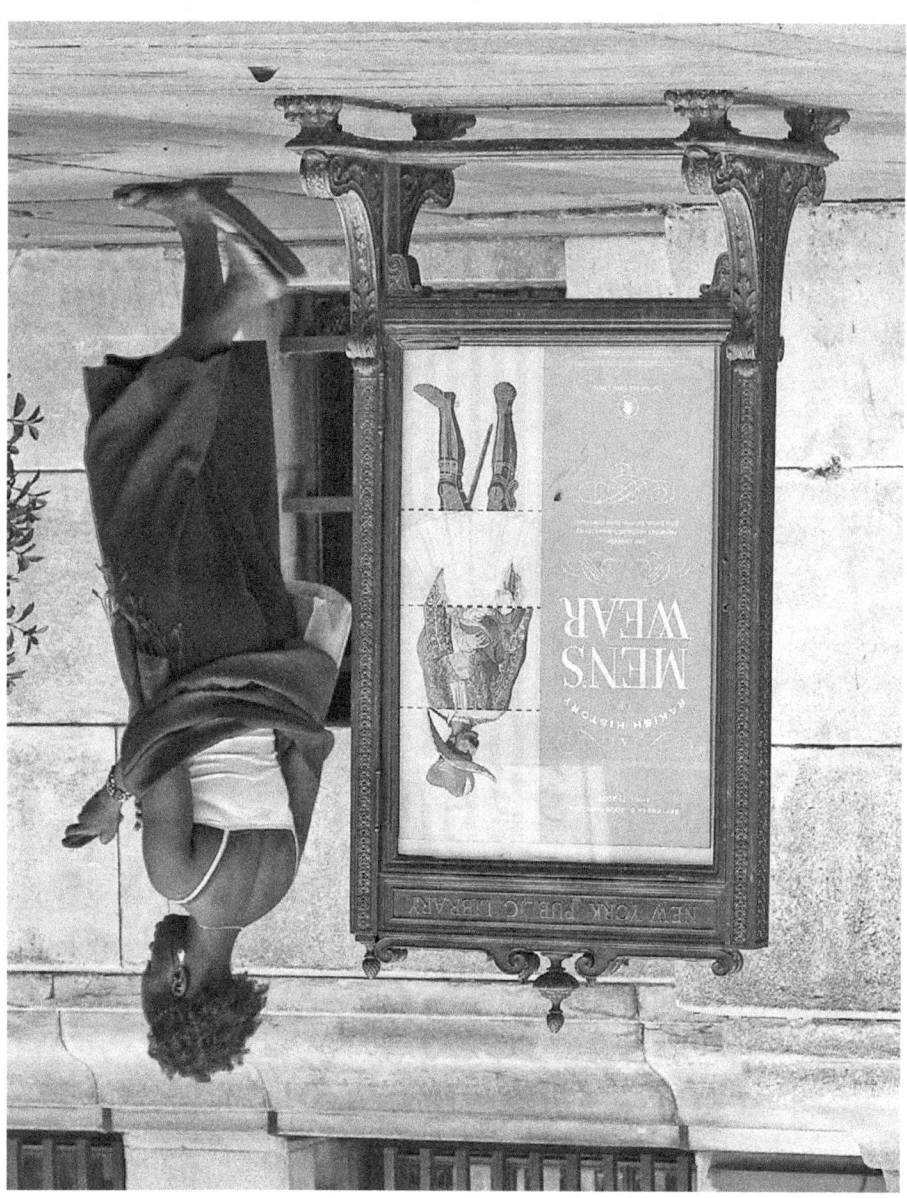

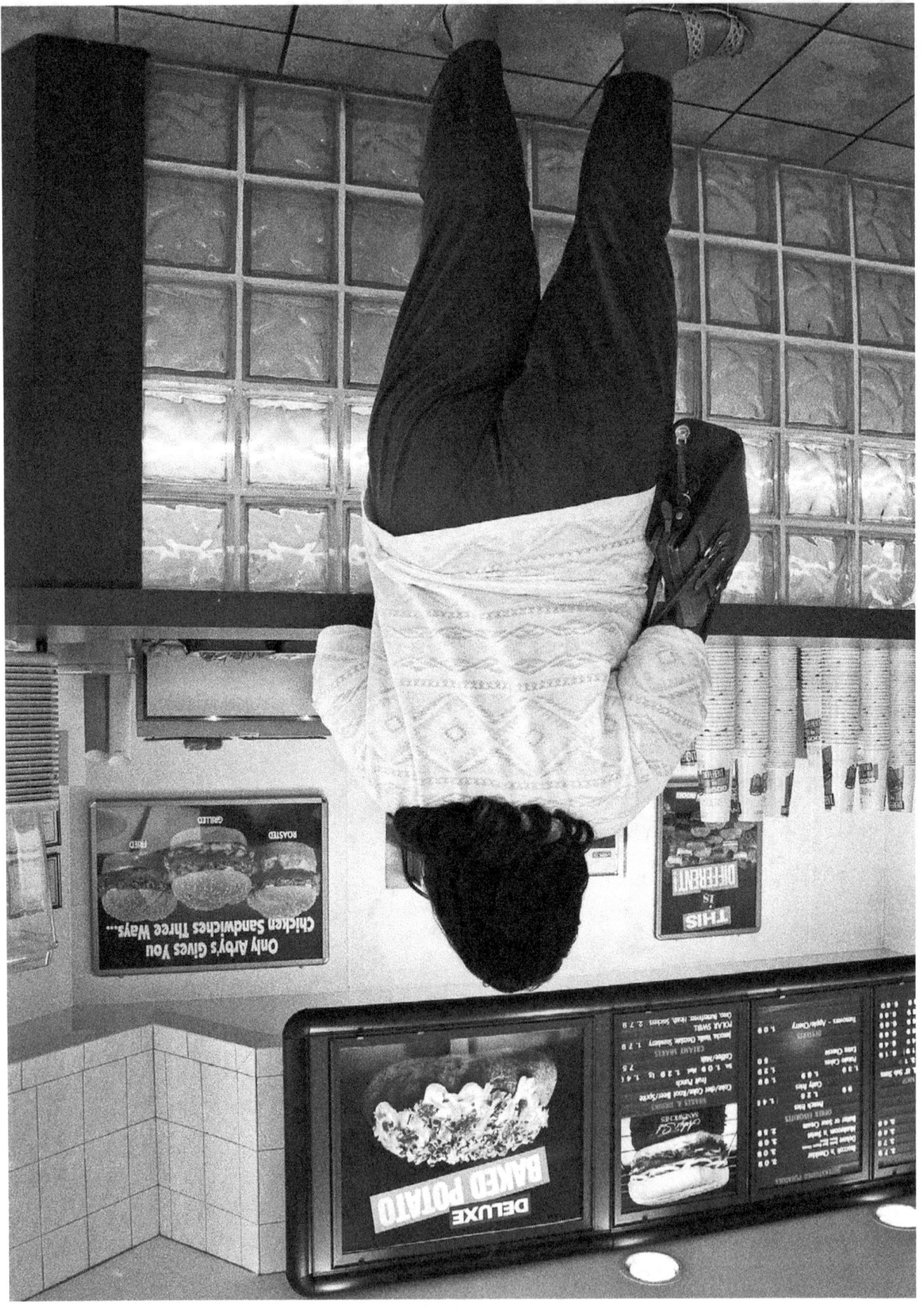

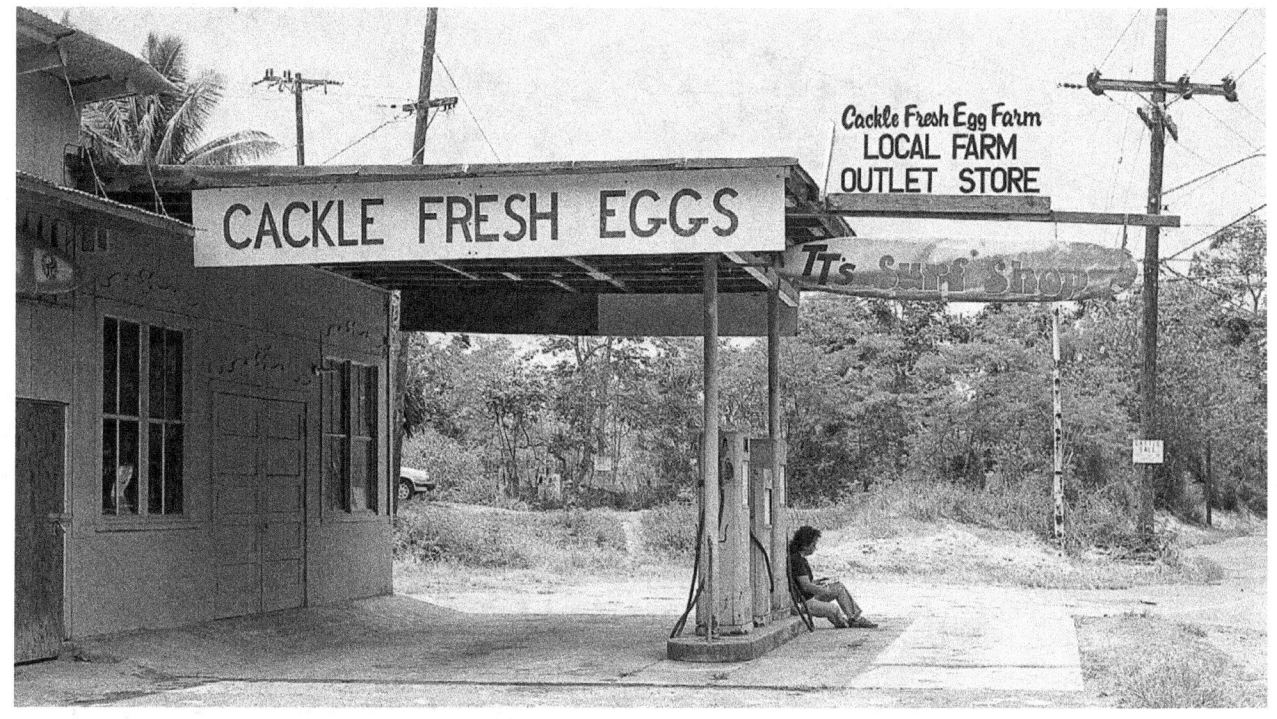

Hawaii, 1988

Maui, Hawaii, 1994

Copenhagen. 1996

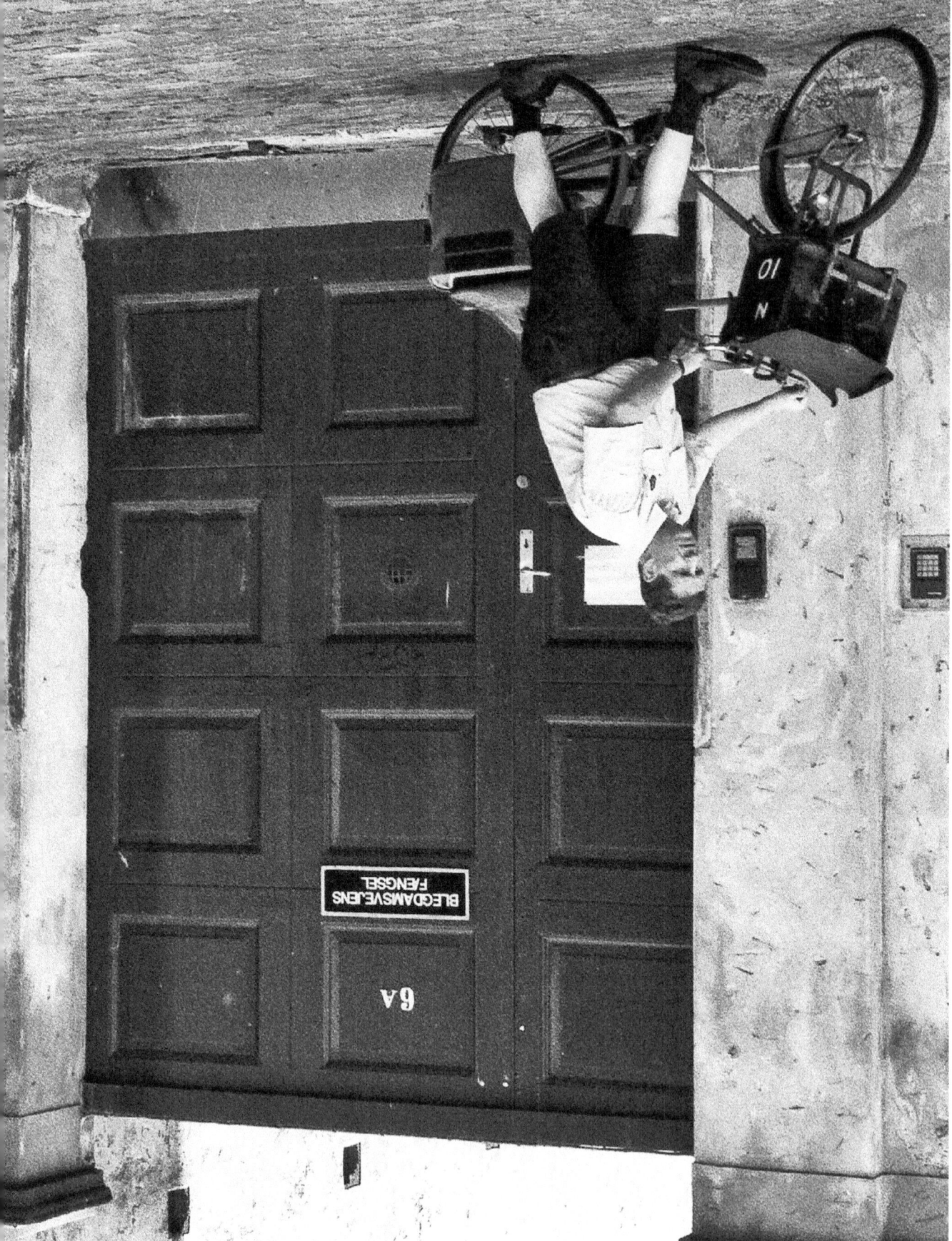

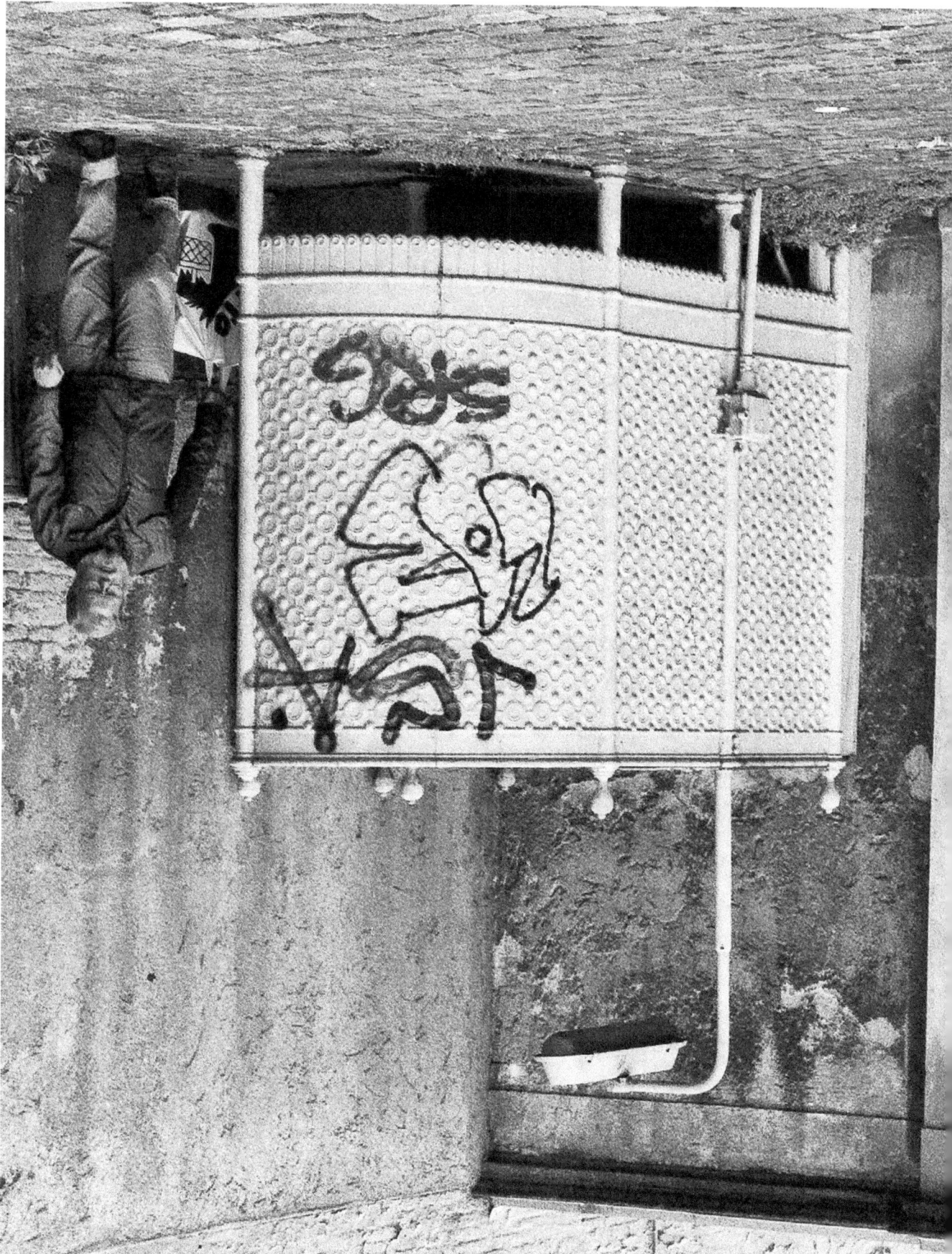

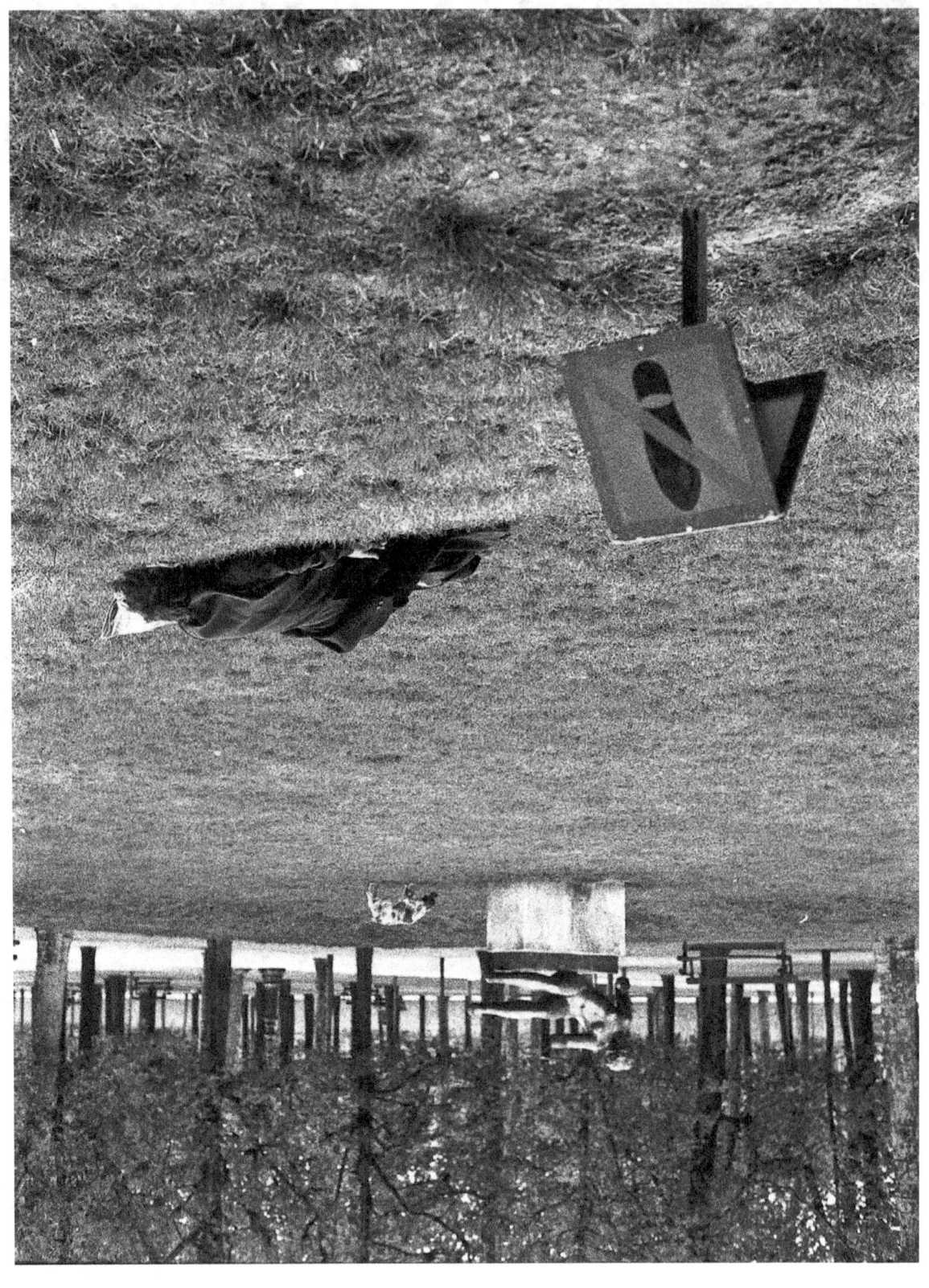

Paris, 1987

Greenland, 2000

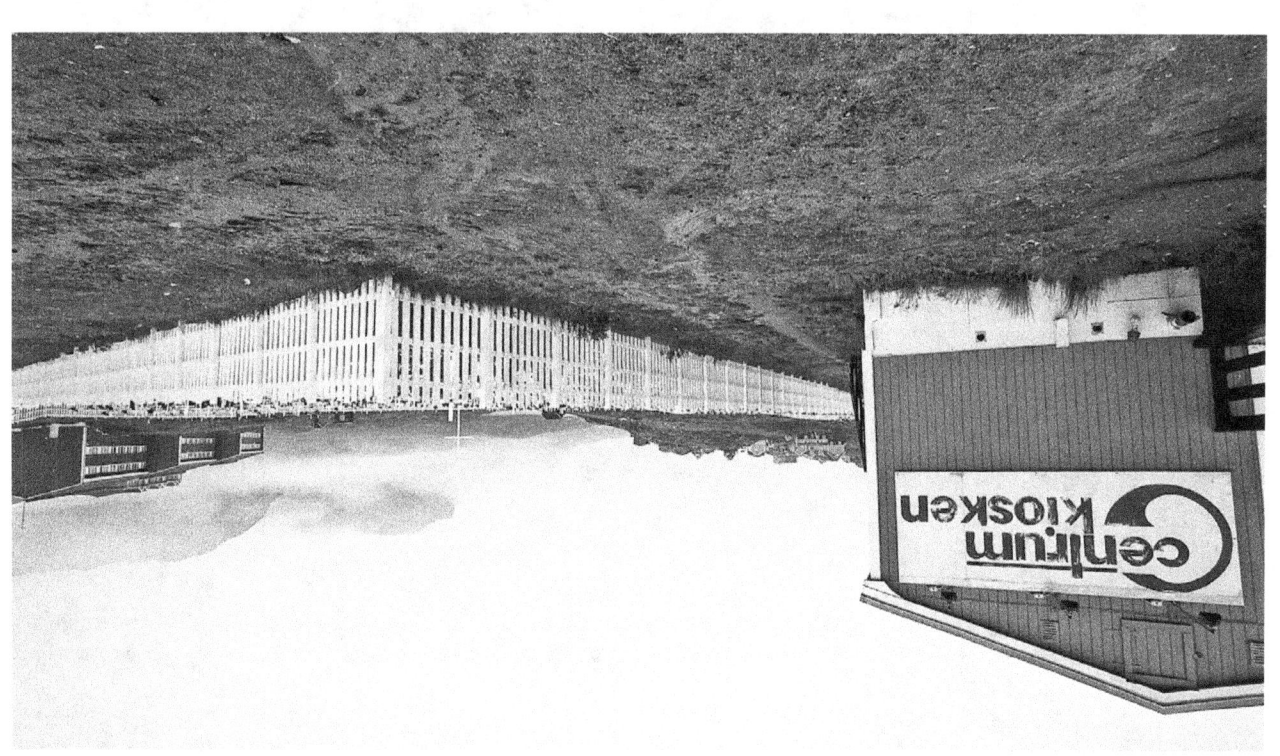

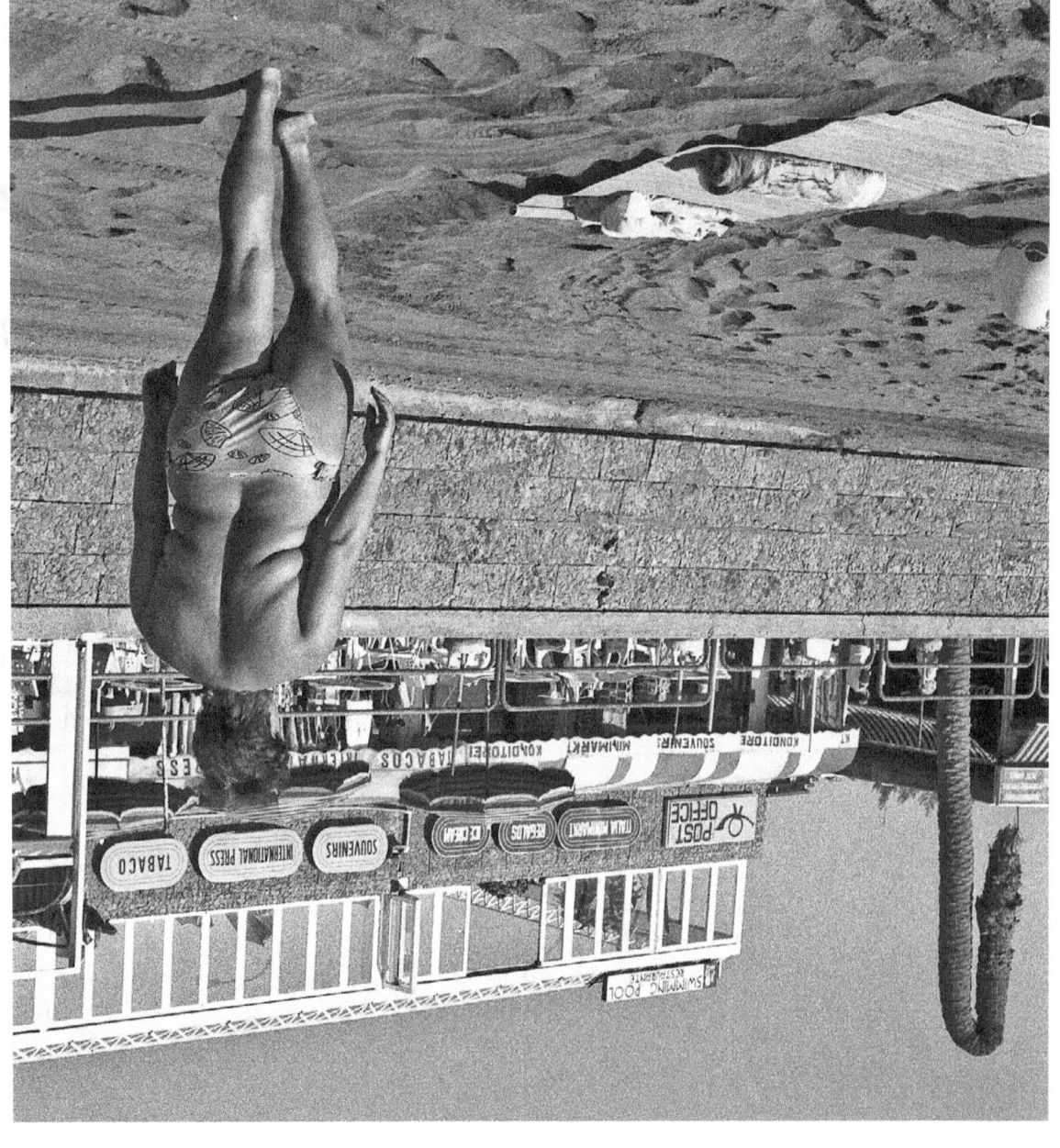

Grand Canaria, Spain, 1989

Murren, Switzerland, 1999

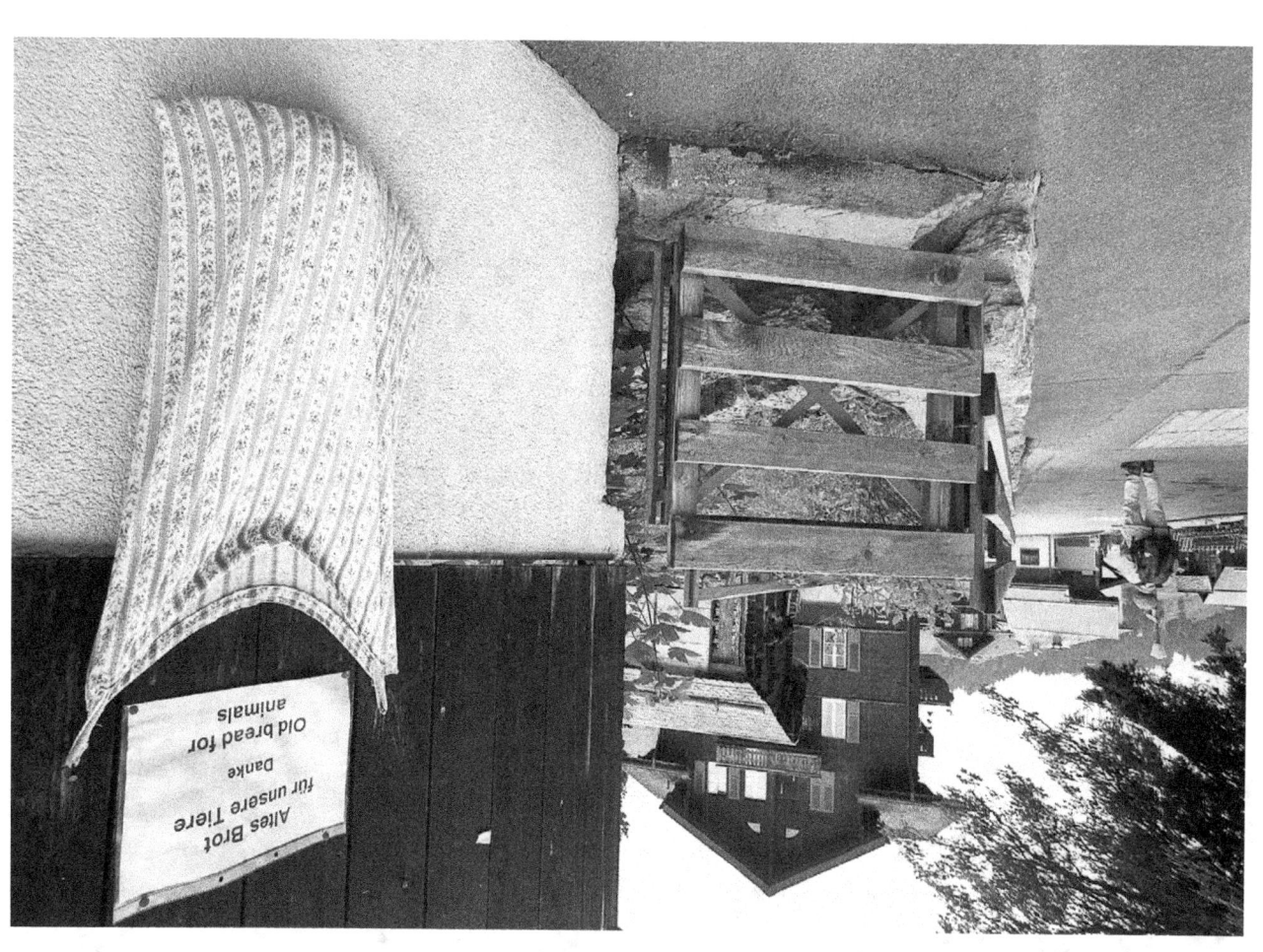

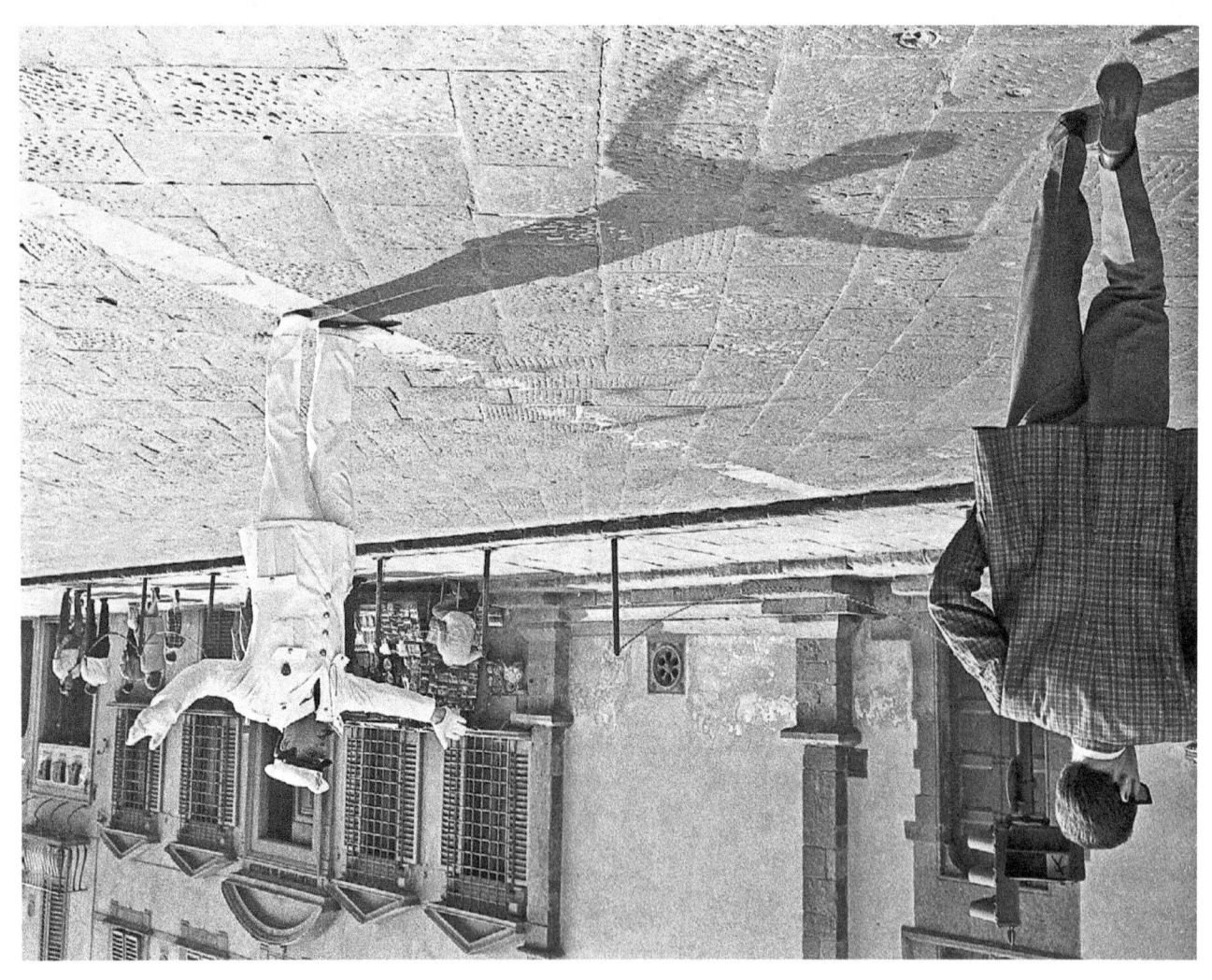

Florence, Italy, 1969

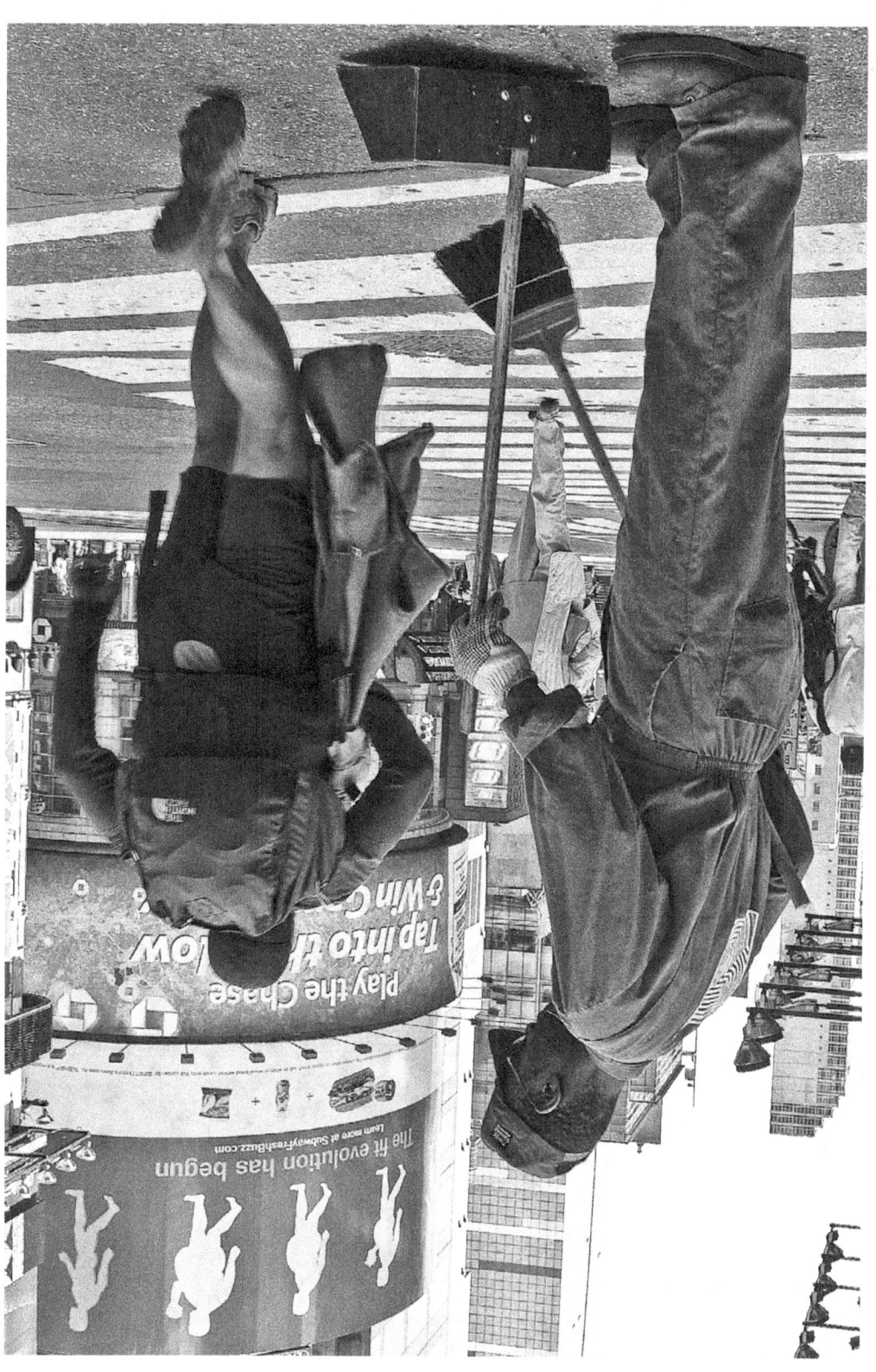

New York, 2007

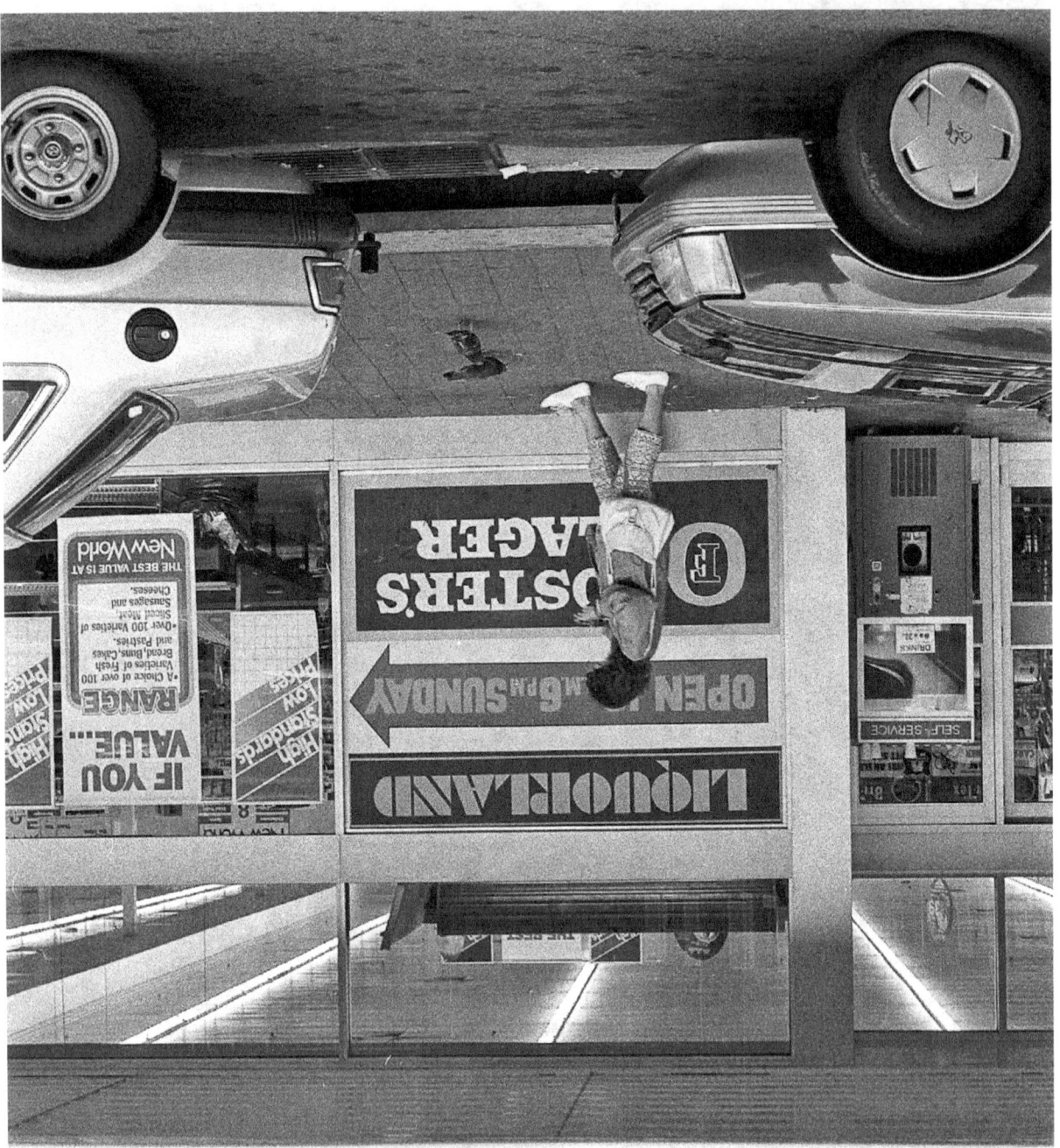

Sidney, Australia, 1988

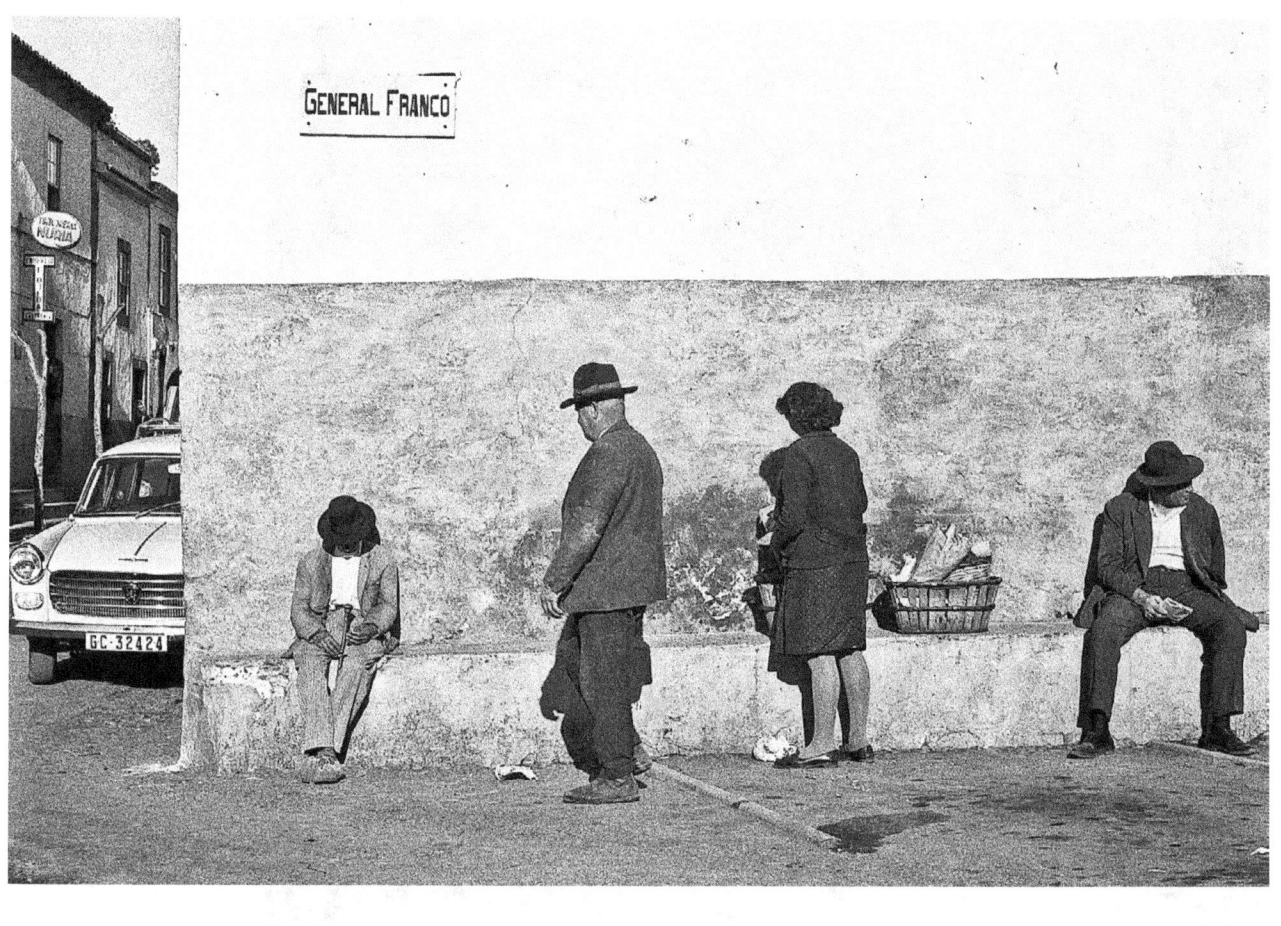

Santa Brigida, Las Palmas, Spain, 1968

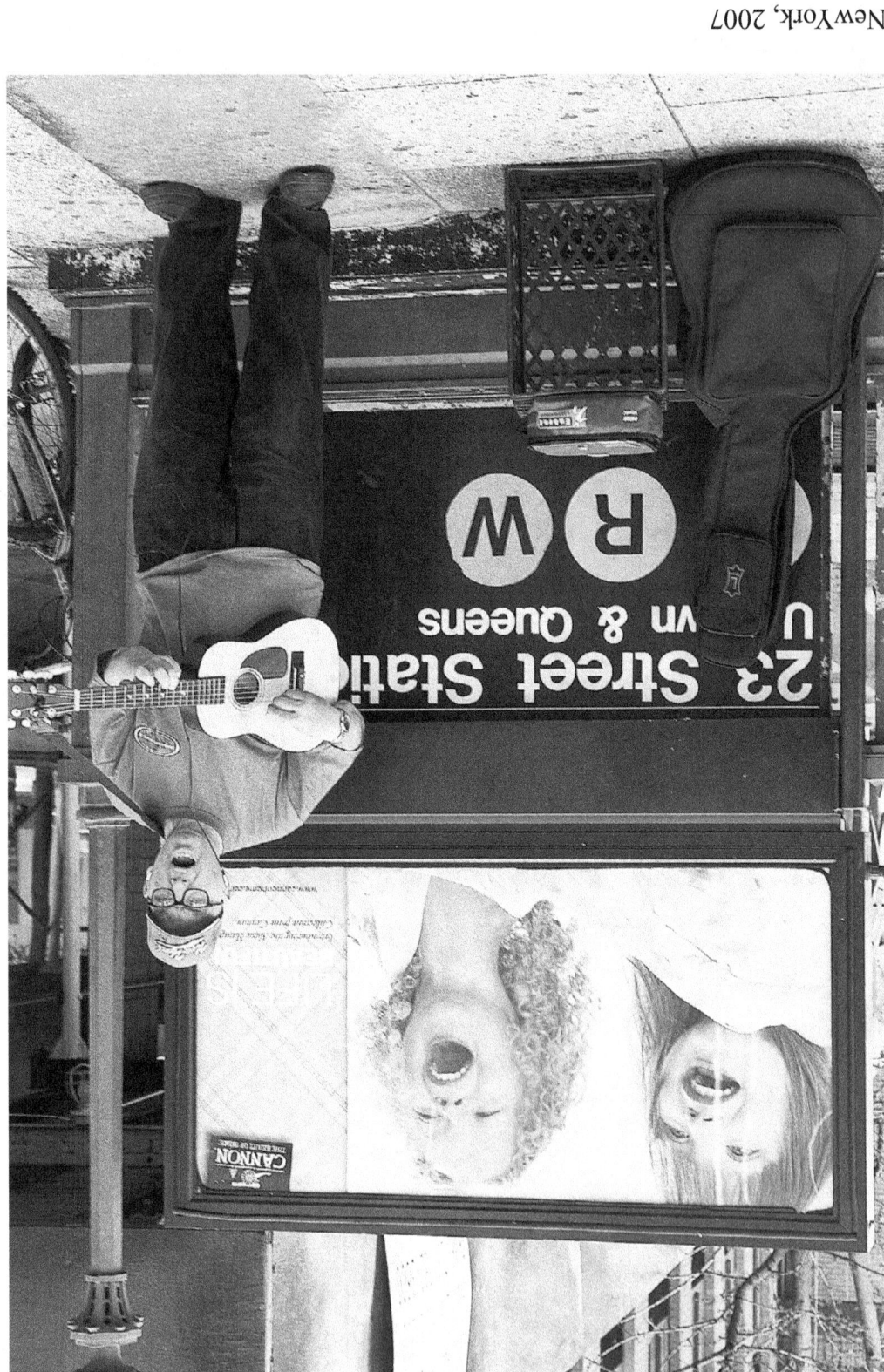

New York, 2007

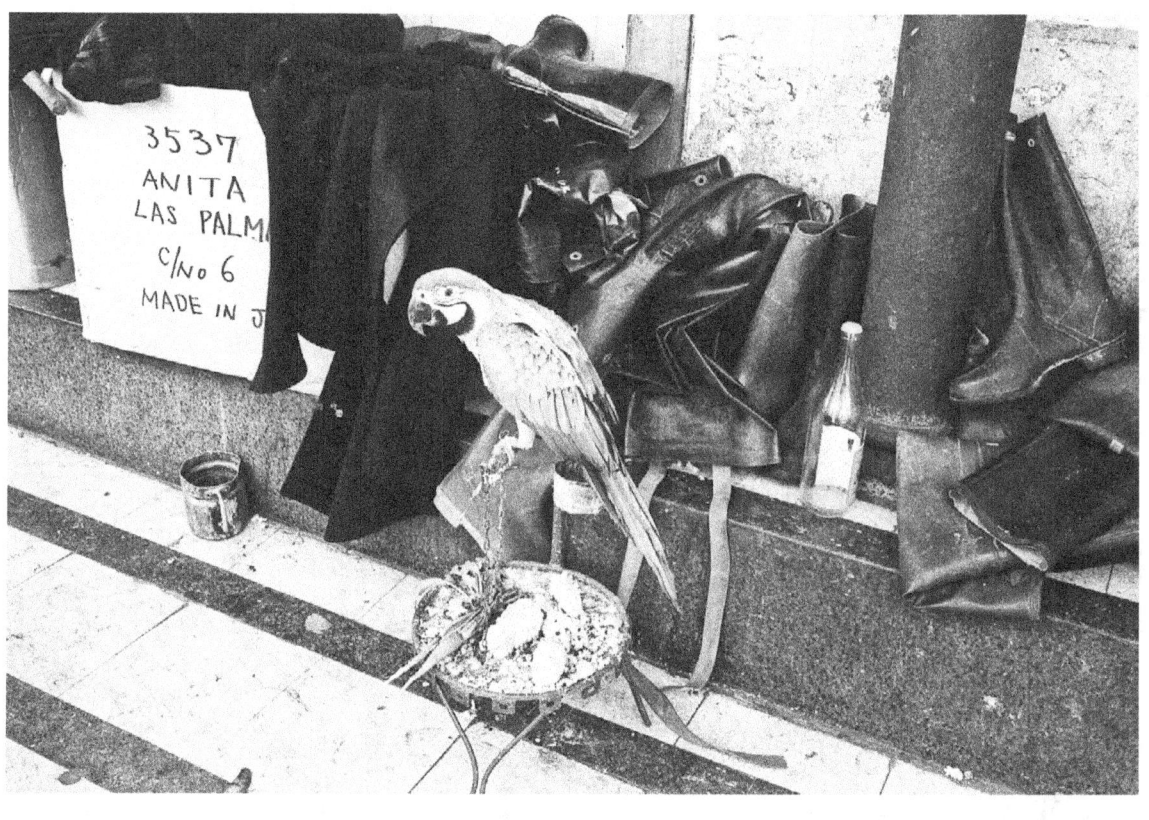

Las Palmas, Grand Canaria, Spain, 1968

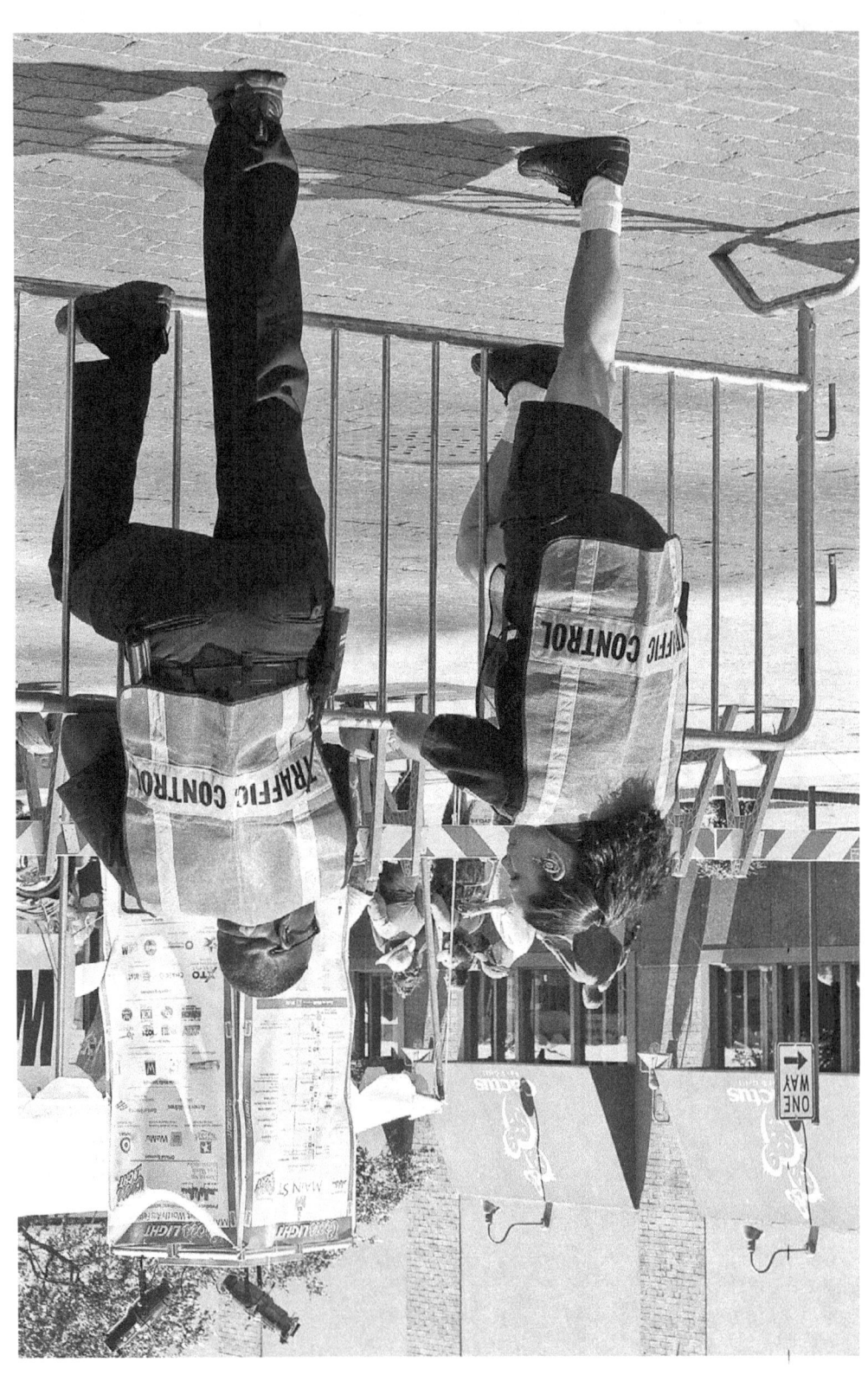

Fort Worth, Texas, 2007

Mammoth, Arizona, 2003

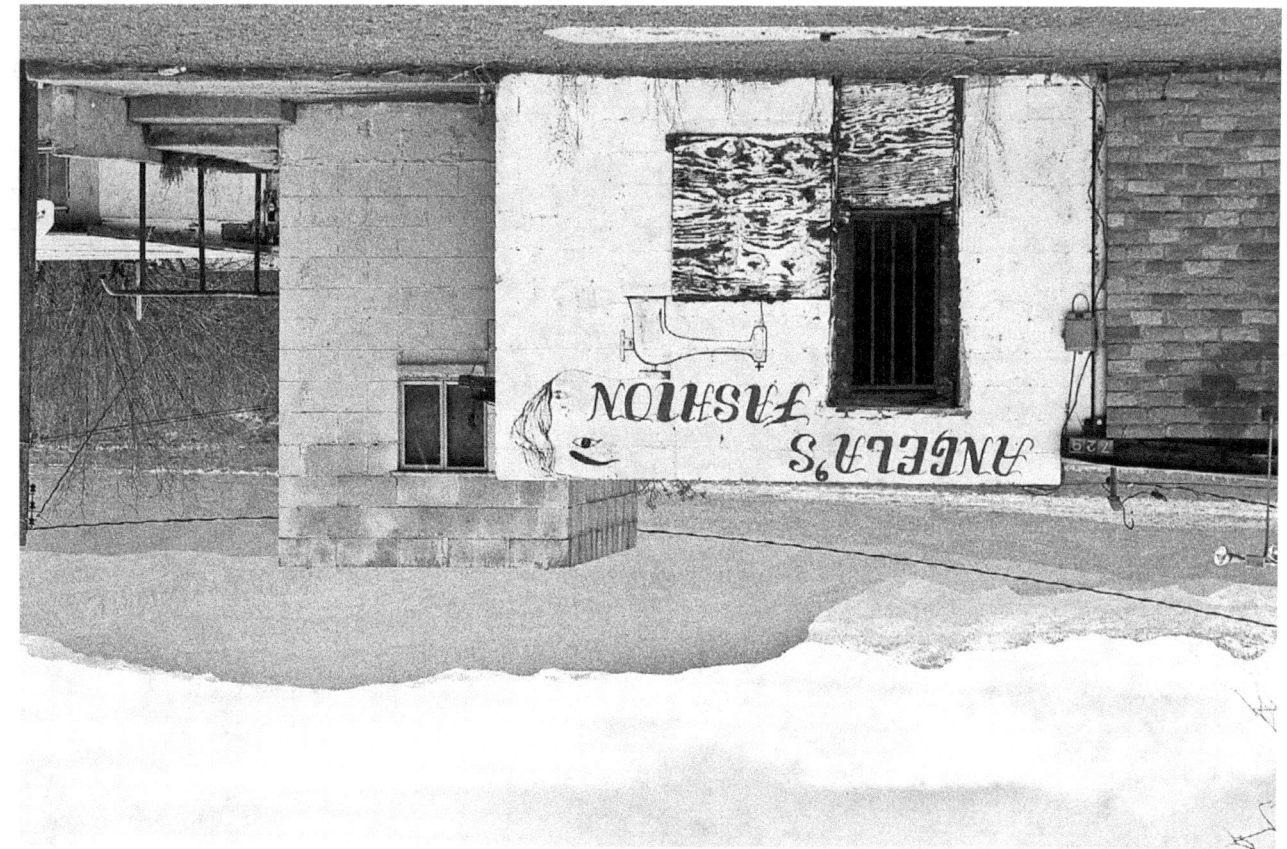

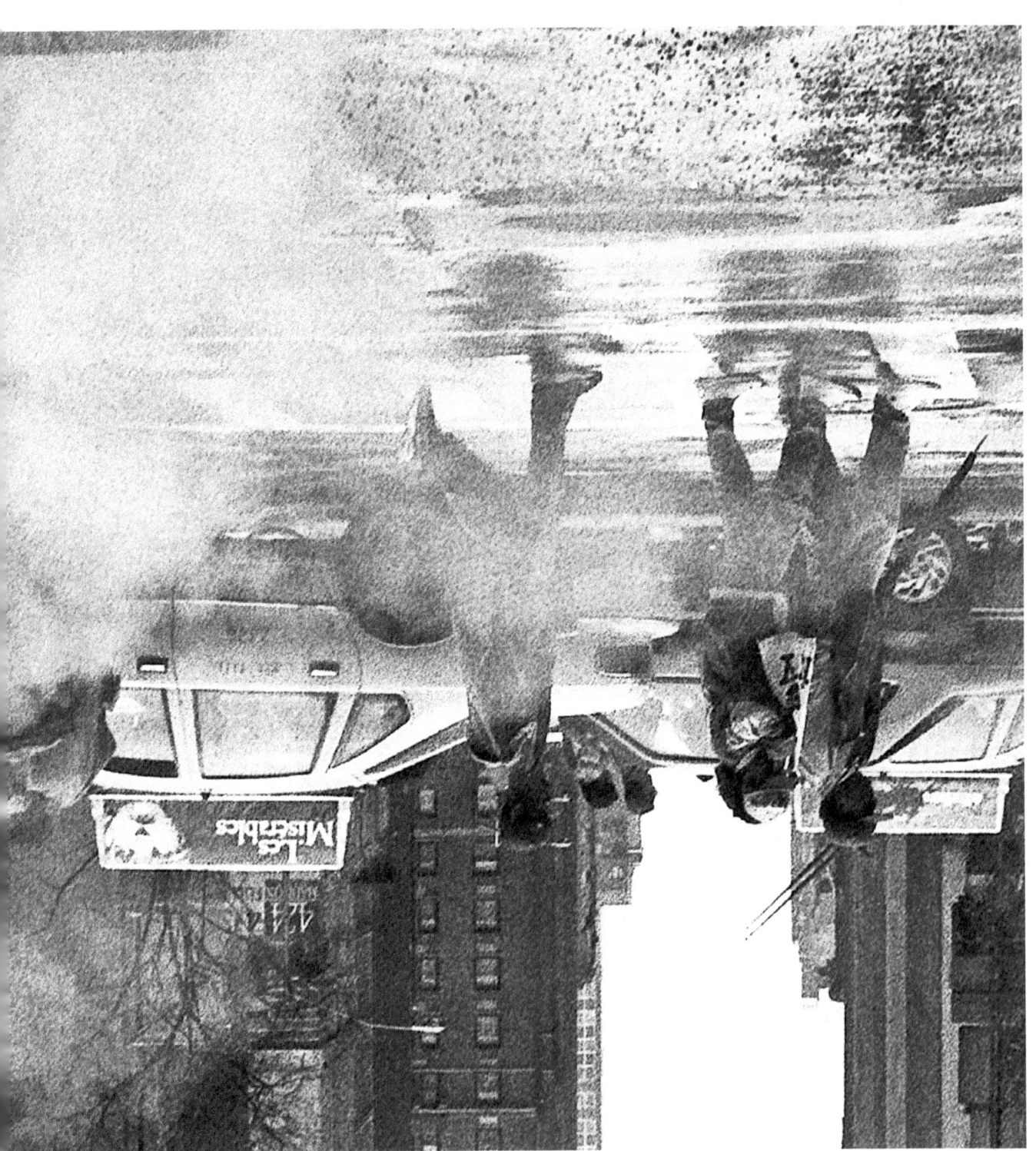

New York, 1998

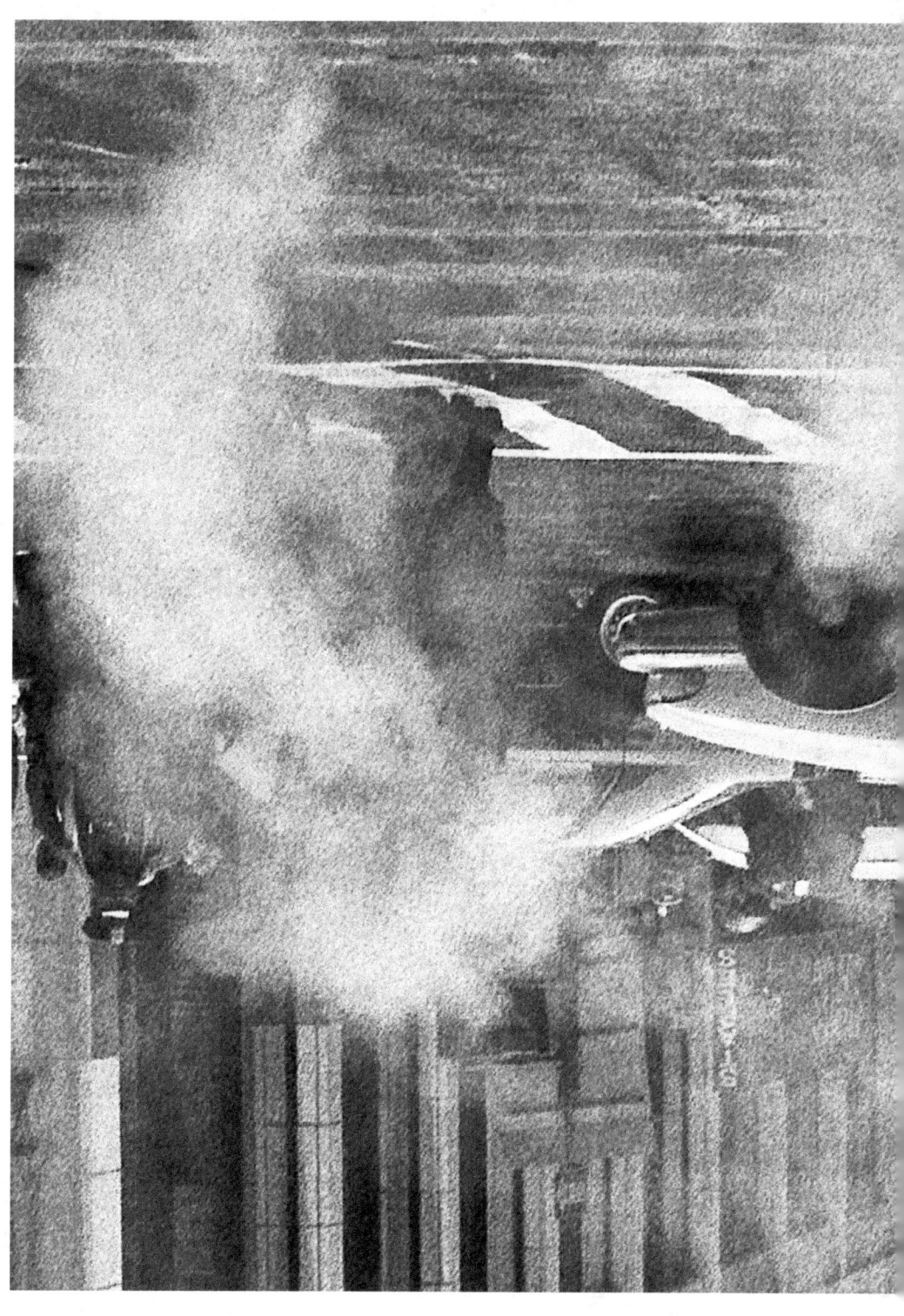

Plage de Pero, Corsica, 2000

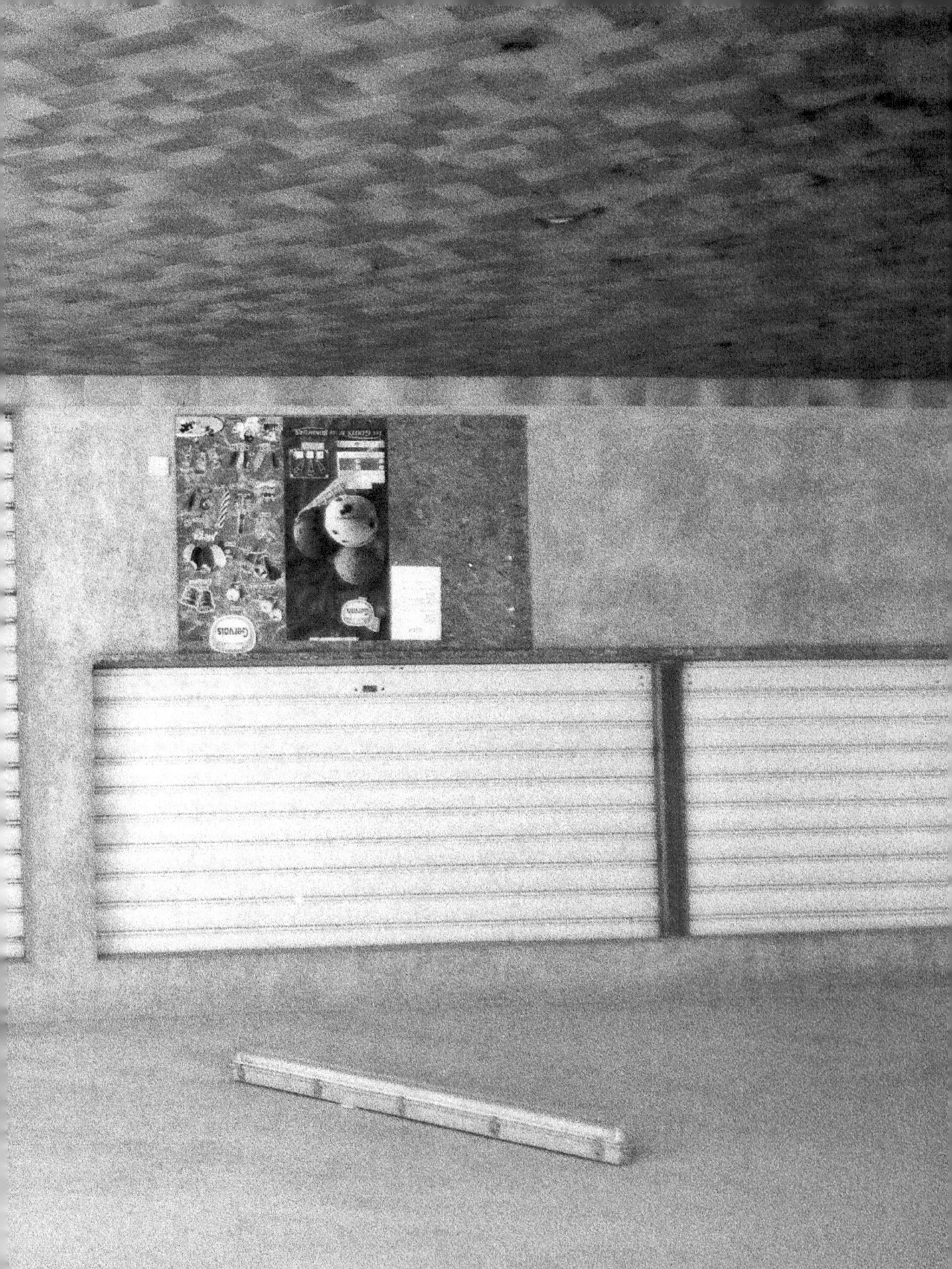

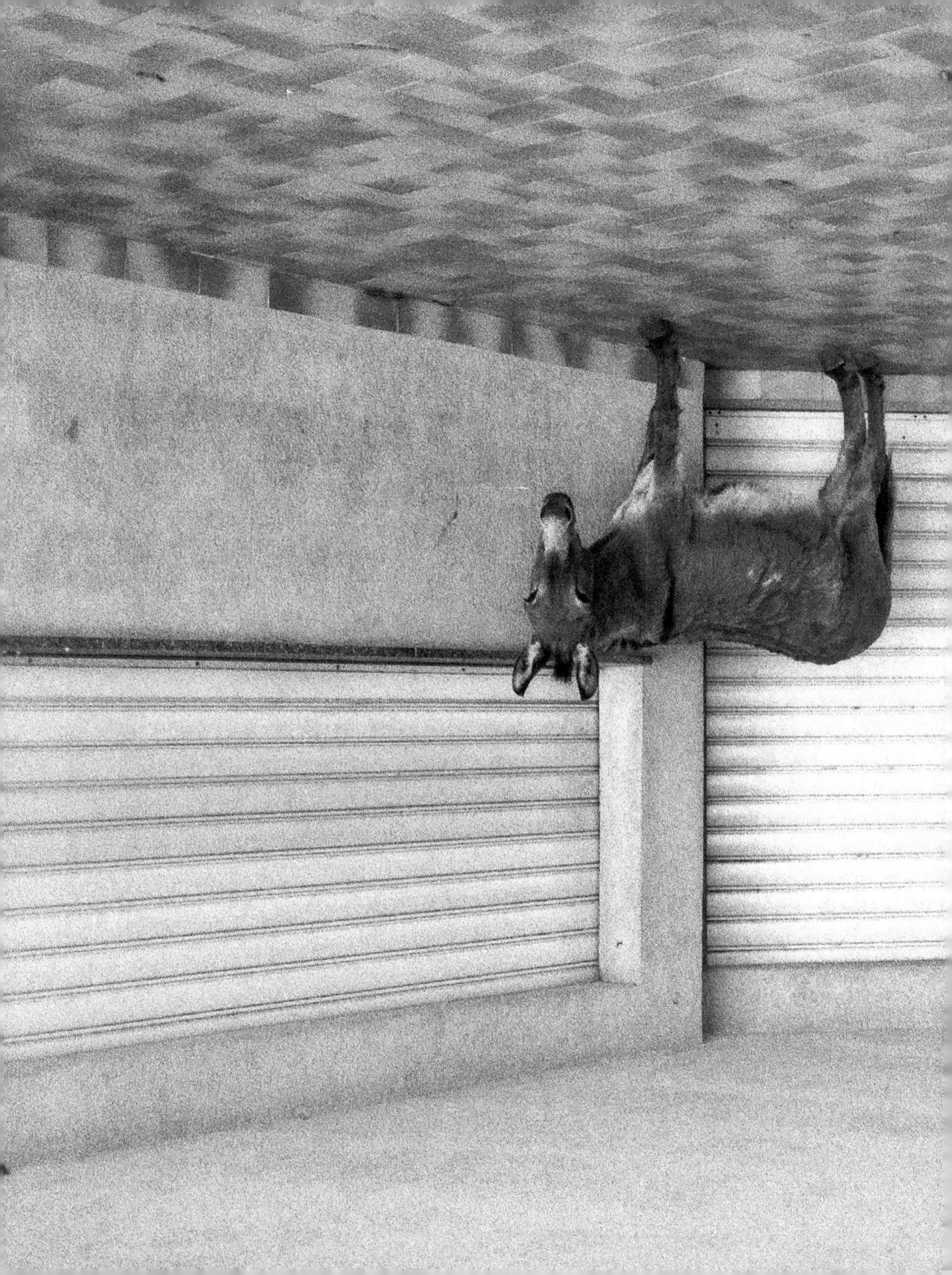

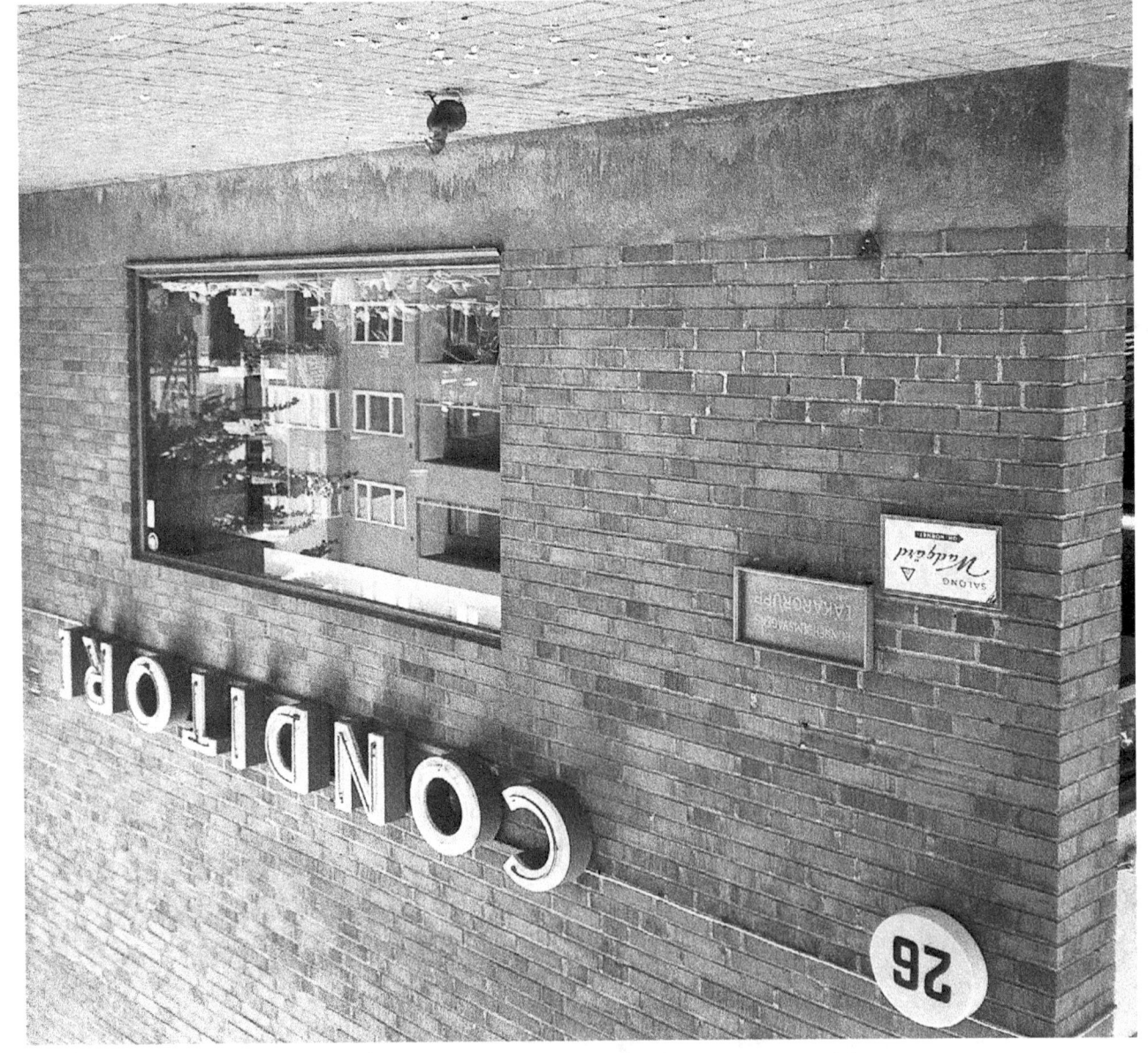

Malmö, Sweden, 1994

Chicago, 1988

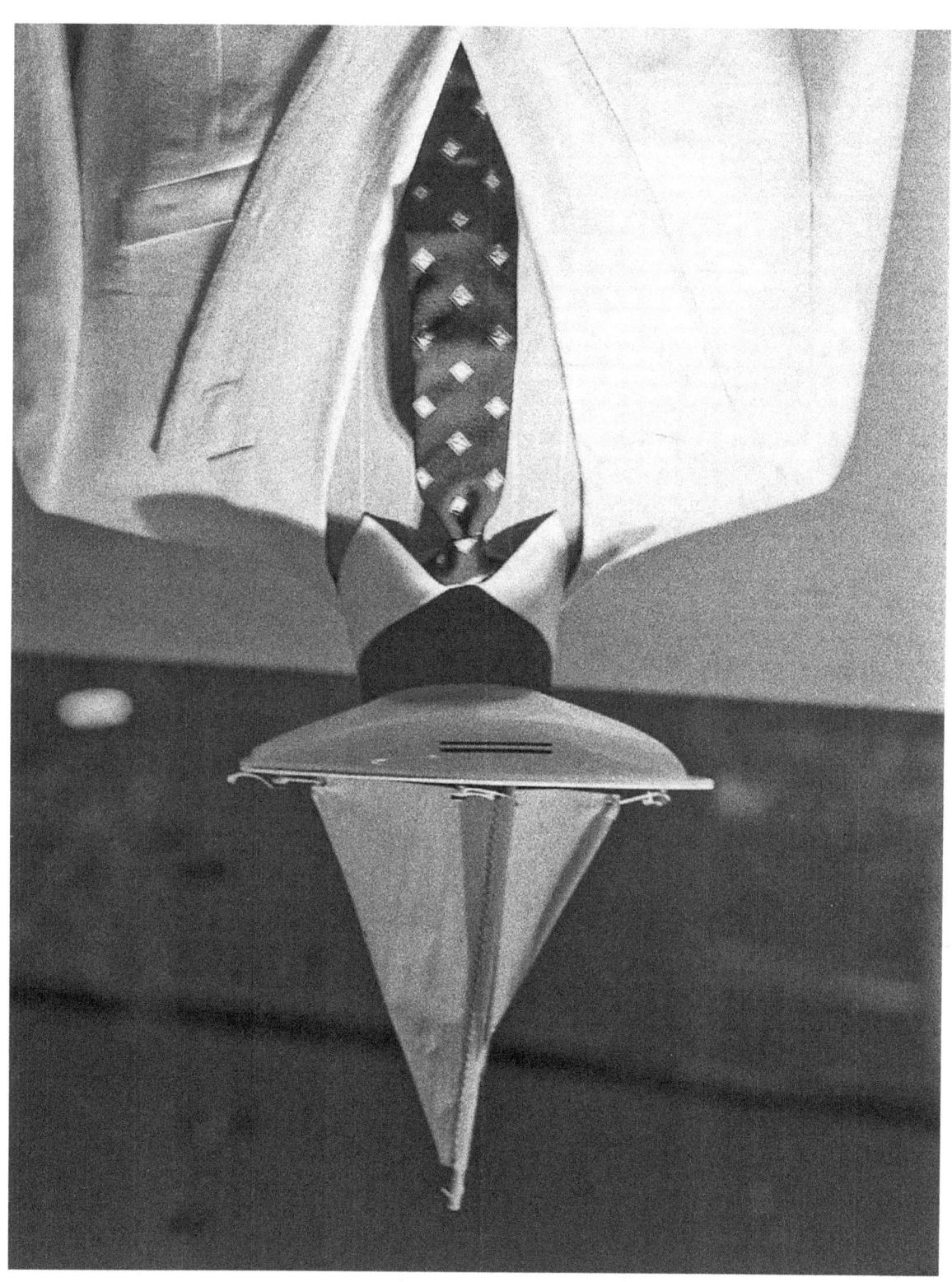

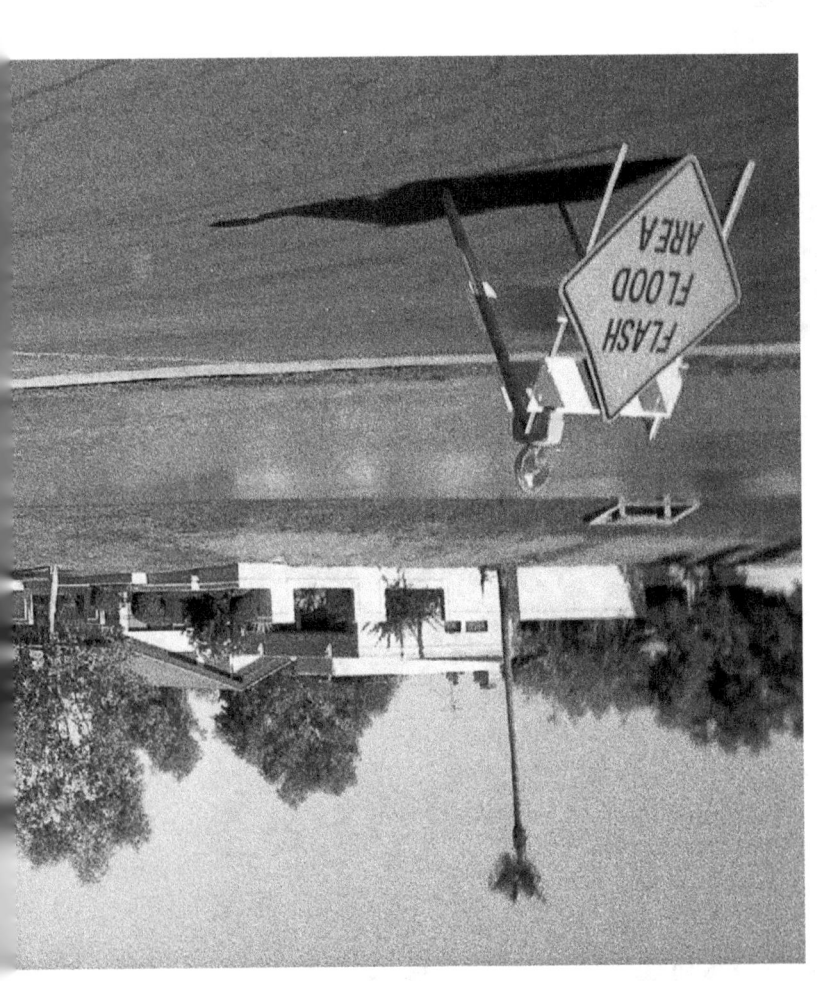

Phoenix, Arizona, 1990

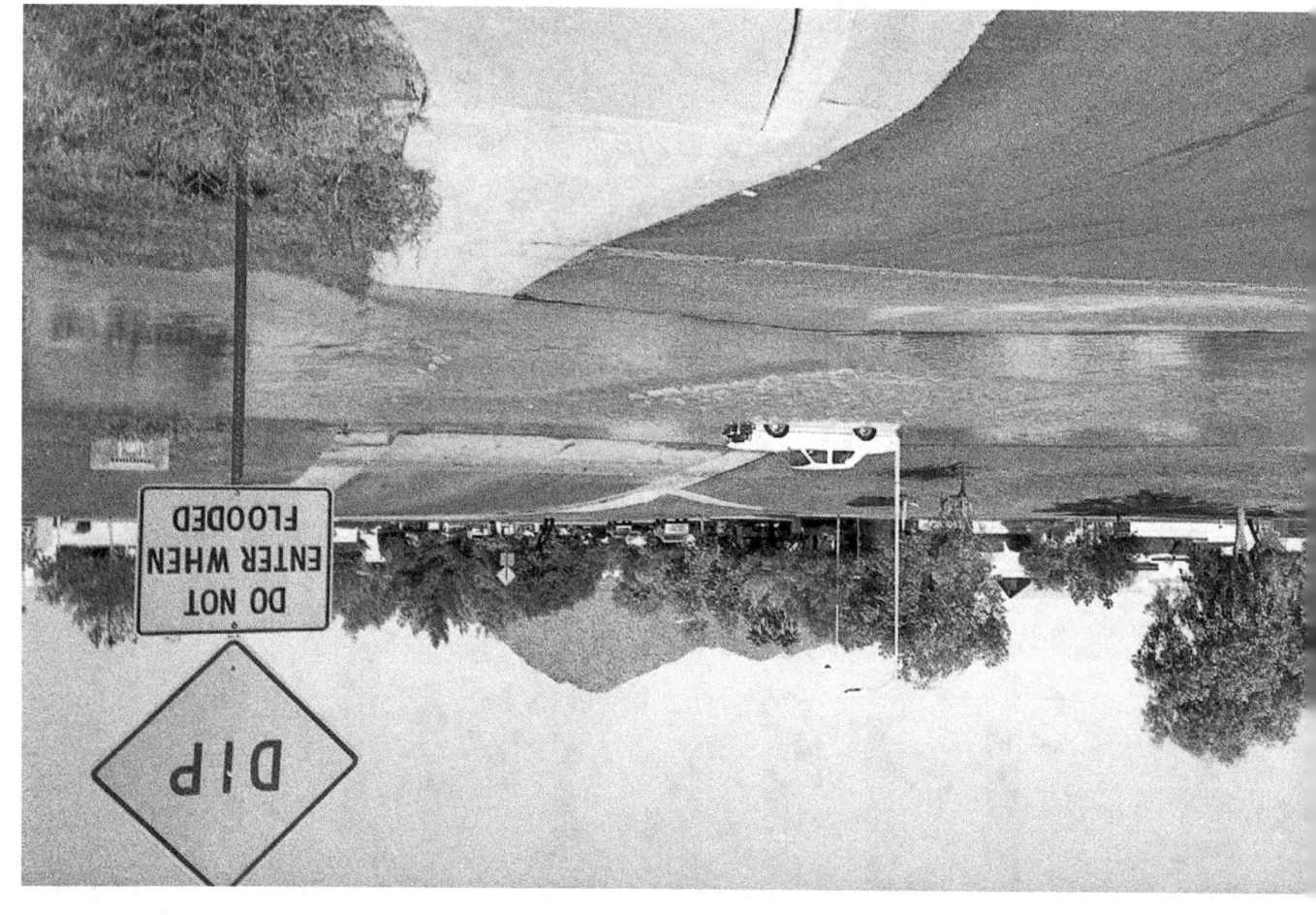

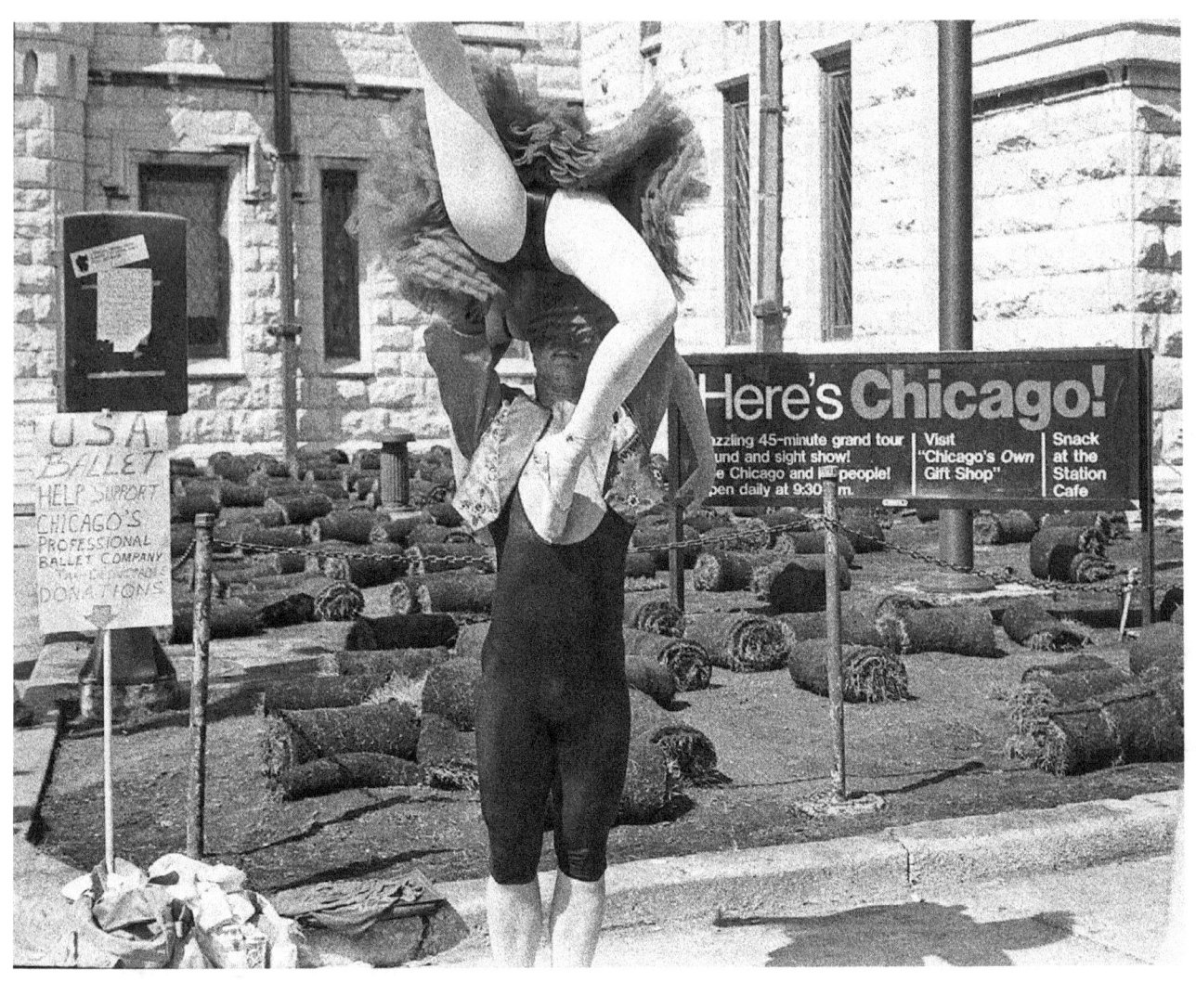

Chicago, 1988

Tokyo, 1988

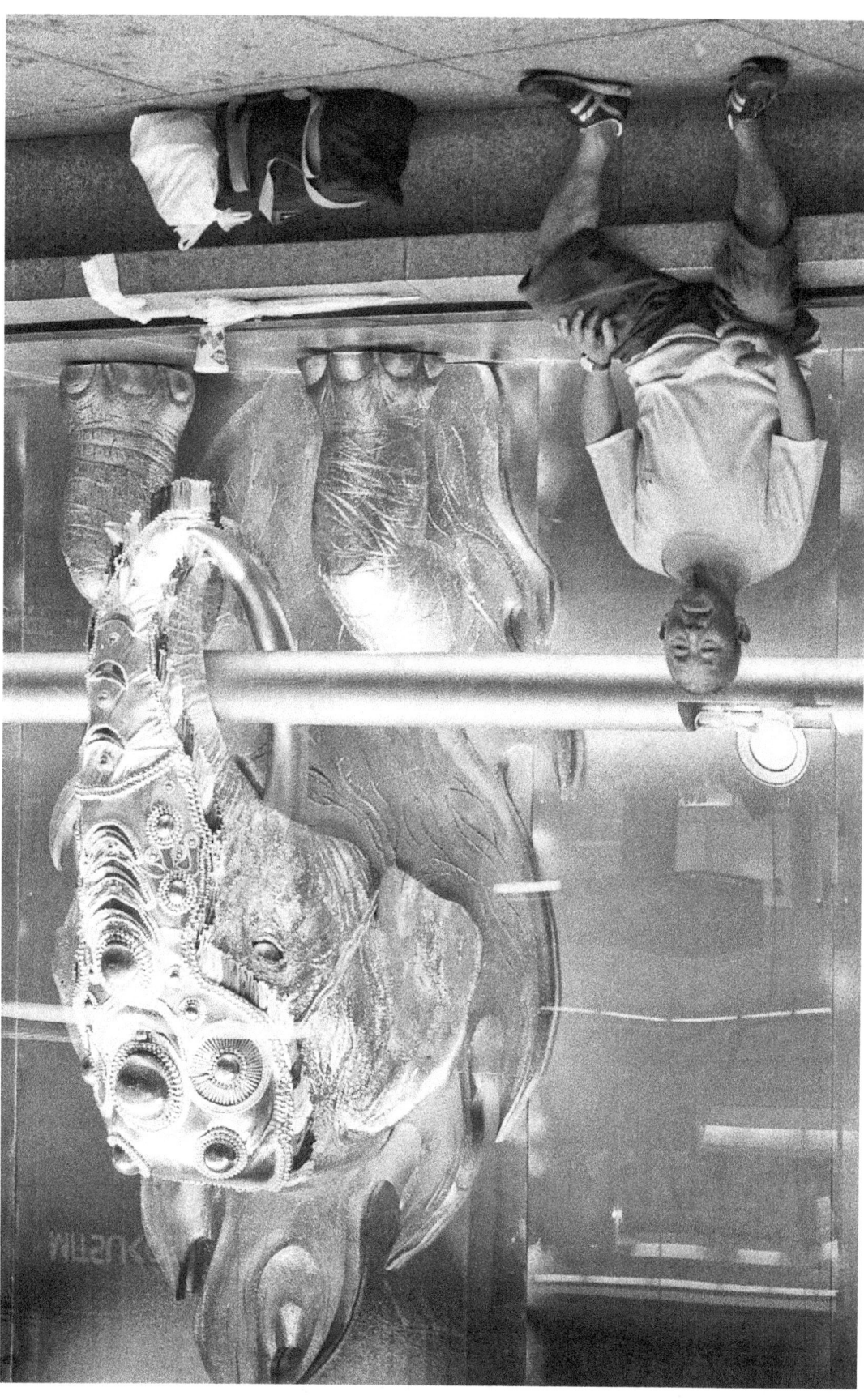

Stockholm, Sweden, 2008

Sidney, 1988

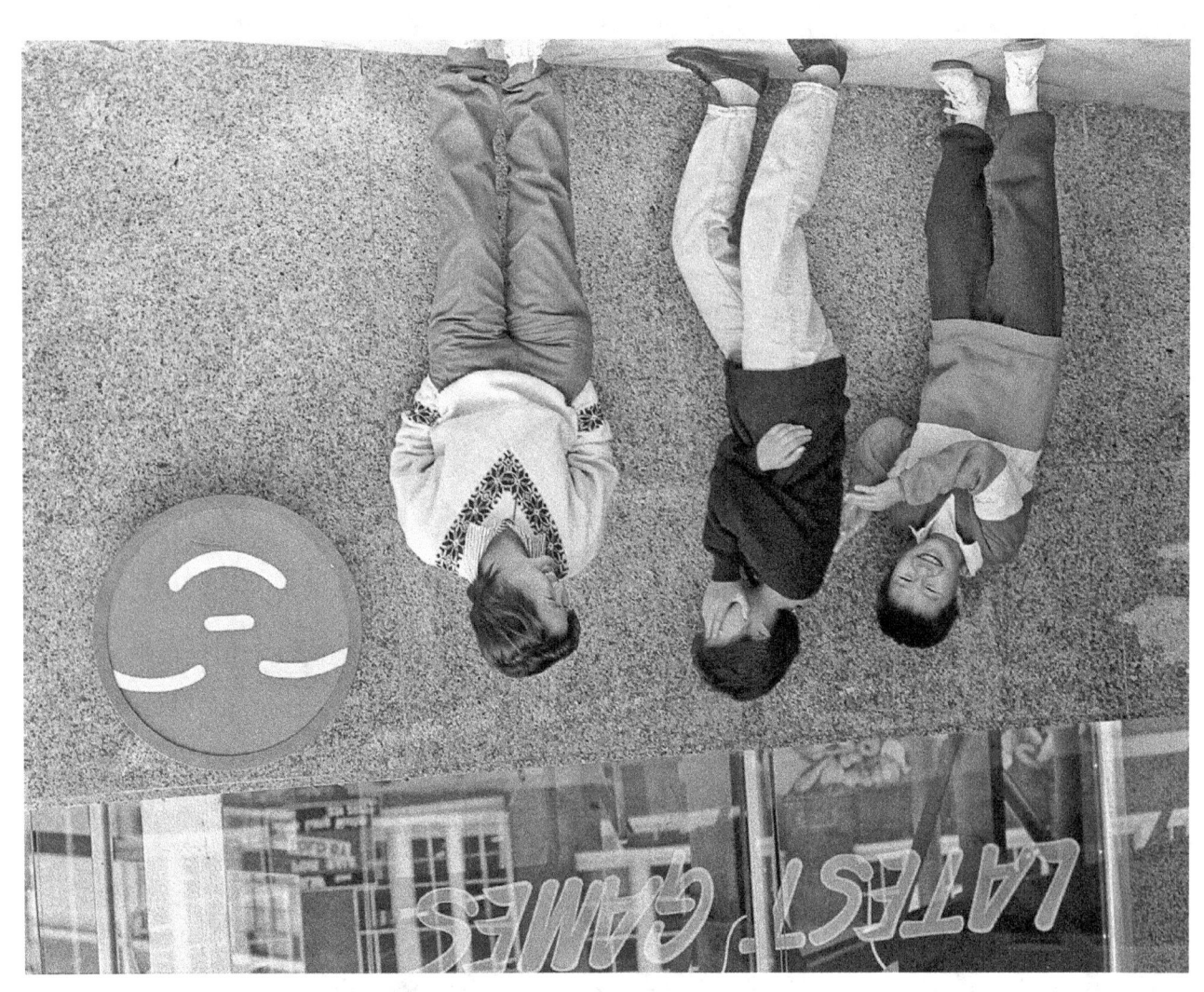

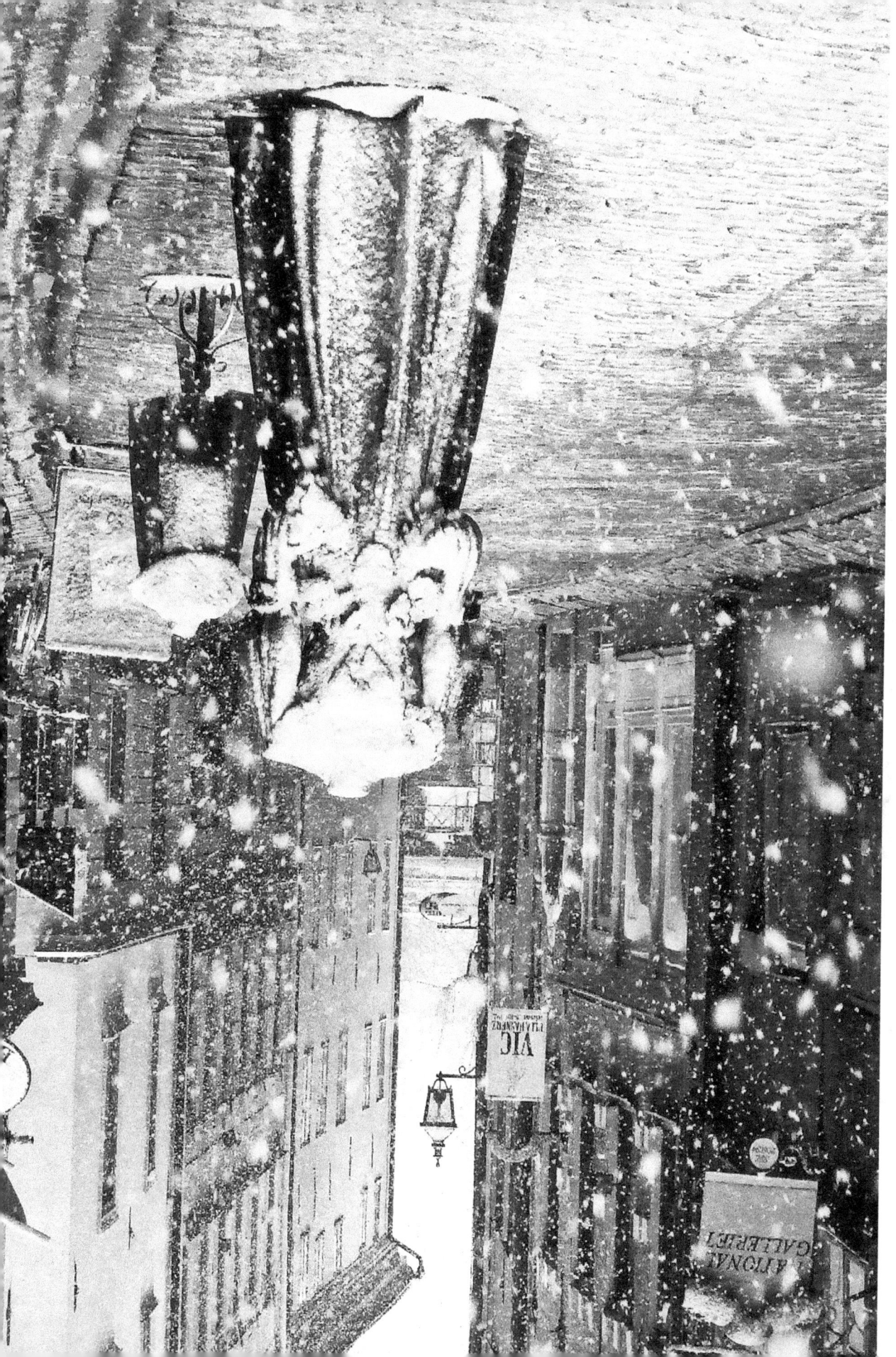

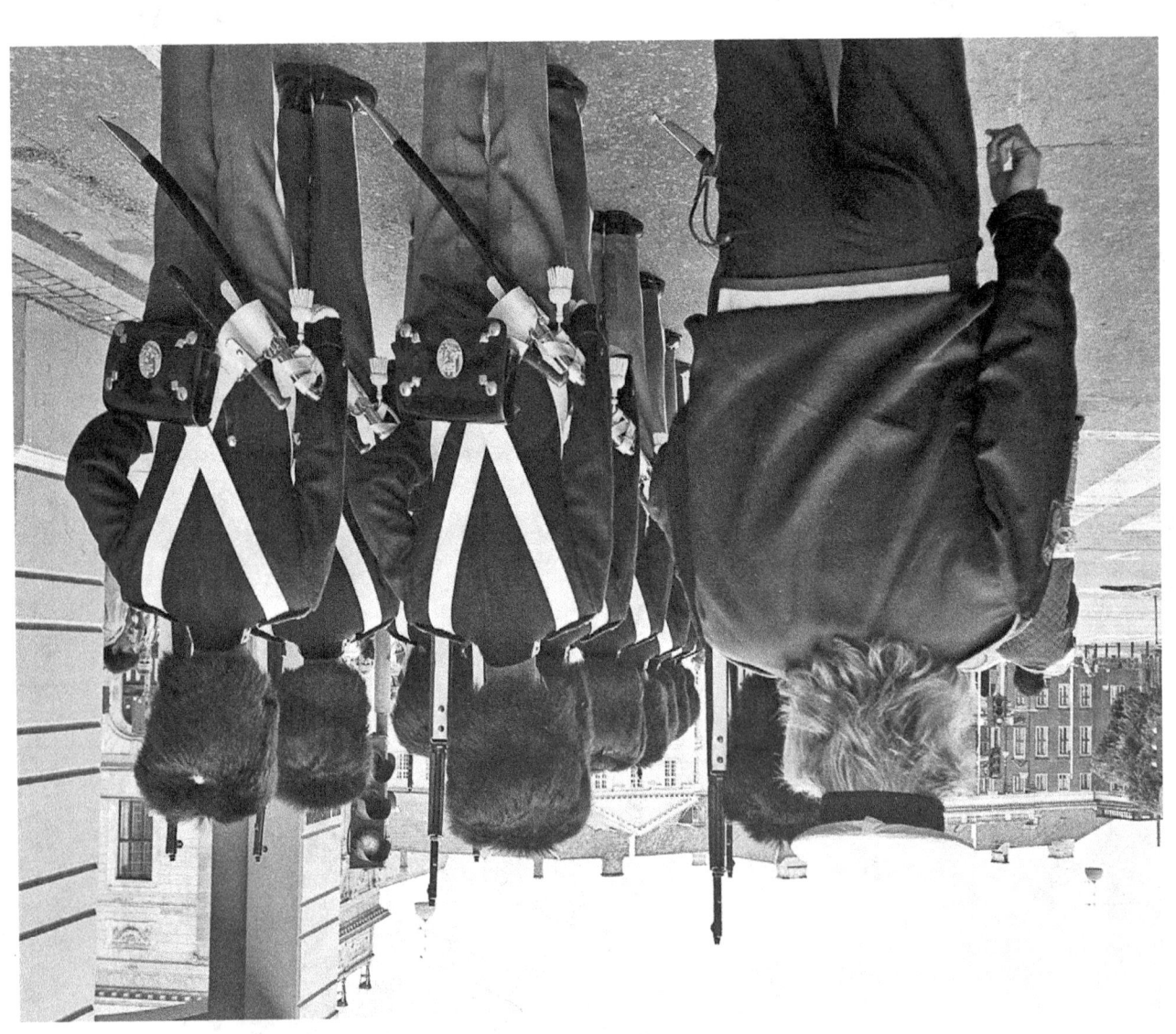

Copenhagen, Denmark, 1995

Kamloops, Canada, 2001

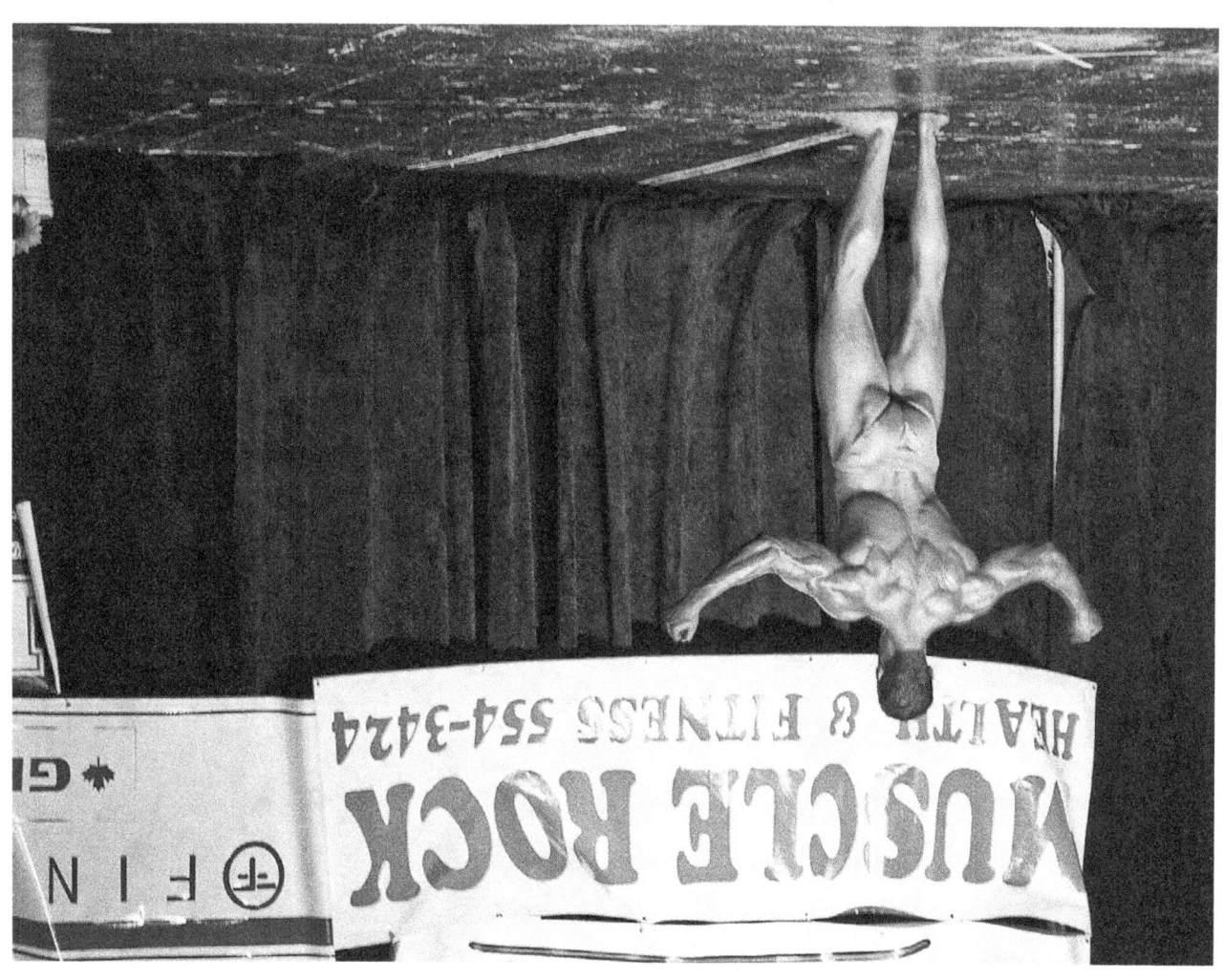

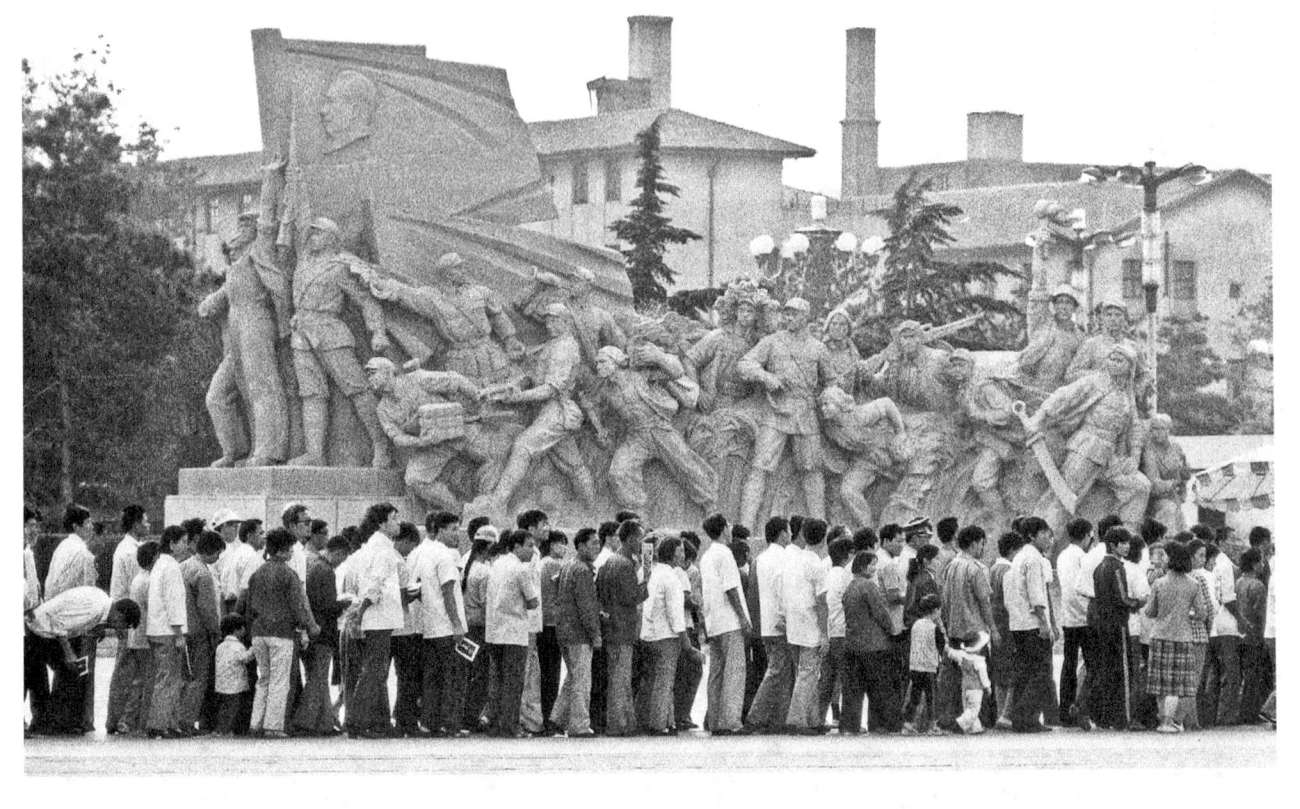

Bejing, 1986

Corsica, France, 2000

BOCCA À SEVE

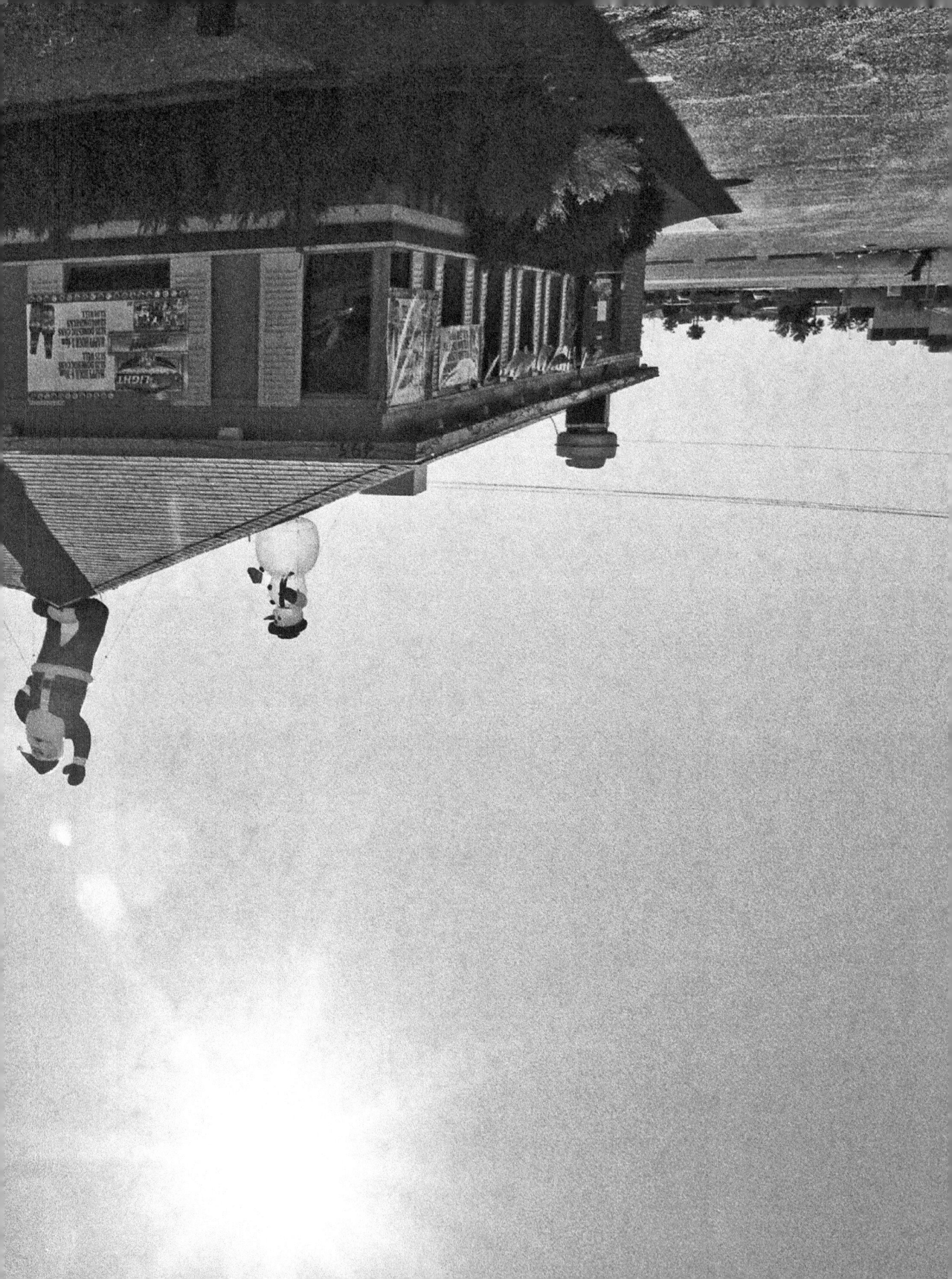

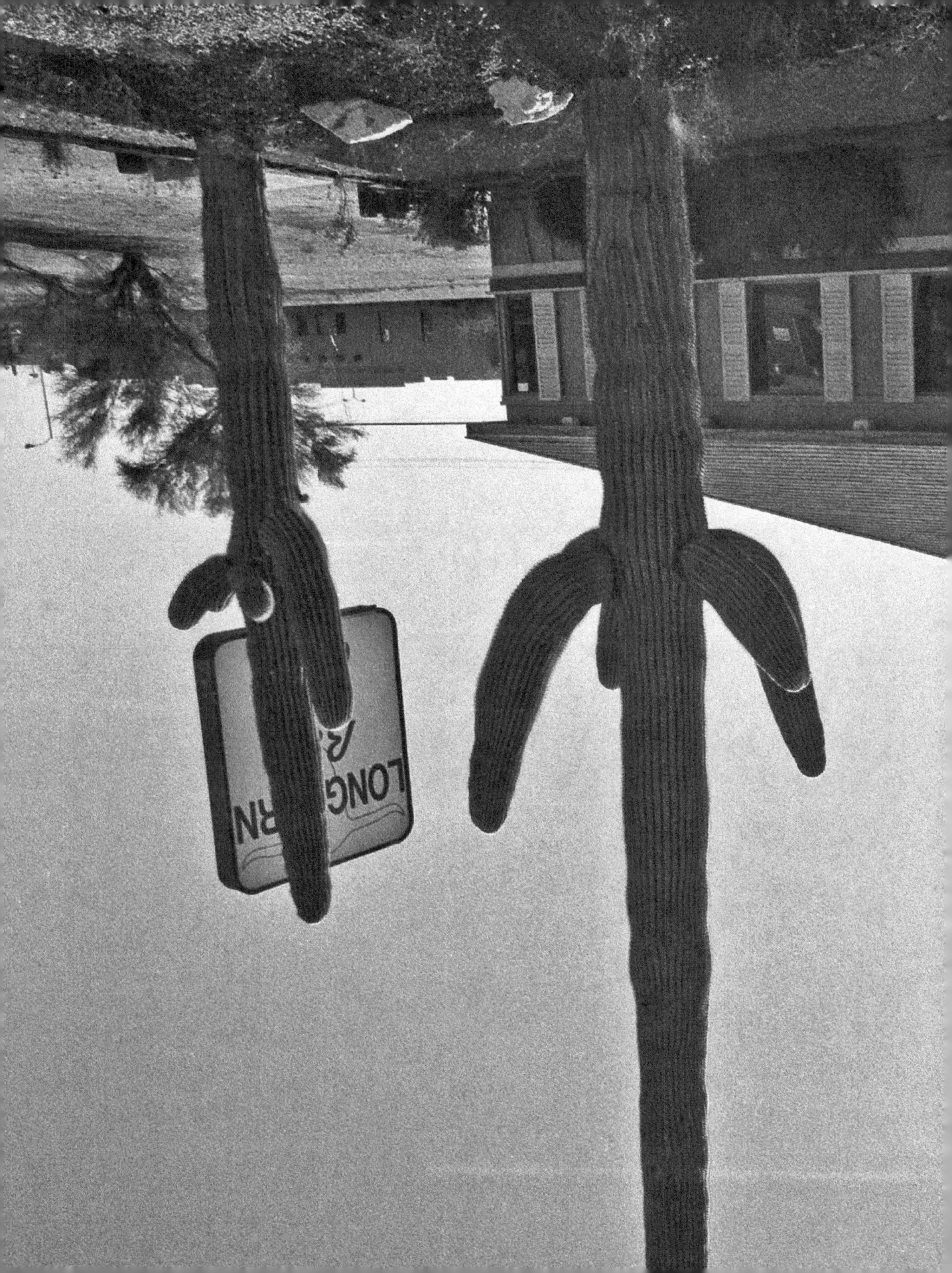

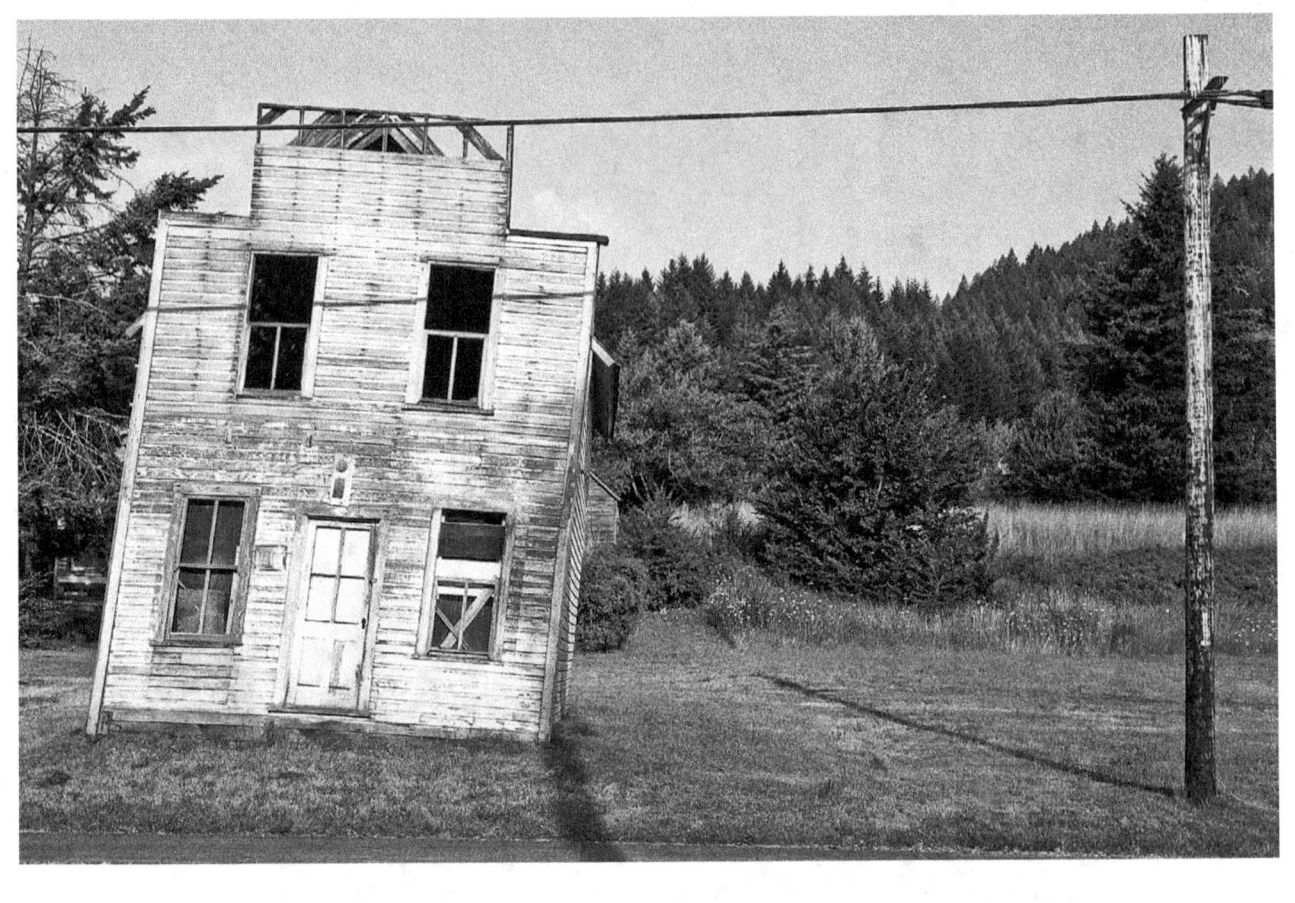

Carson, Washington, 1999

Apache Junction, Arizona, 2002

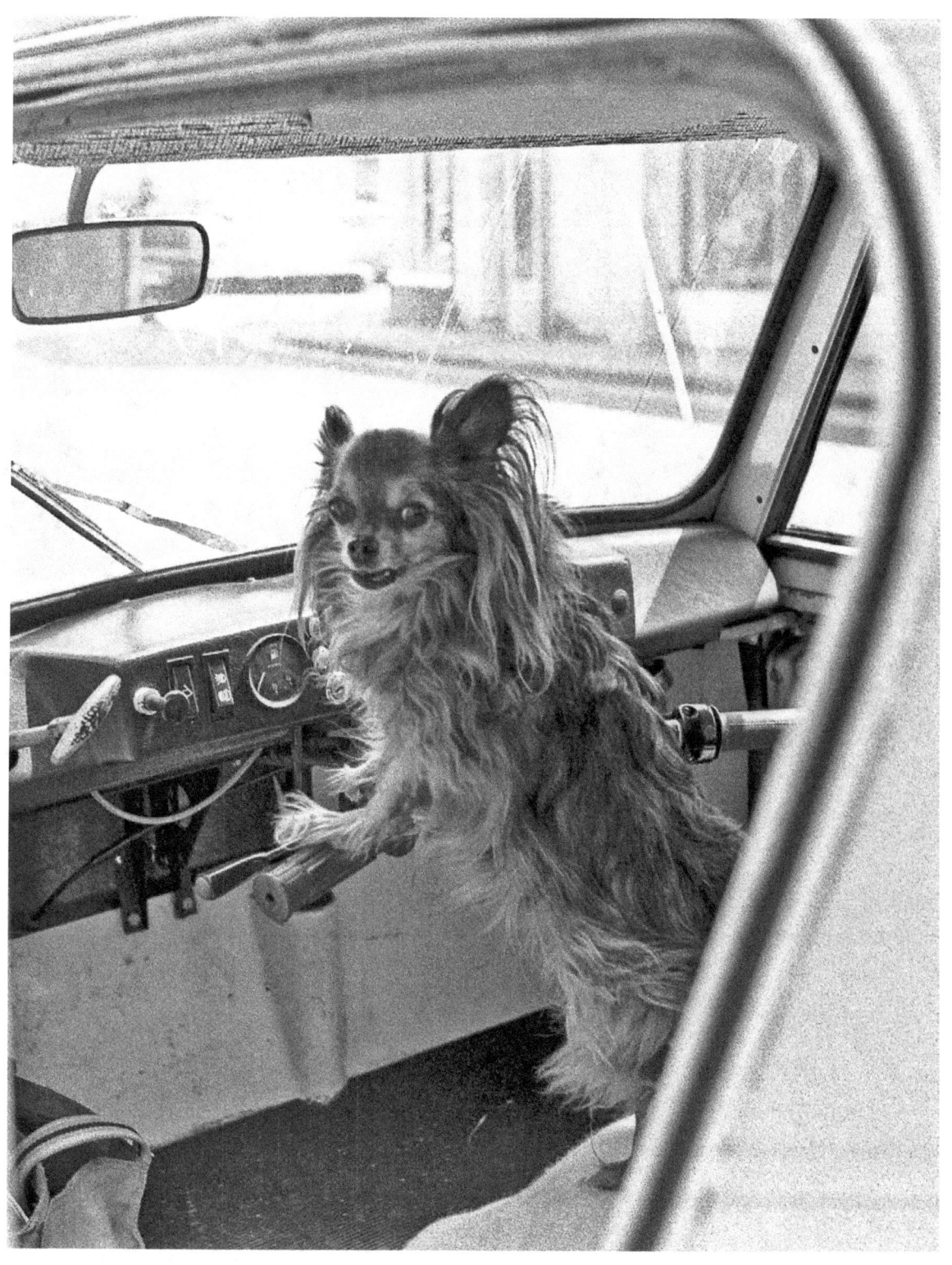

Penzance Cornwall, 1992

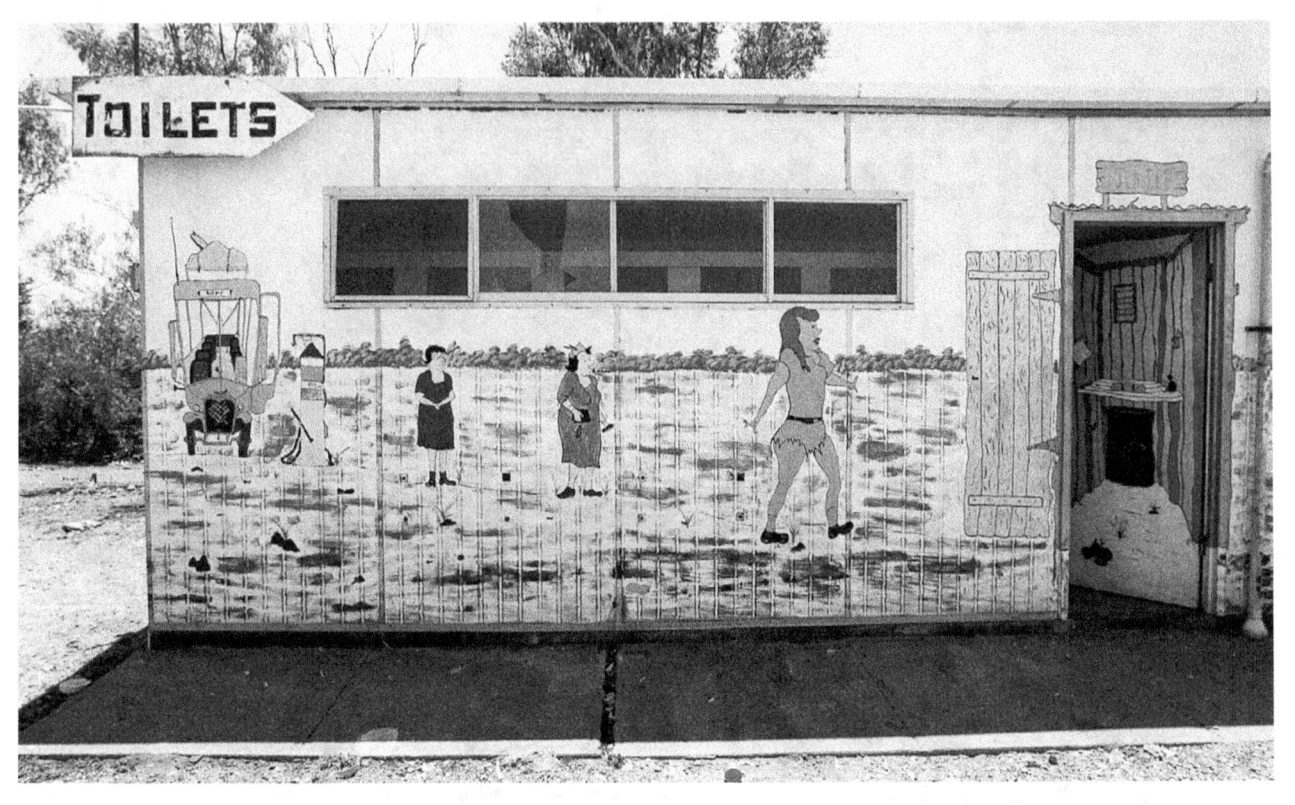

Alice Spring, Australia, 1996

New York, 2007

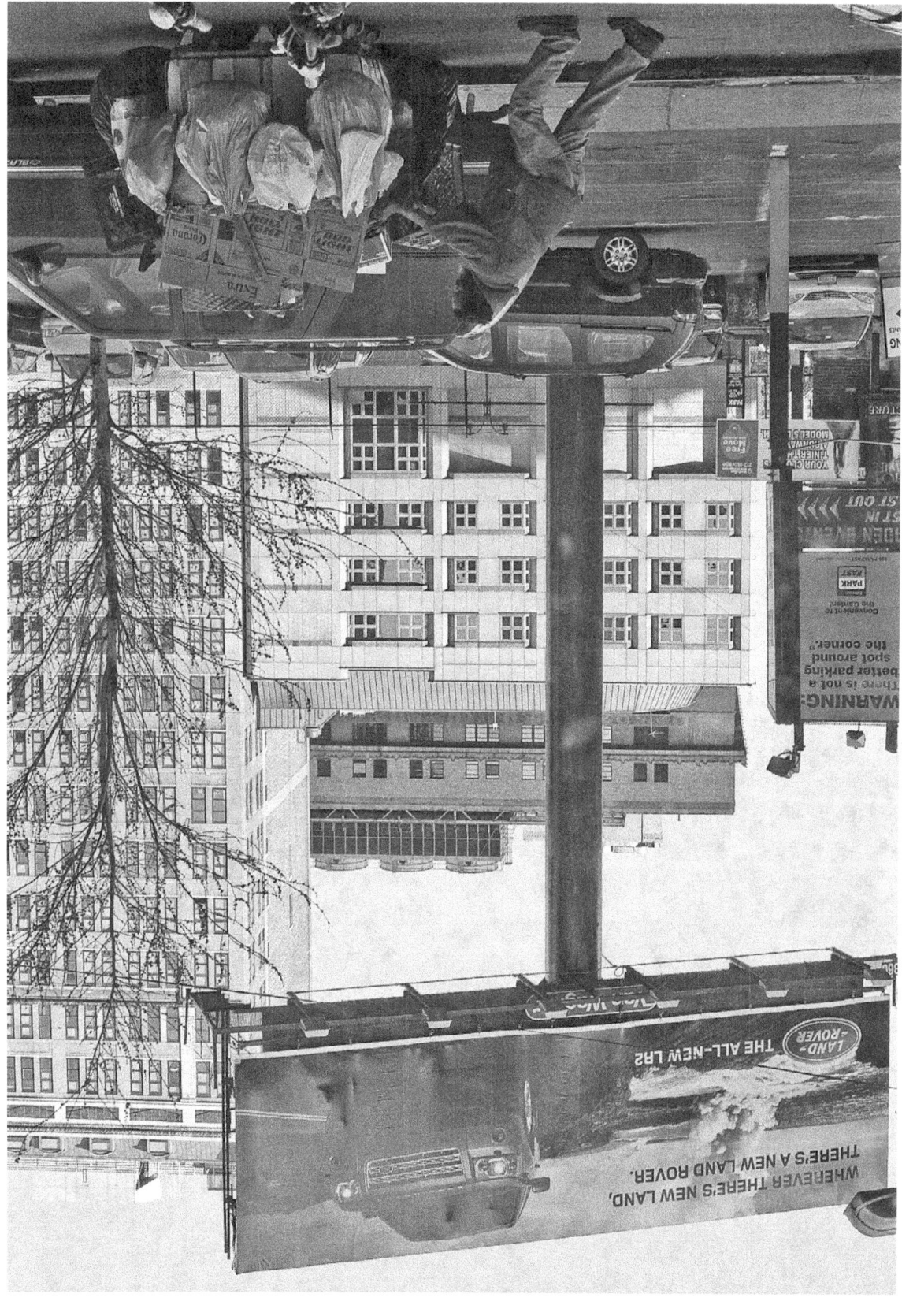

Eilat, Israel, 1999

Phoenix, Arizona, 1990

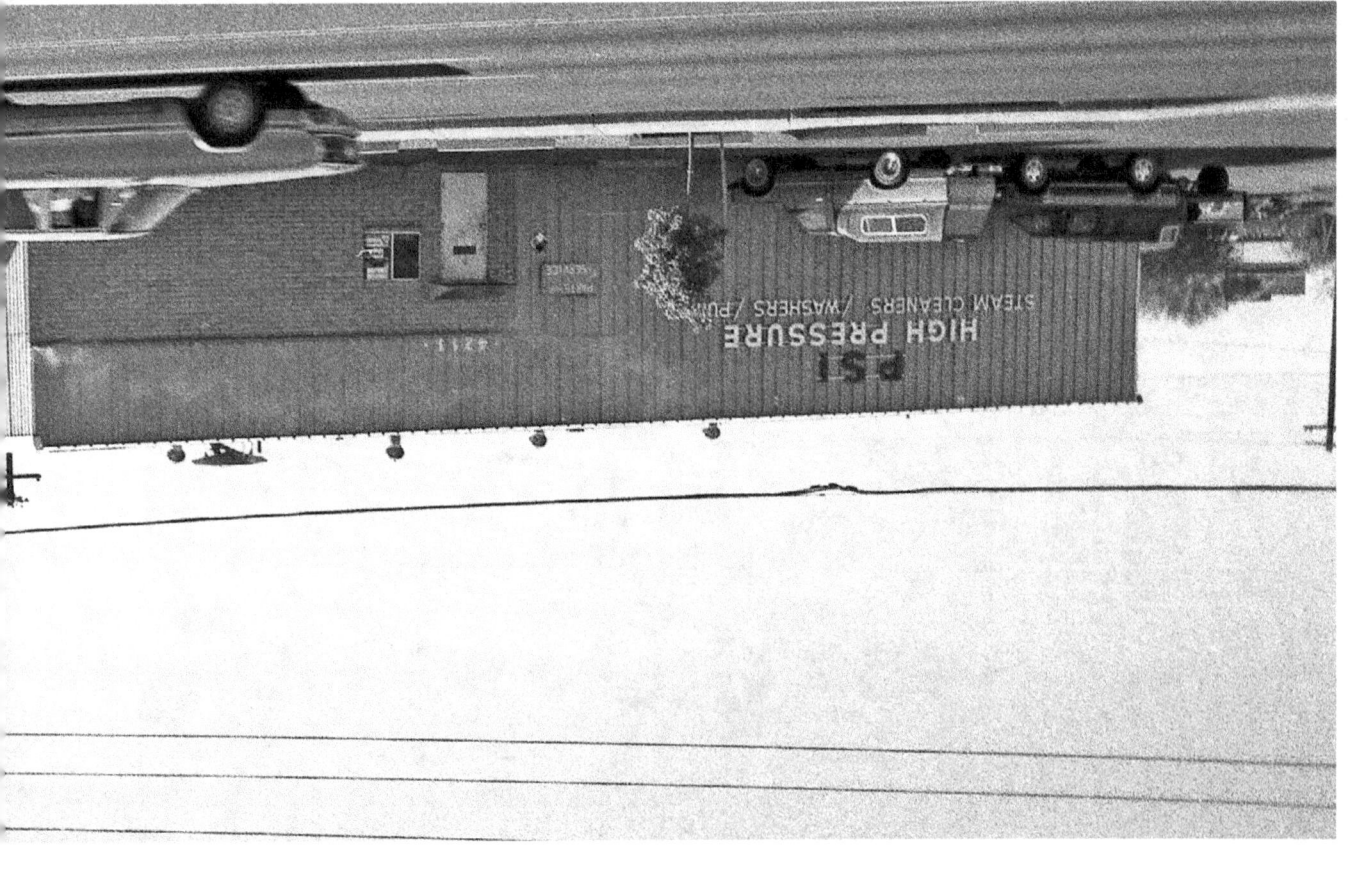

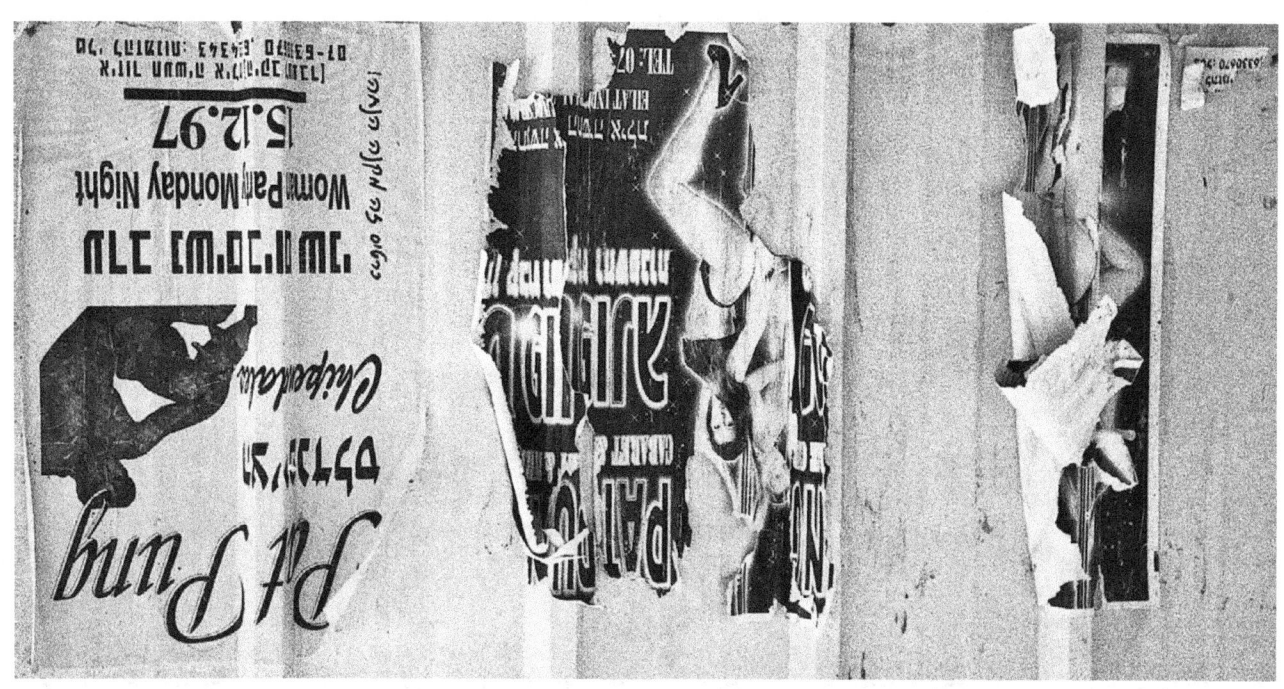

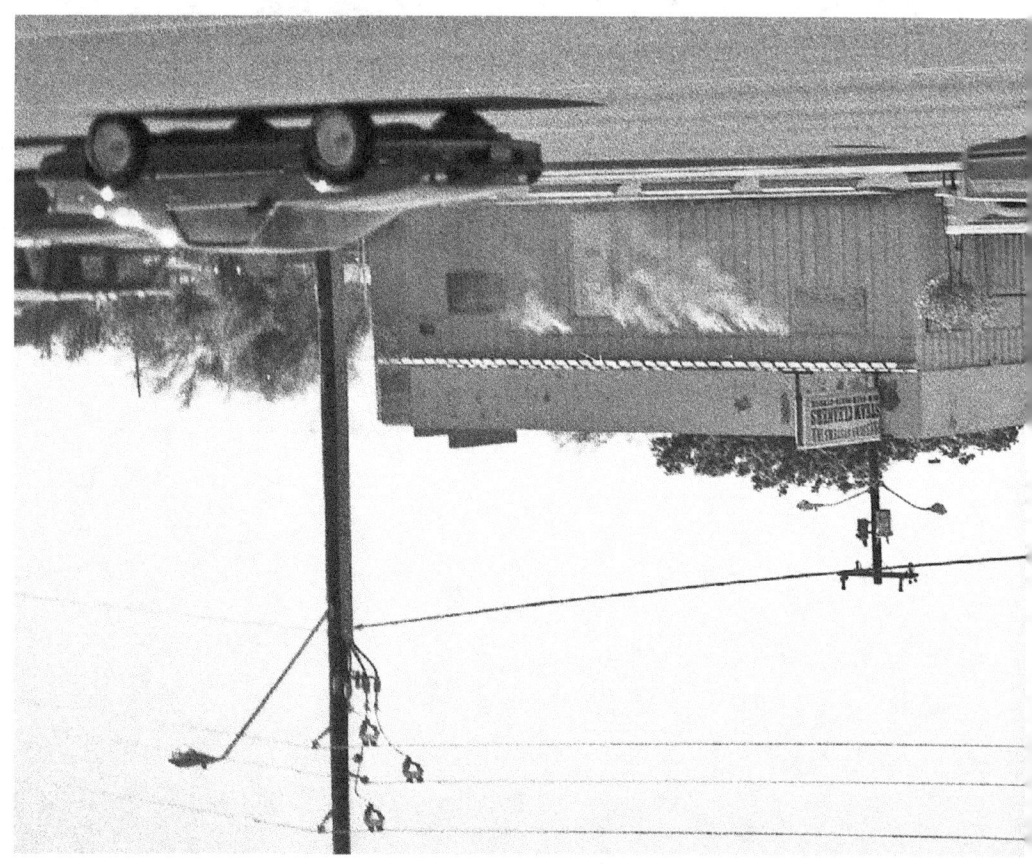

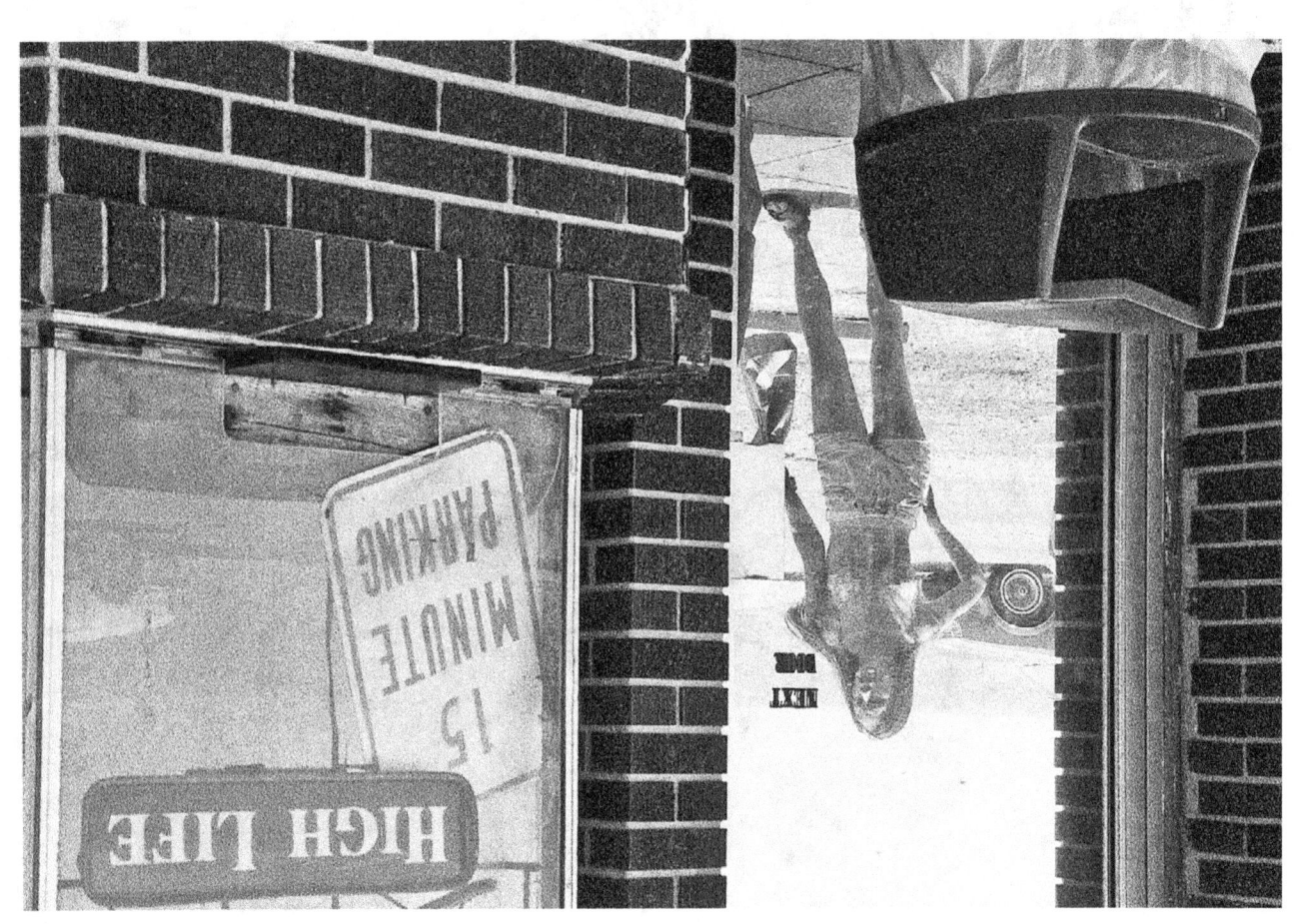

Gulfport, Mississippi, 1994

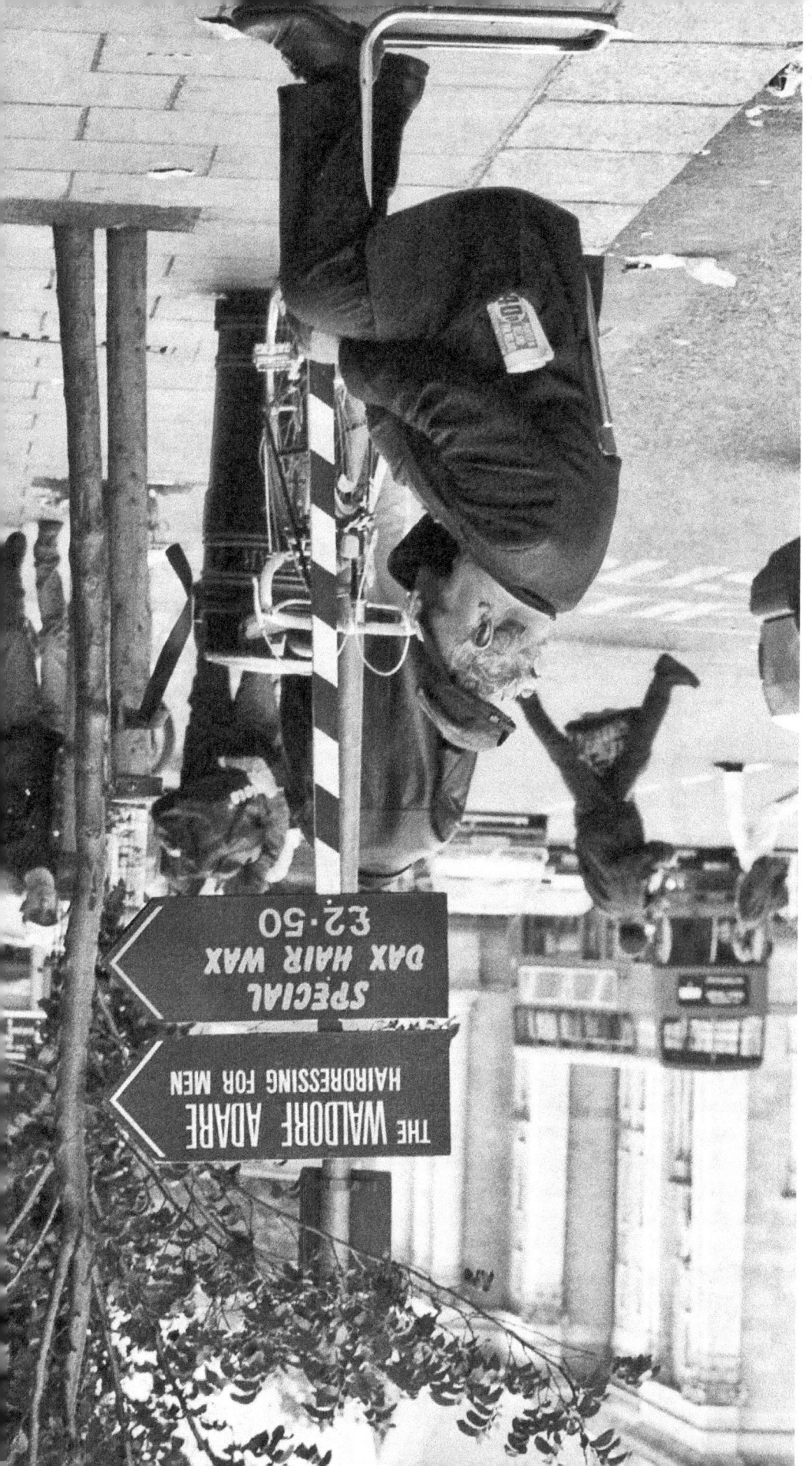

Dublin, Ireland, 1996

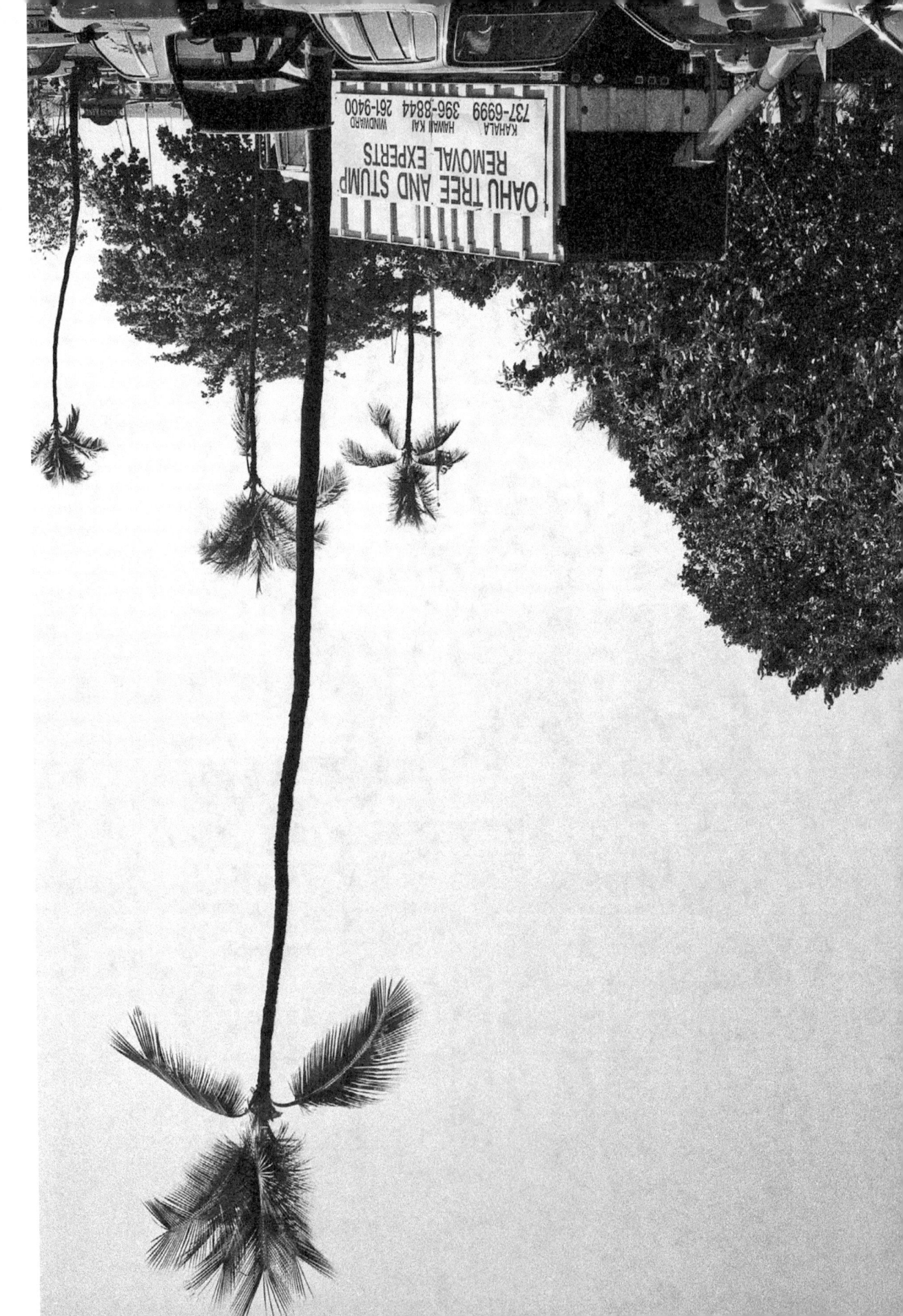

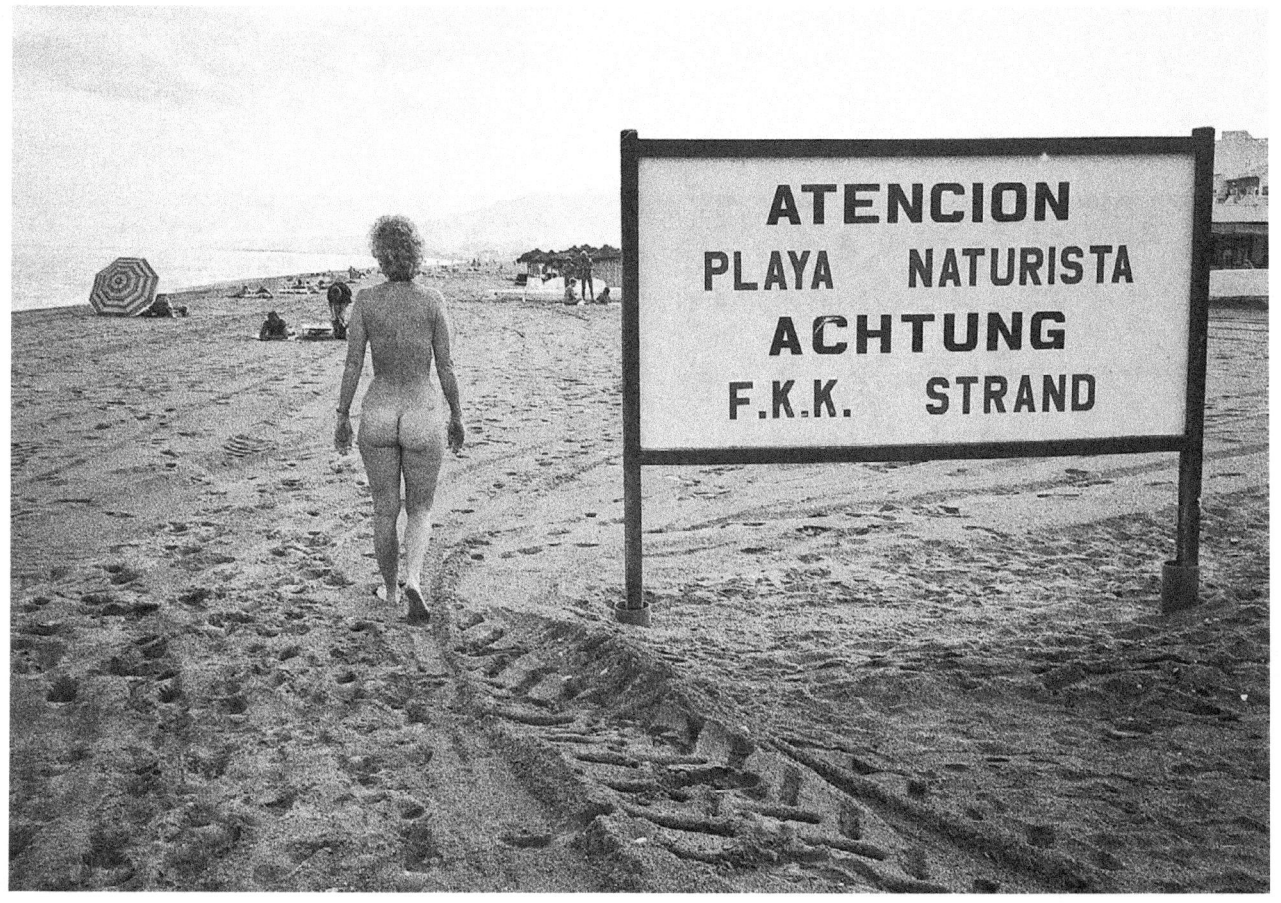

Playa Vera, Spain, 1992

Maui, Hawaii, 1994

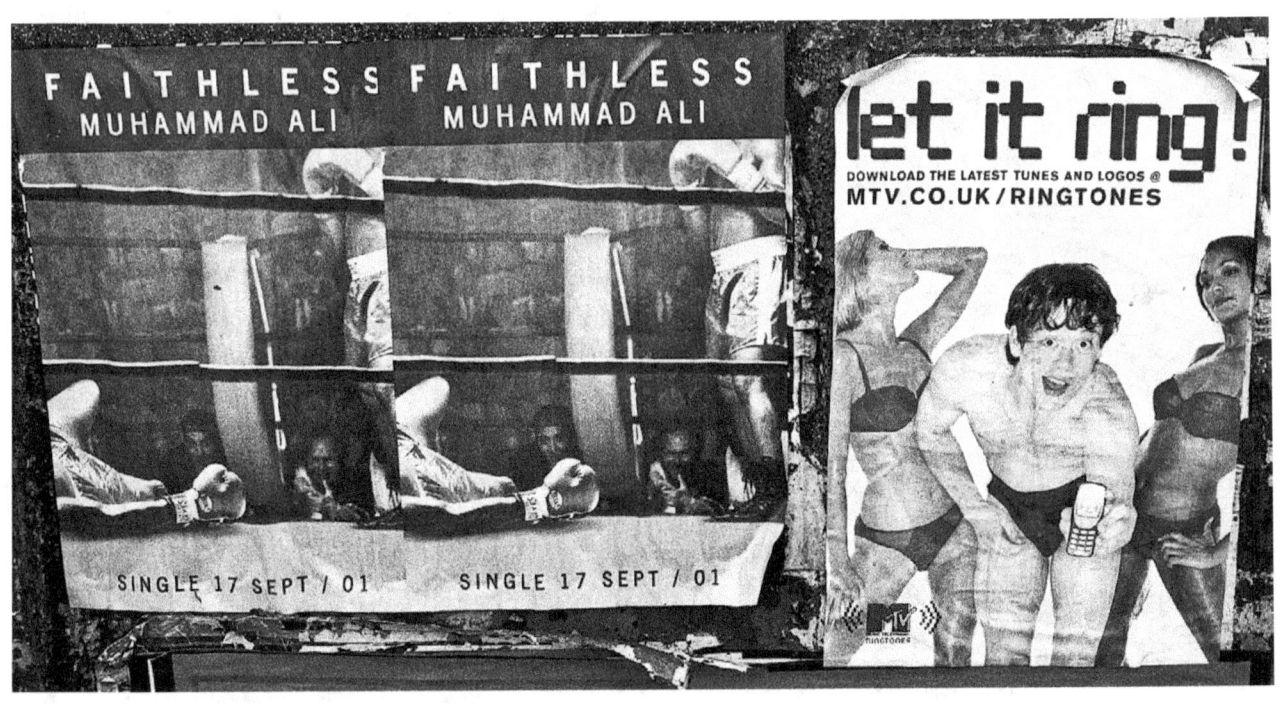

London, 2001

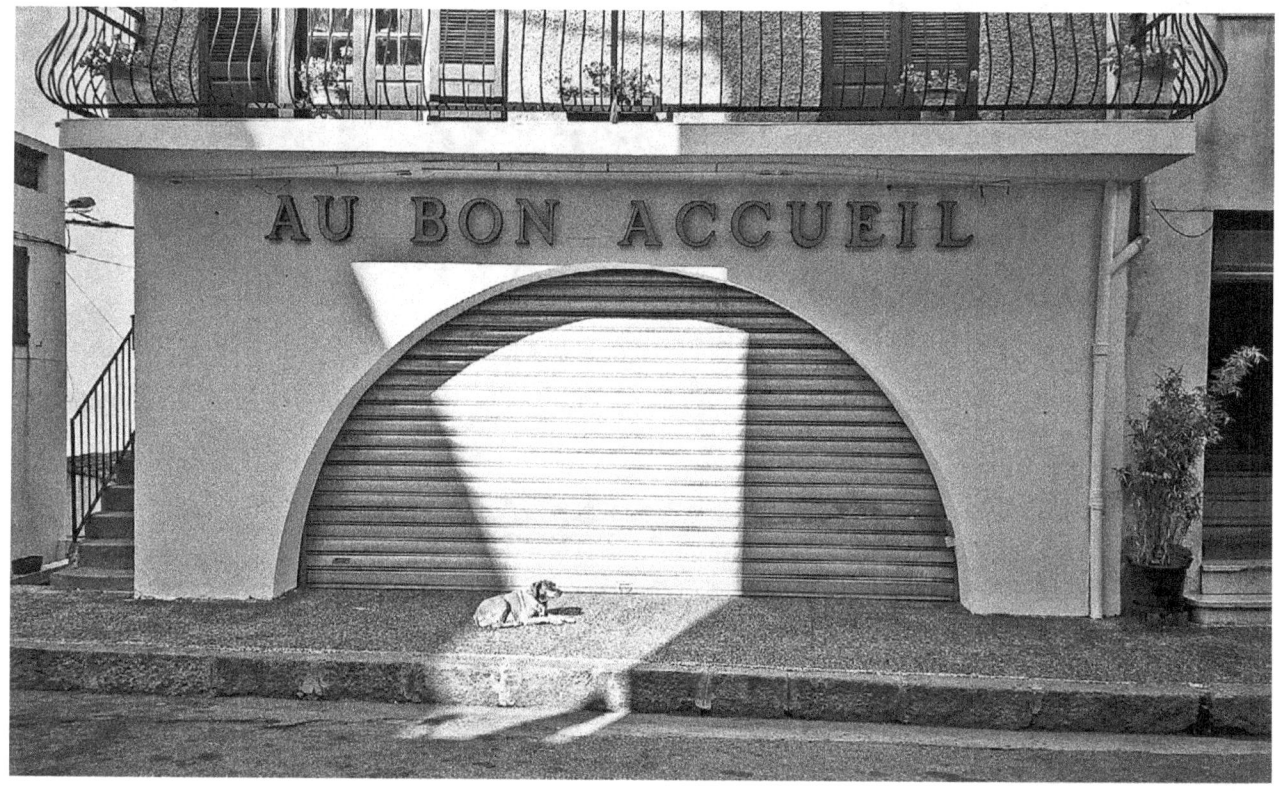

Cargése, Corsica, 2000

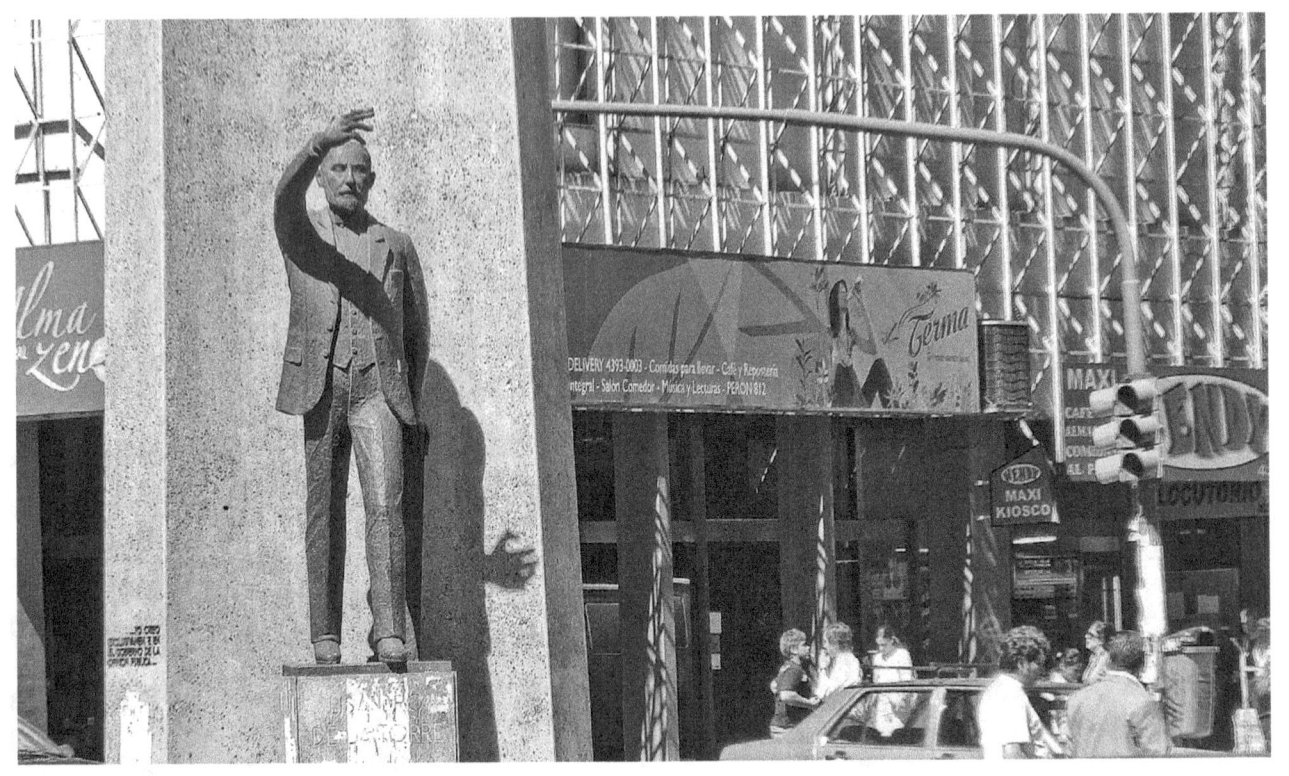

Buenos Aires, 2007

New York, 2007

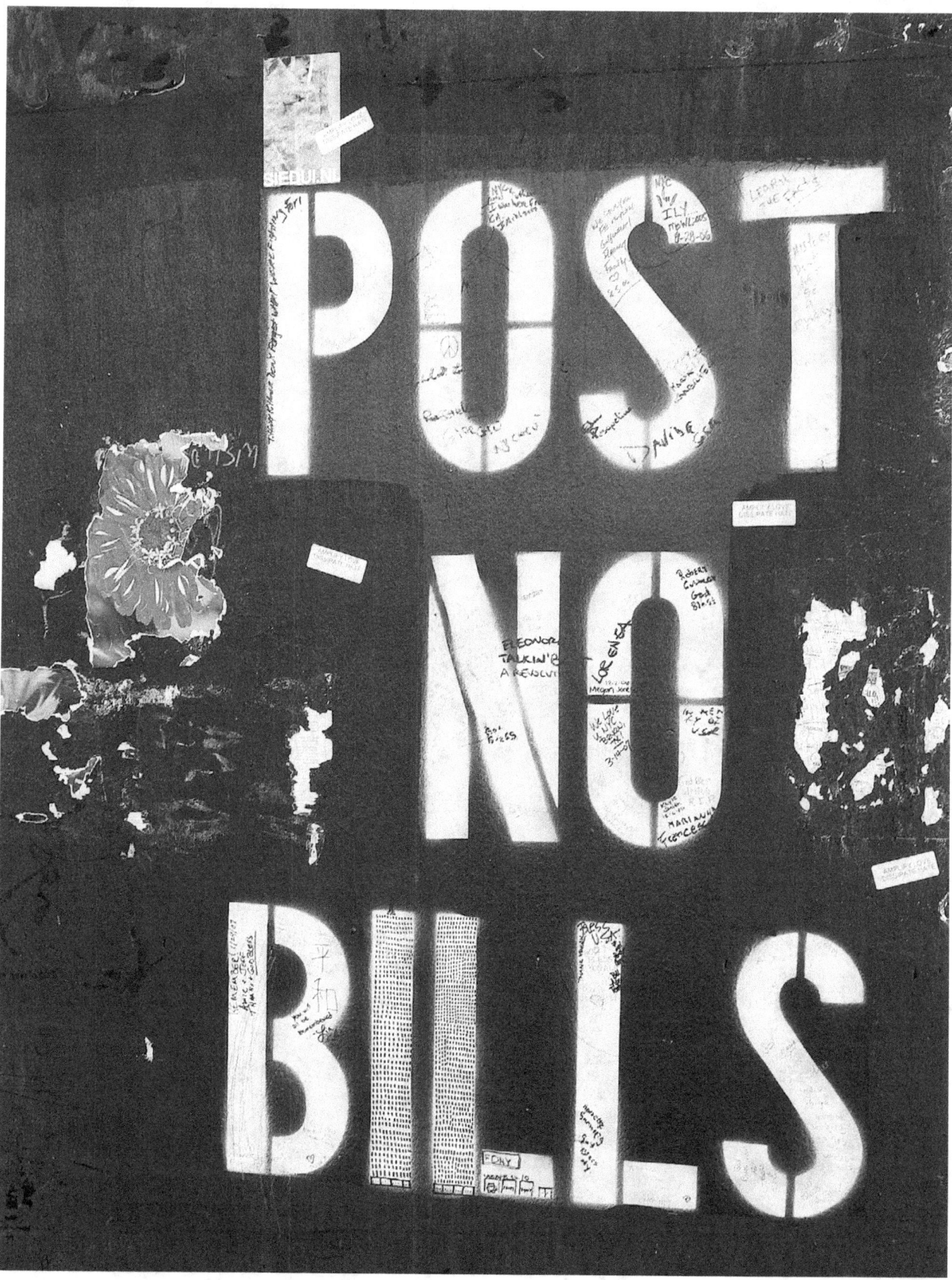

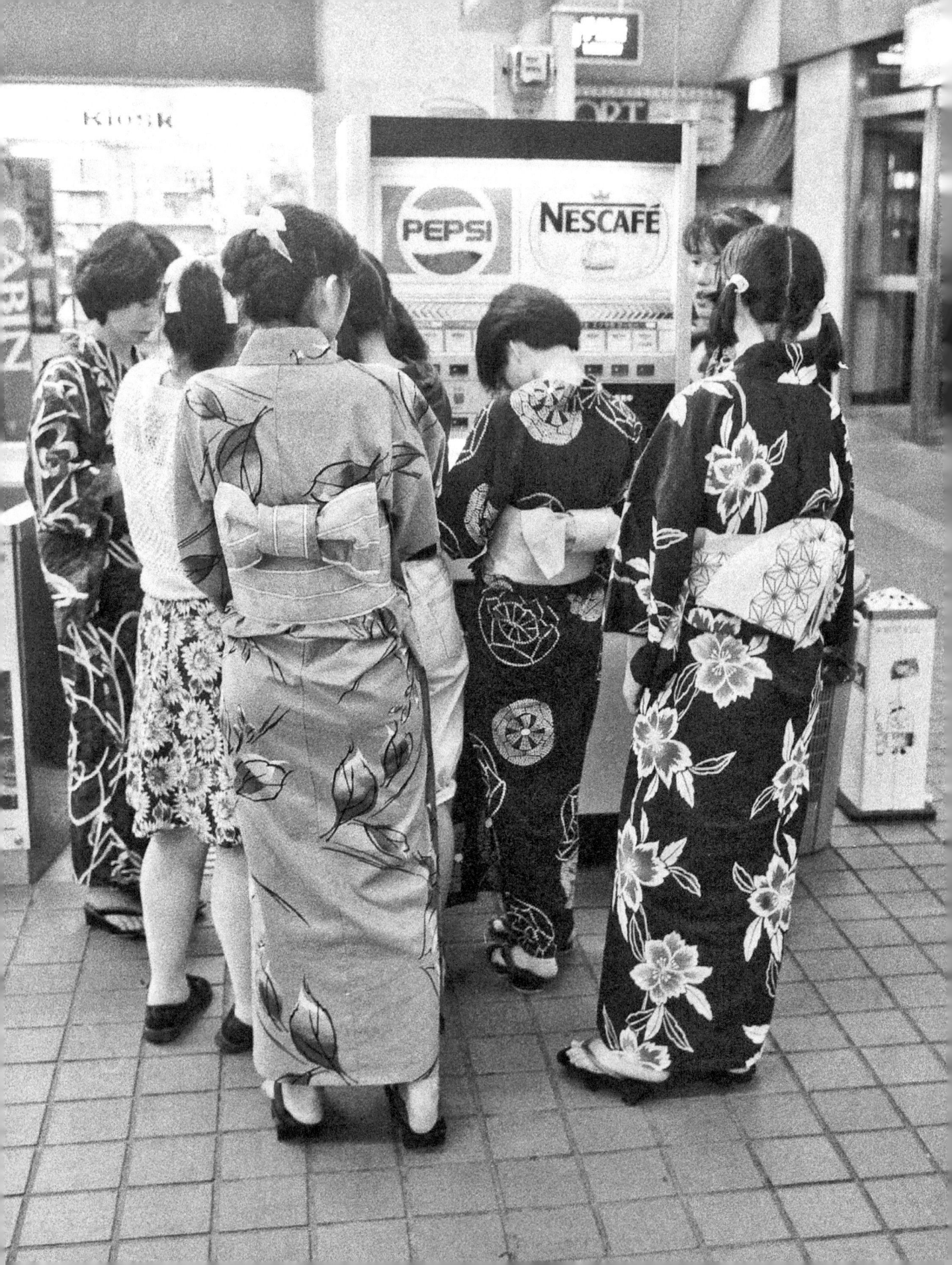

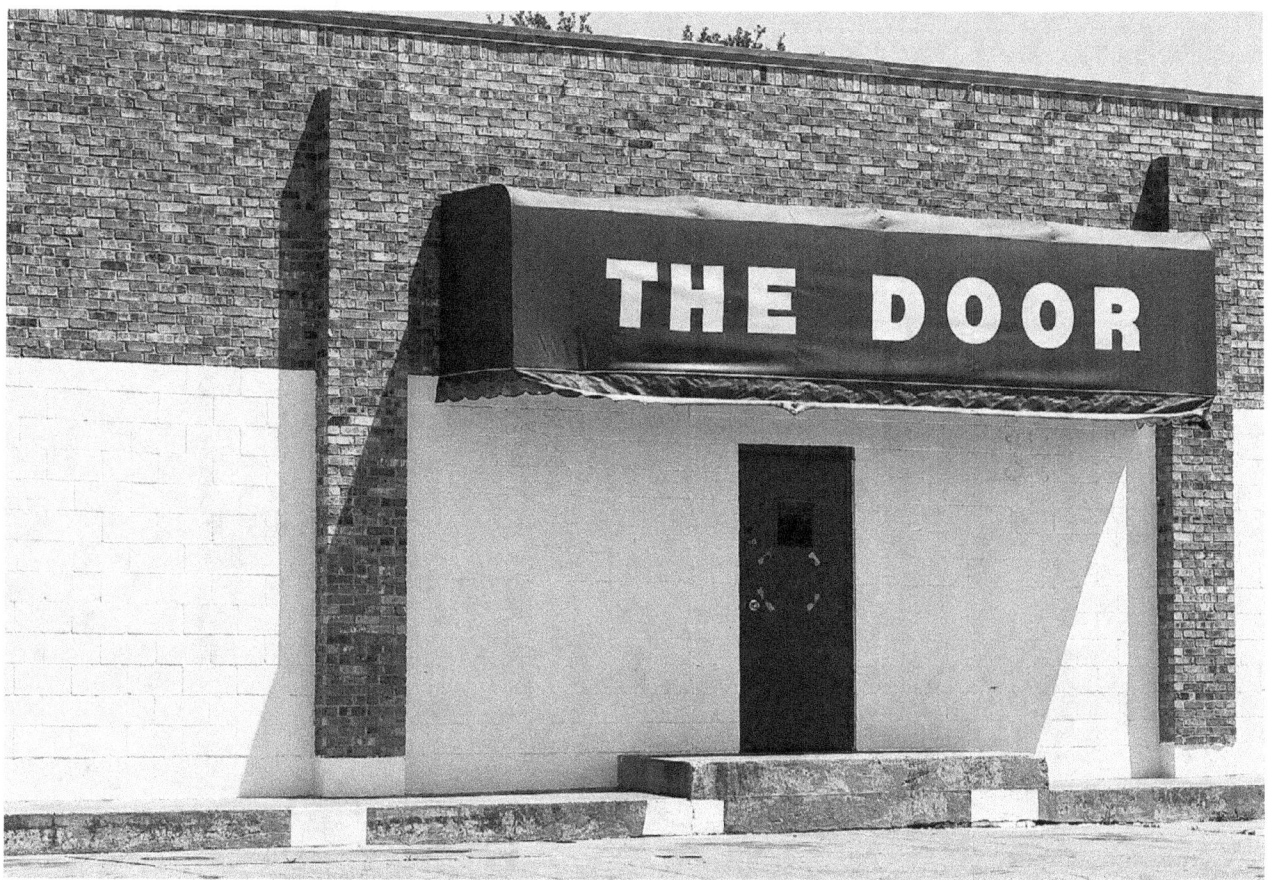

FortWorth, Texas, 2007

Sendai, Japan, 1988

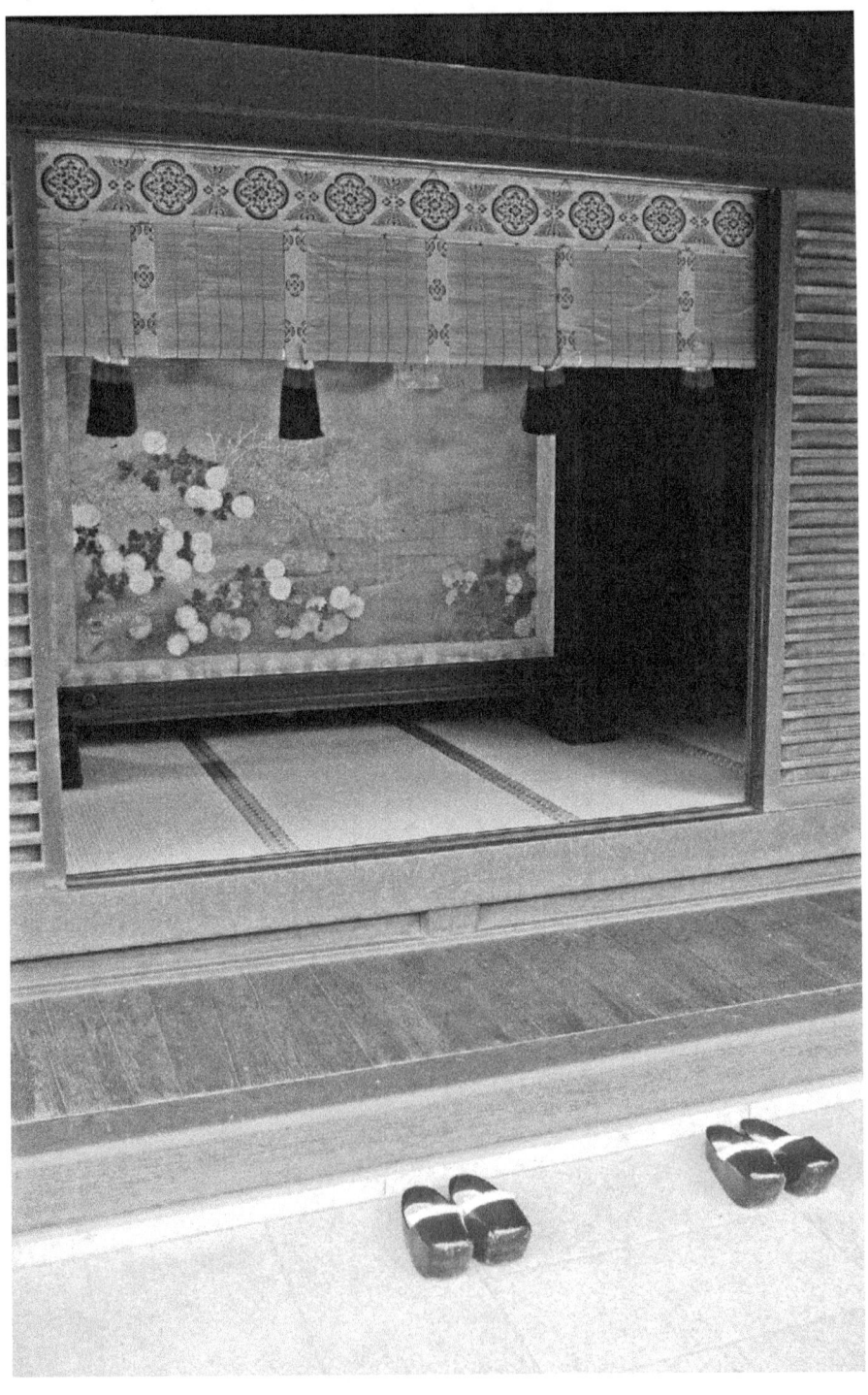

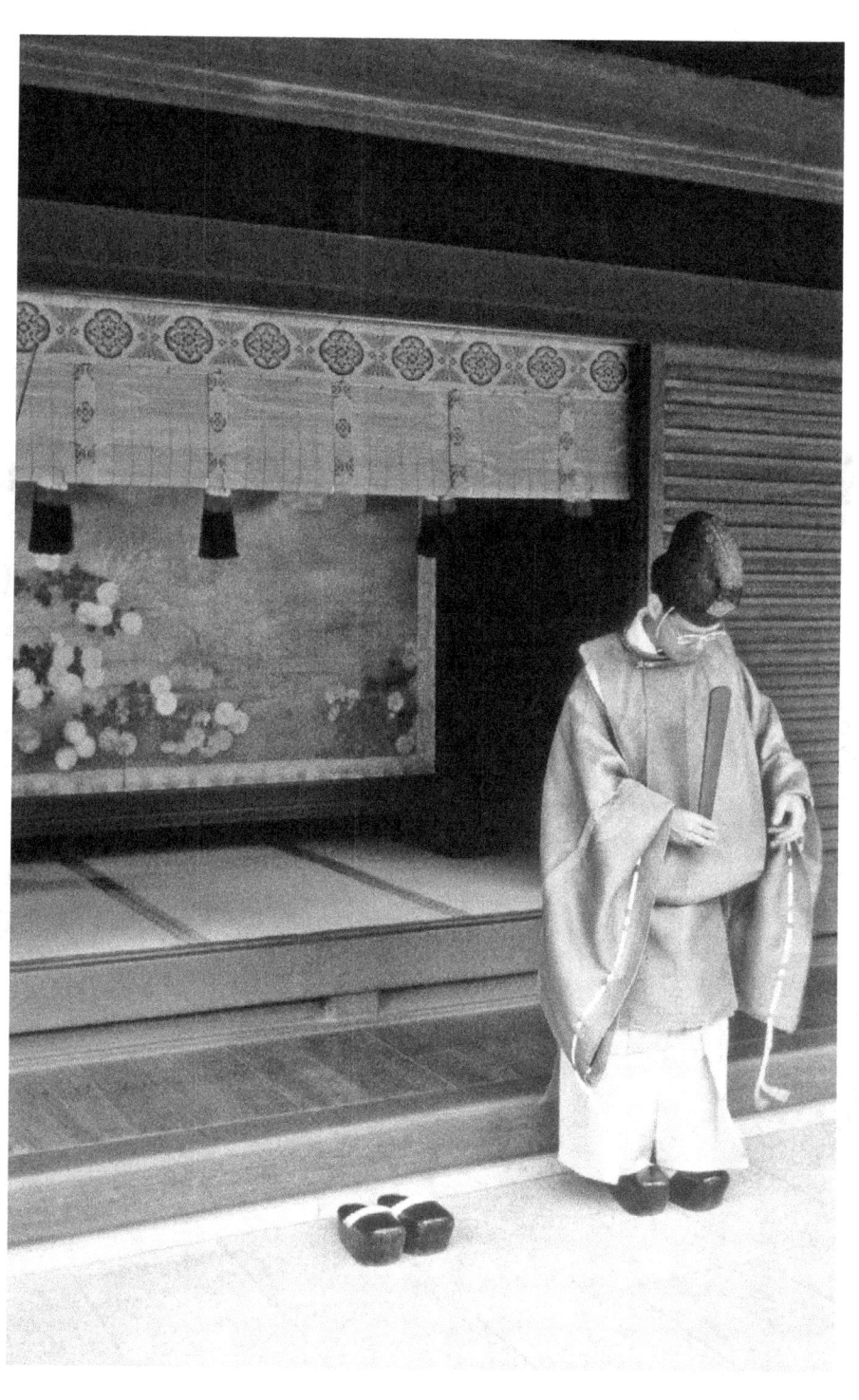

Sendai, Japan, 1988

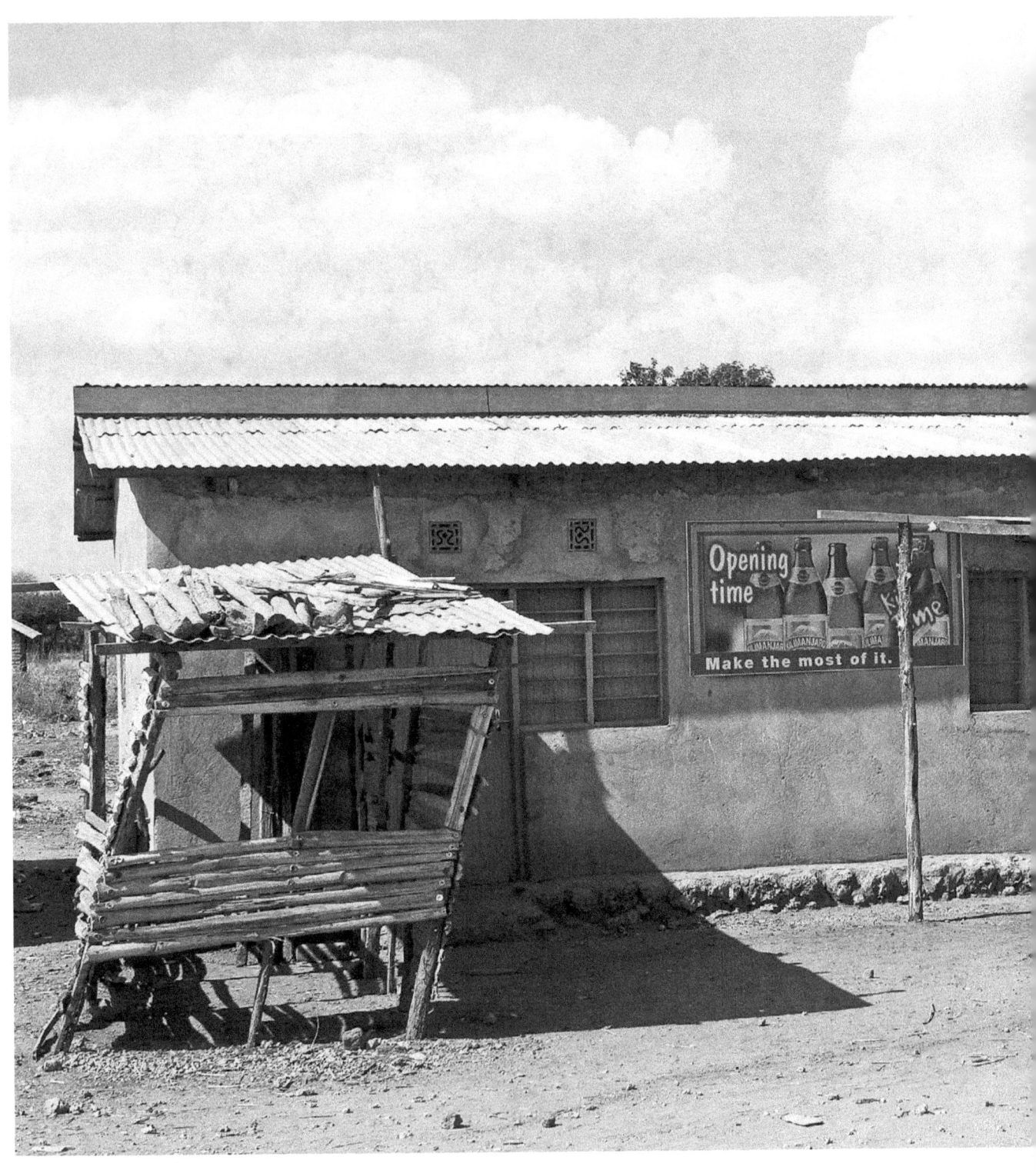

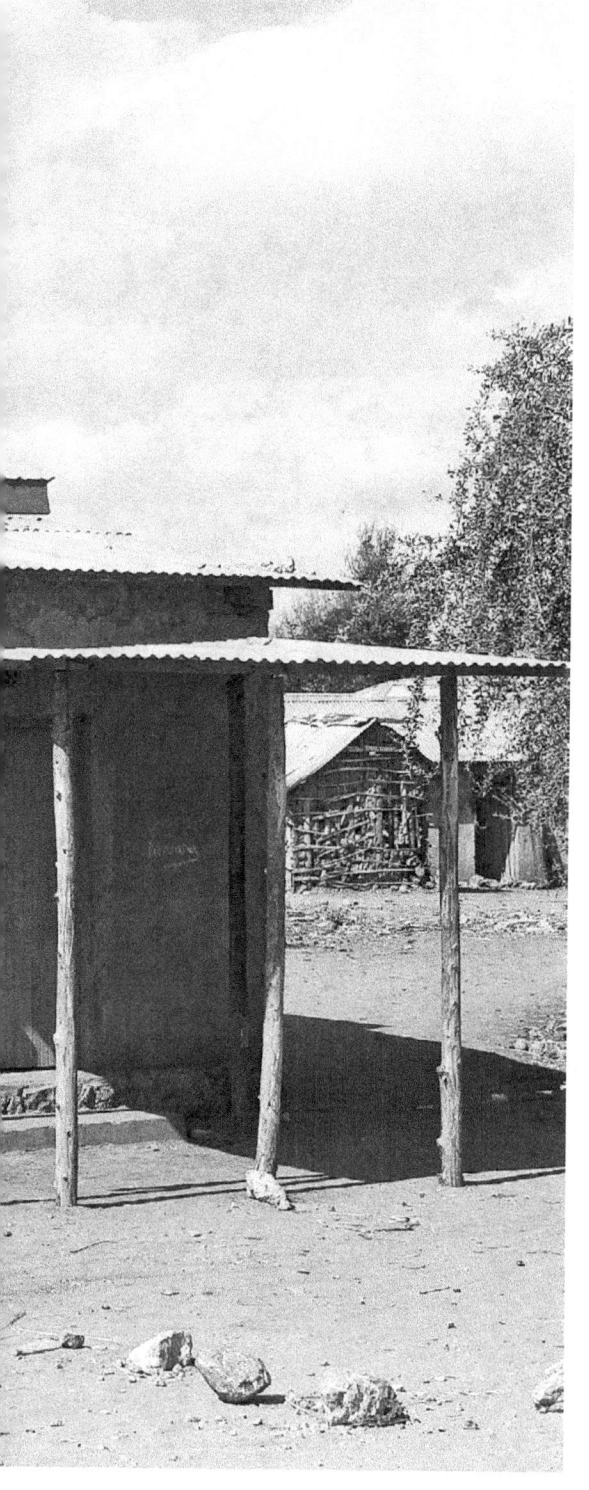

Tarangire, Tanzania, 2005

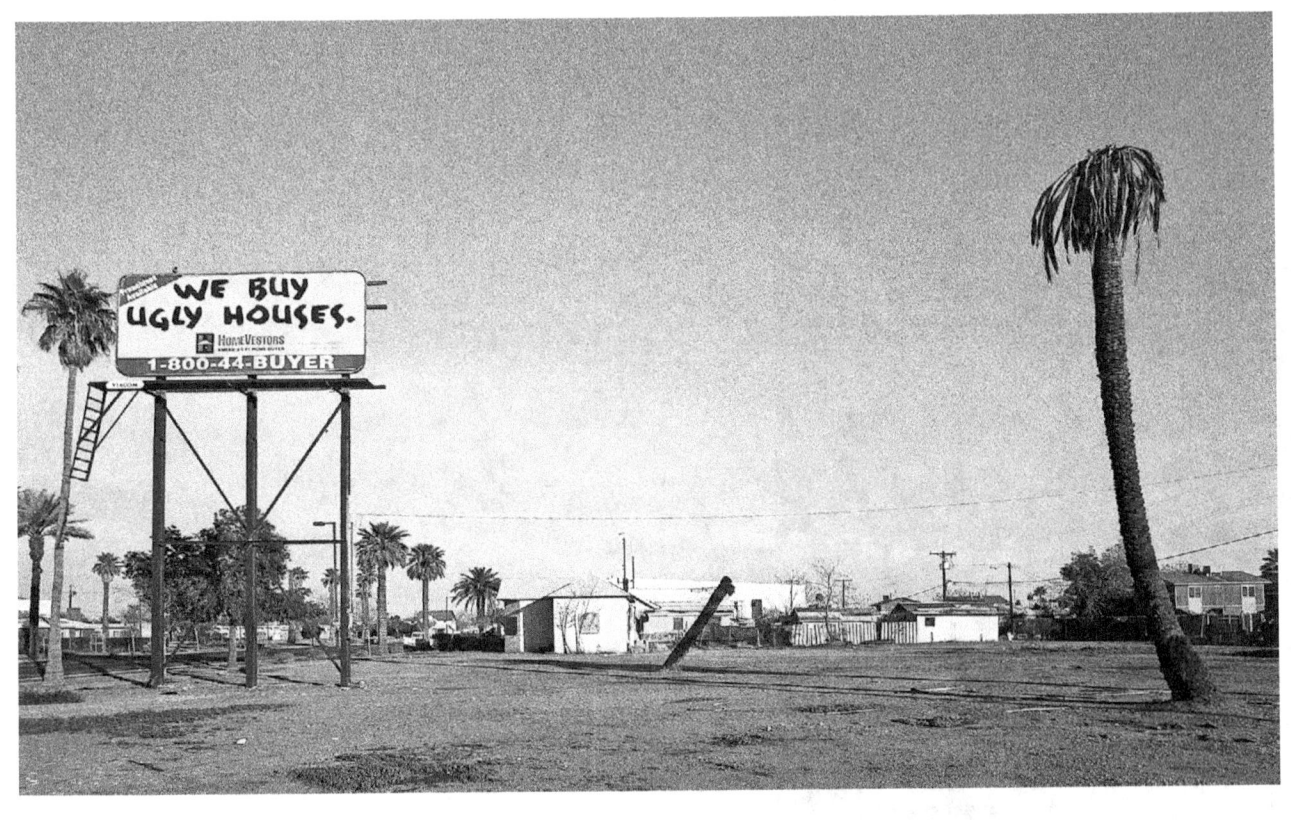

Phoenix, Arizona, 2003

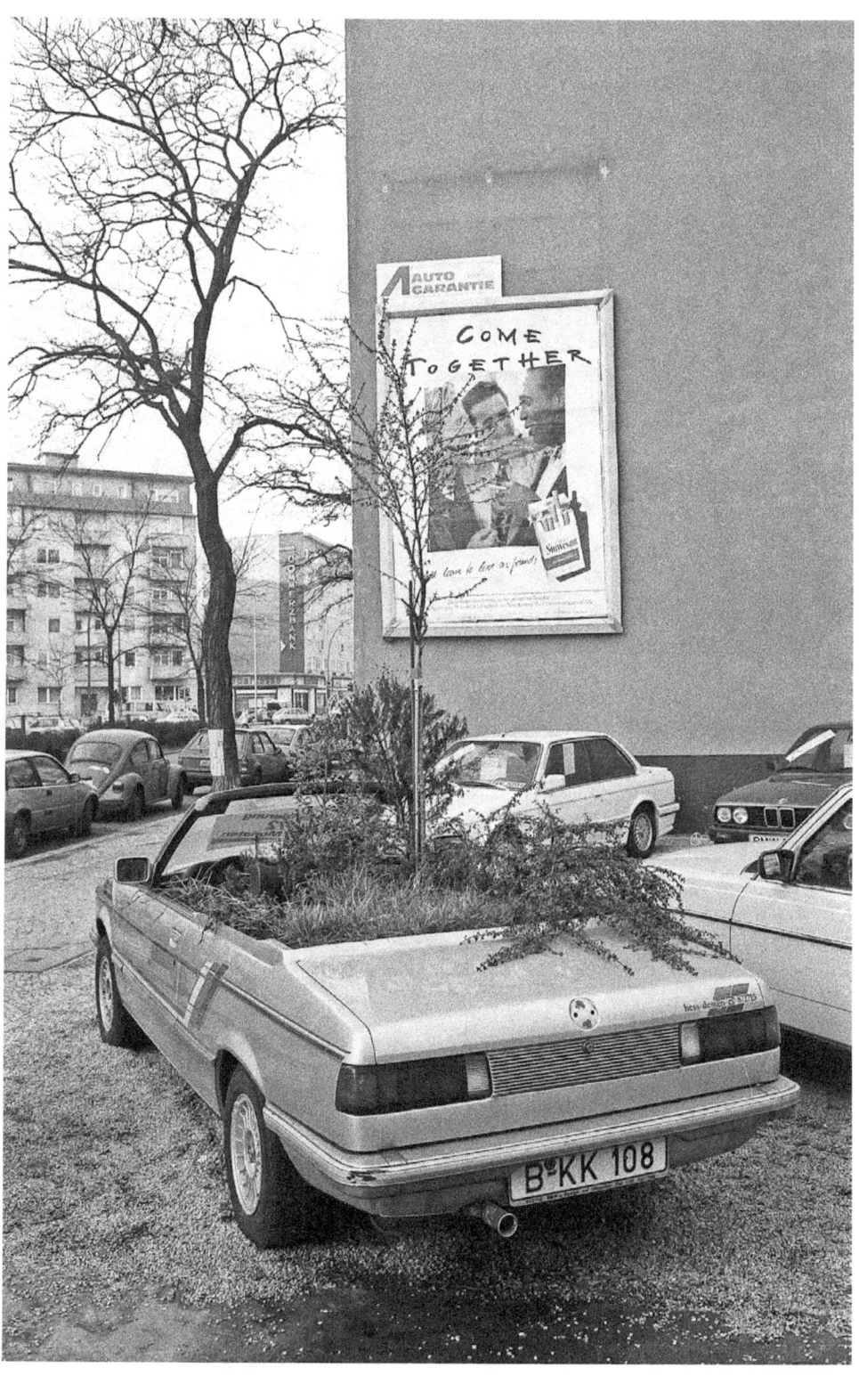

Berlin, 1990

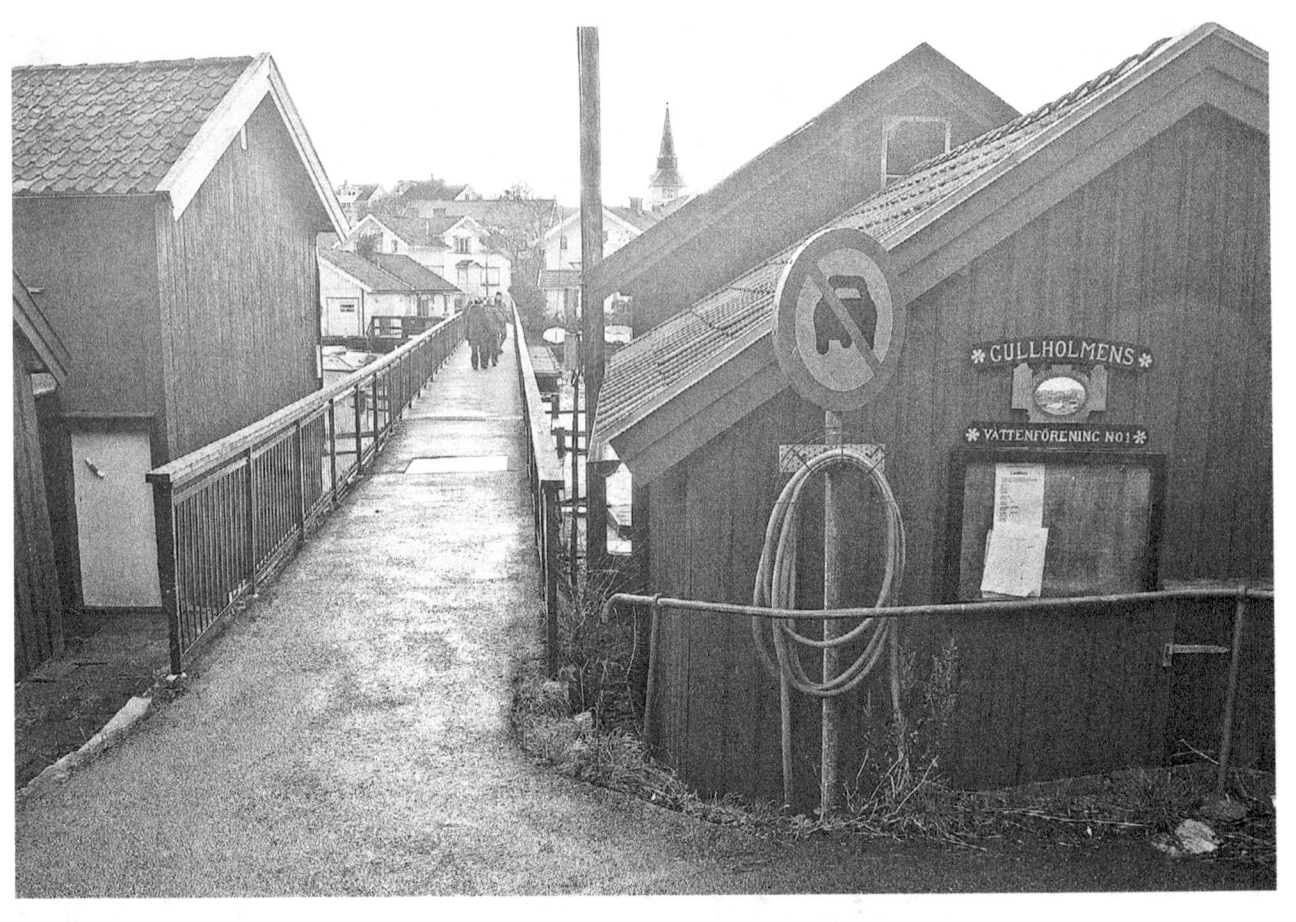

Gullholmen, Sweden, 2008

Portland, Oregon, 1999

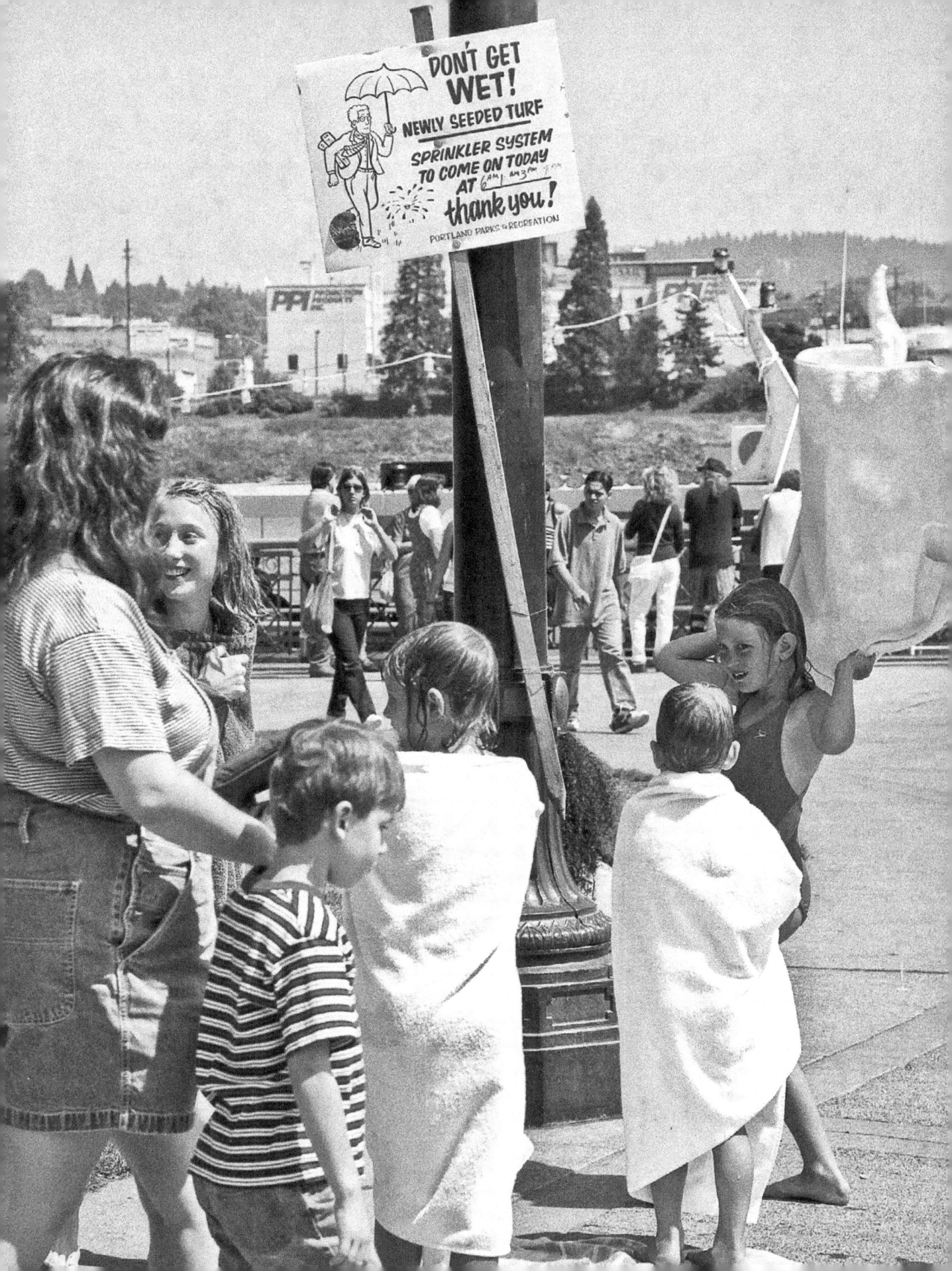

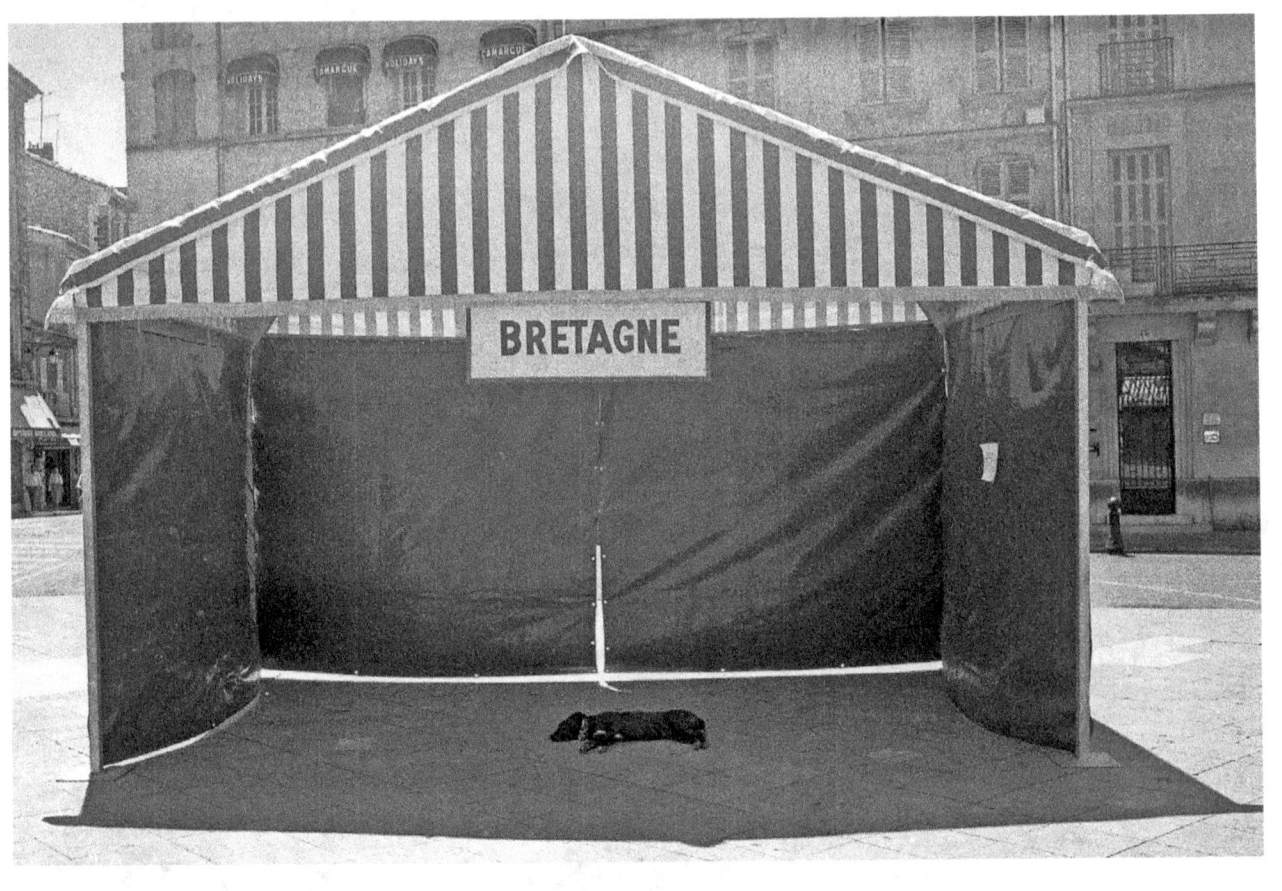

Arles, France, 1989

Buenos Aires, 2007

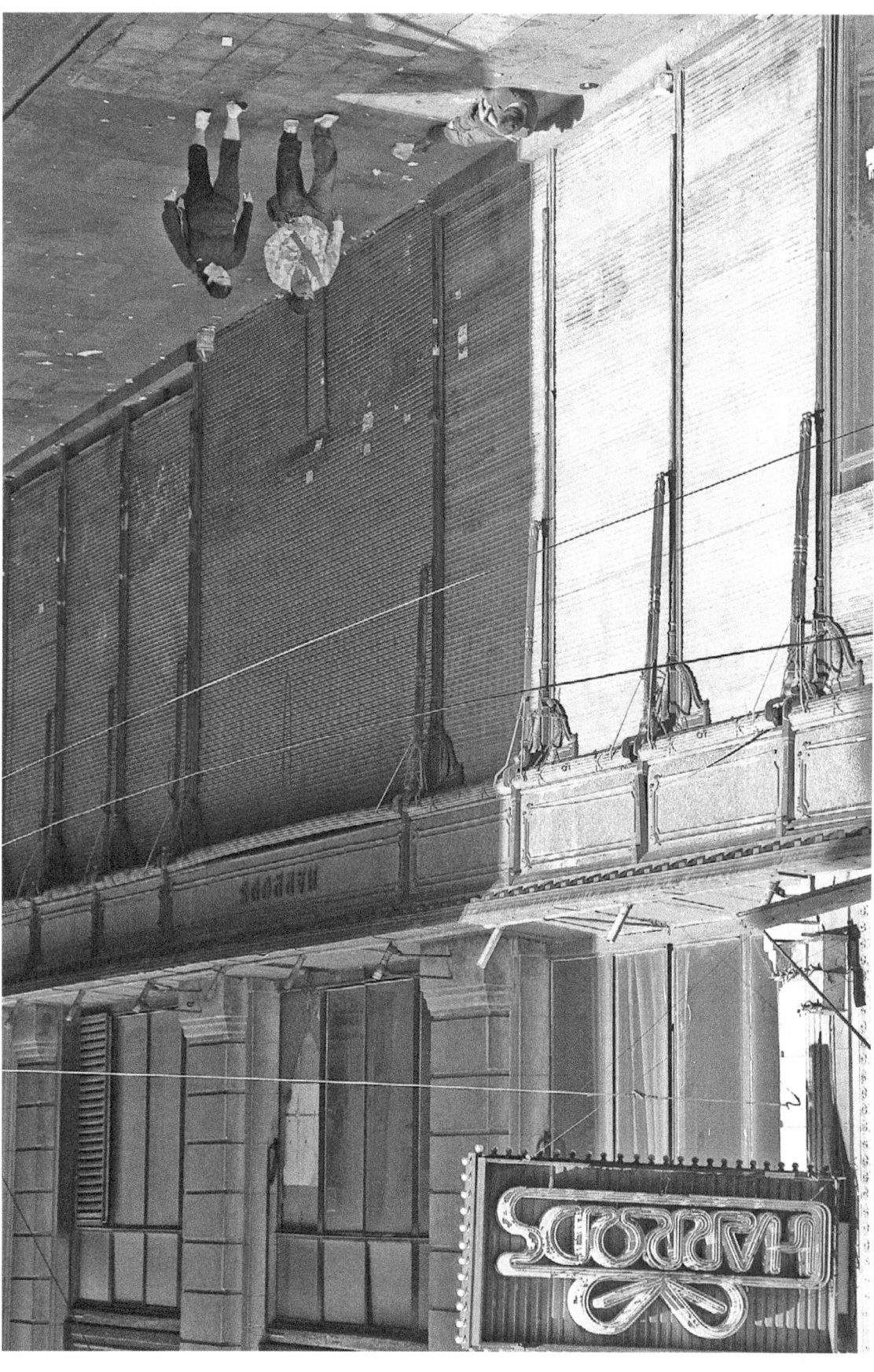

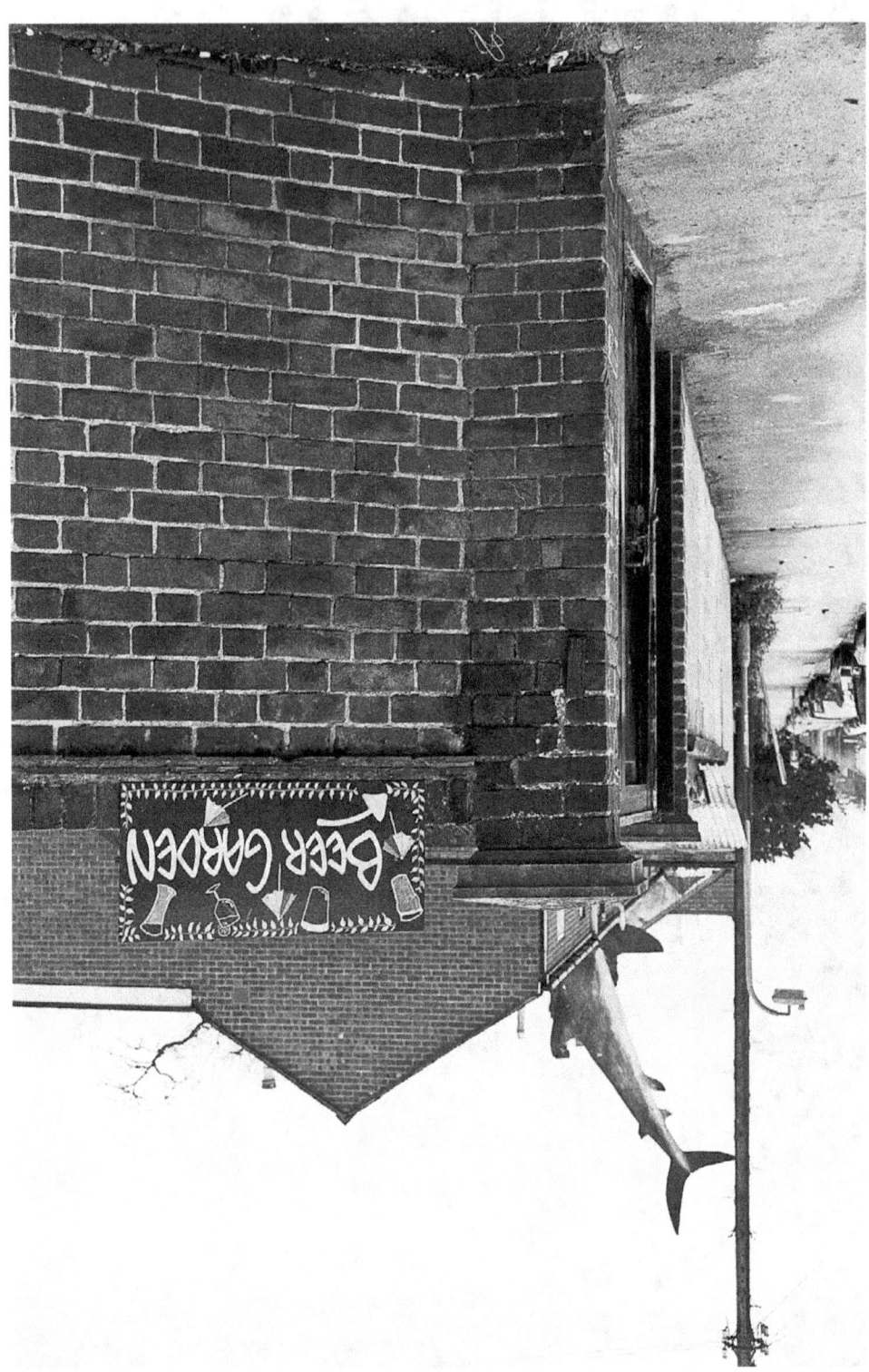

Oxford, 1994

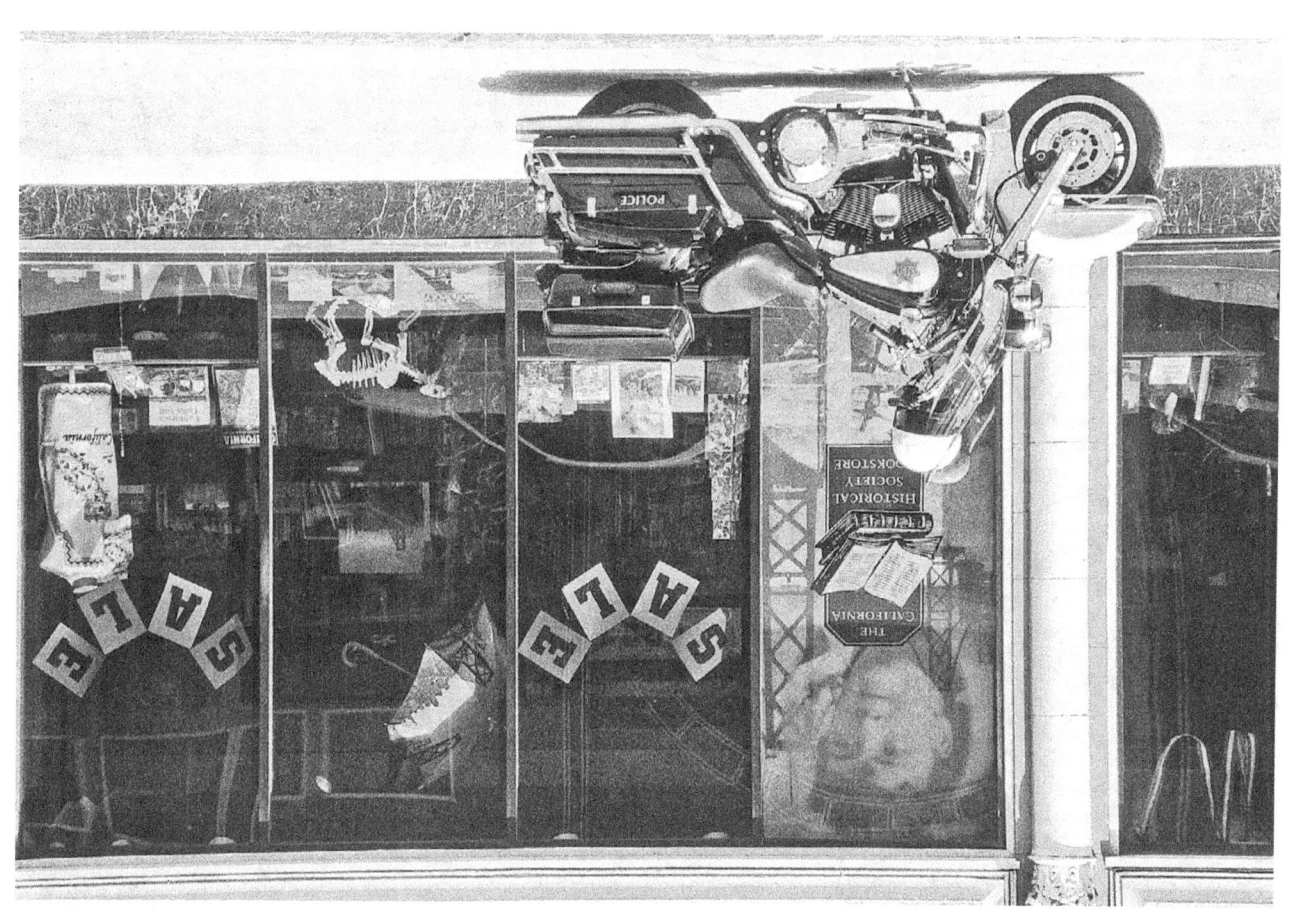

San Fransico, 2001

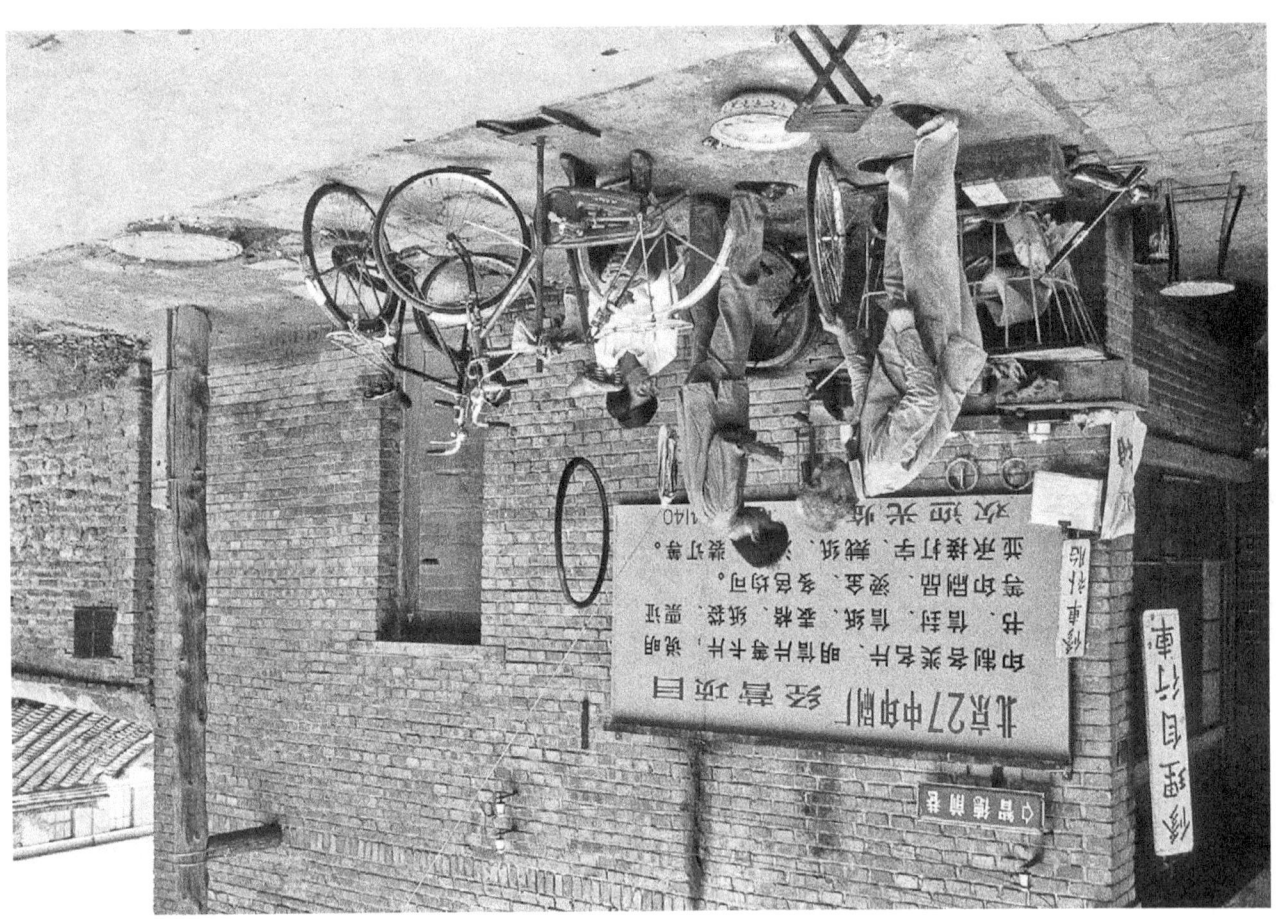

Beijing, 1986

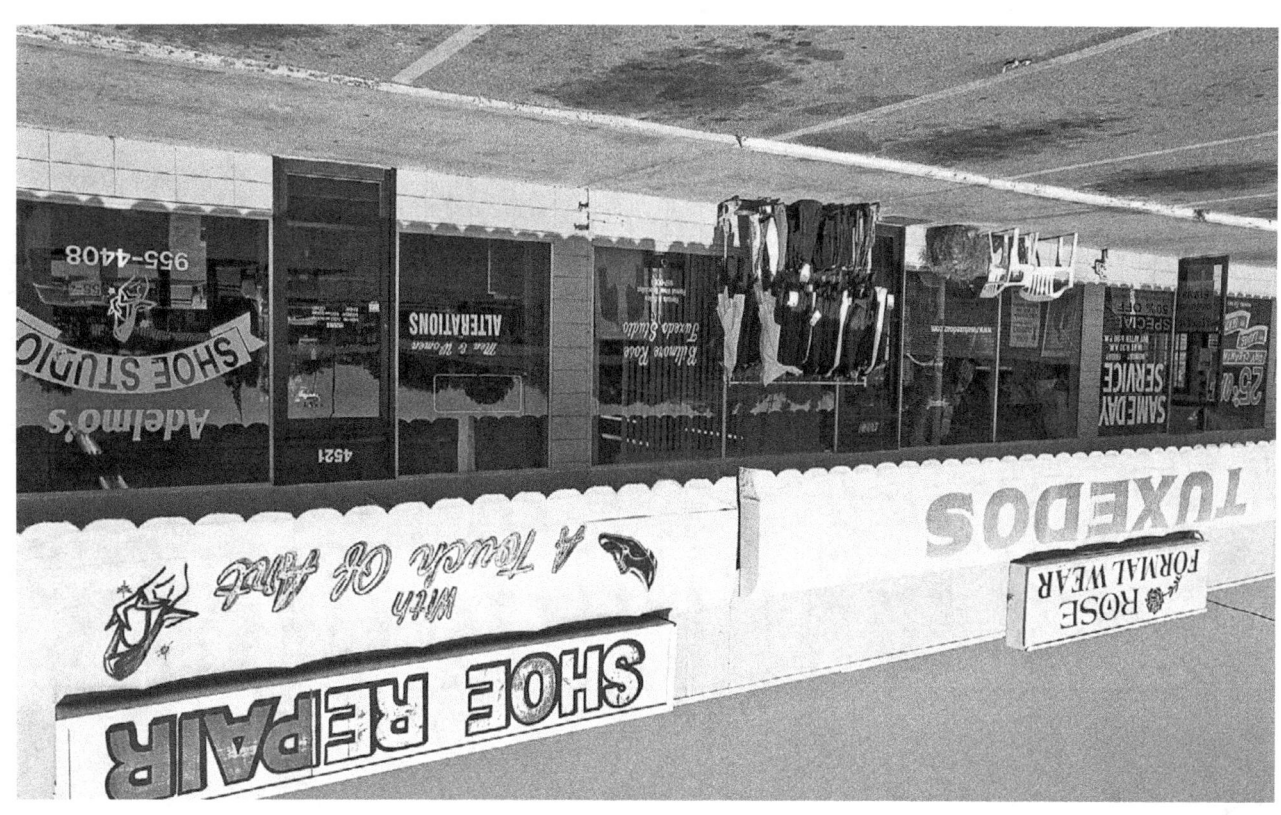

Phoenix, Arizona, 2003

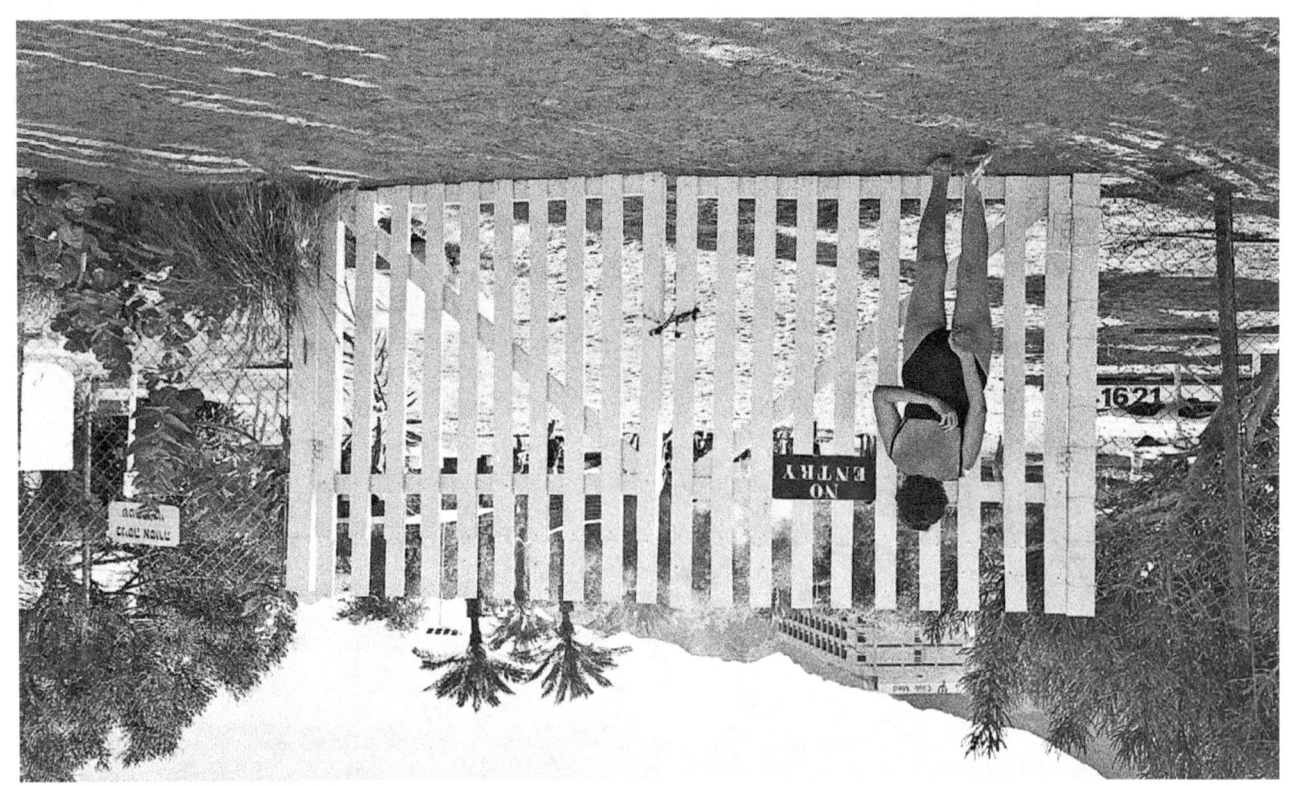

Eilat, Israel, 1999

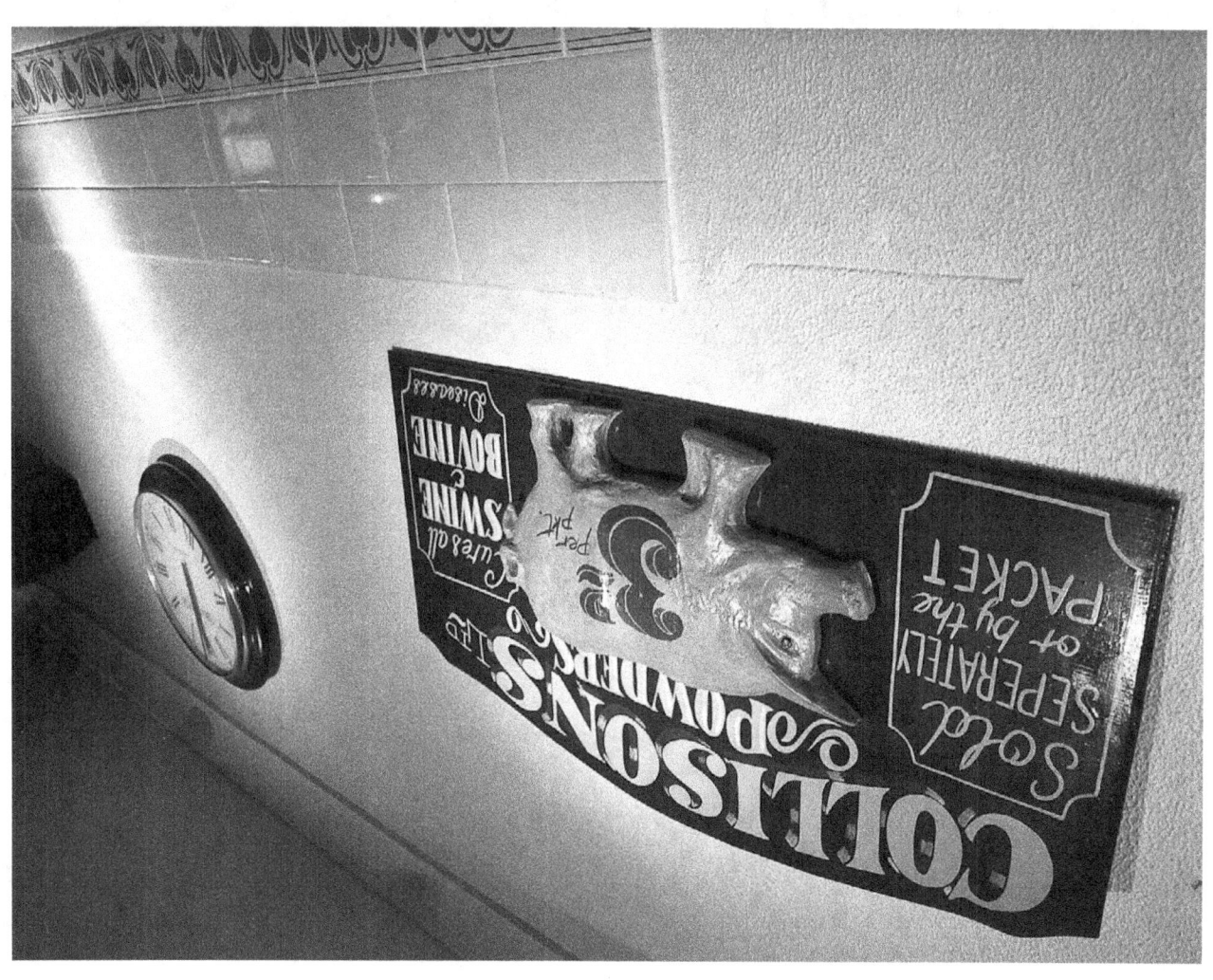

Adeleid, Australia, 1996

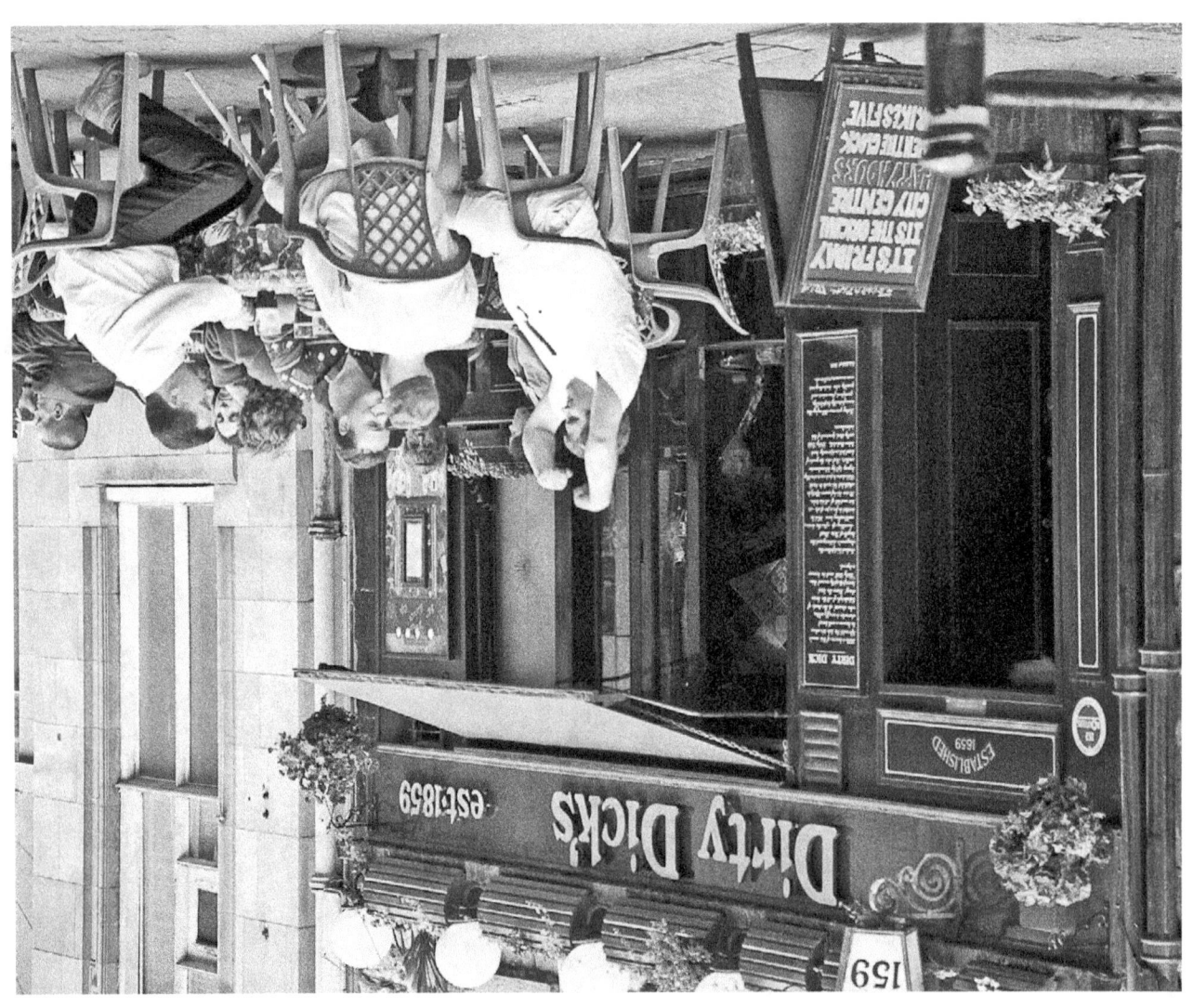

Oban, Scotland, 1998

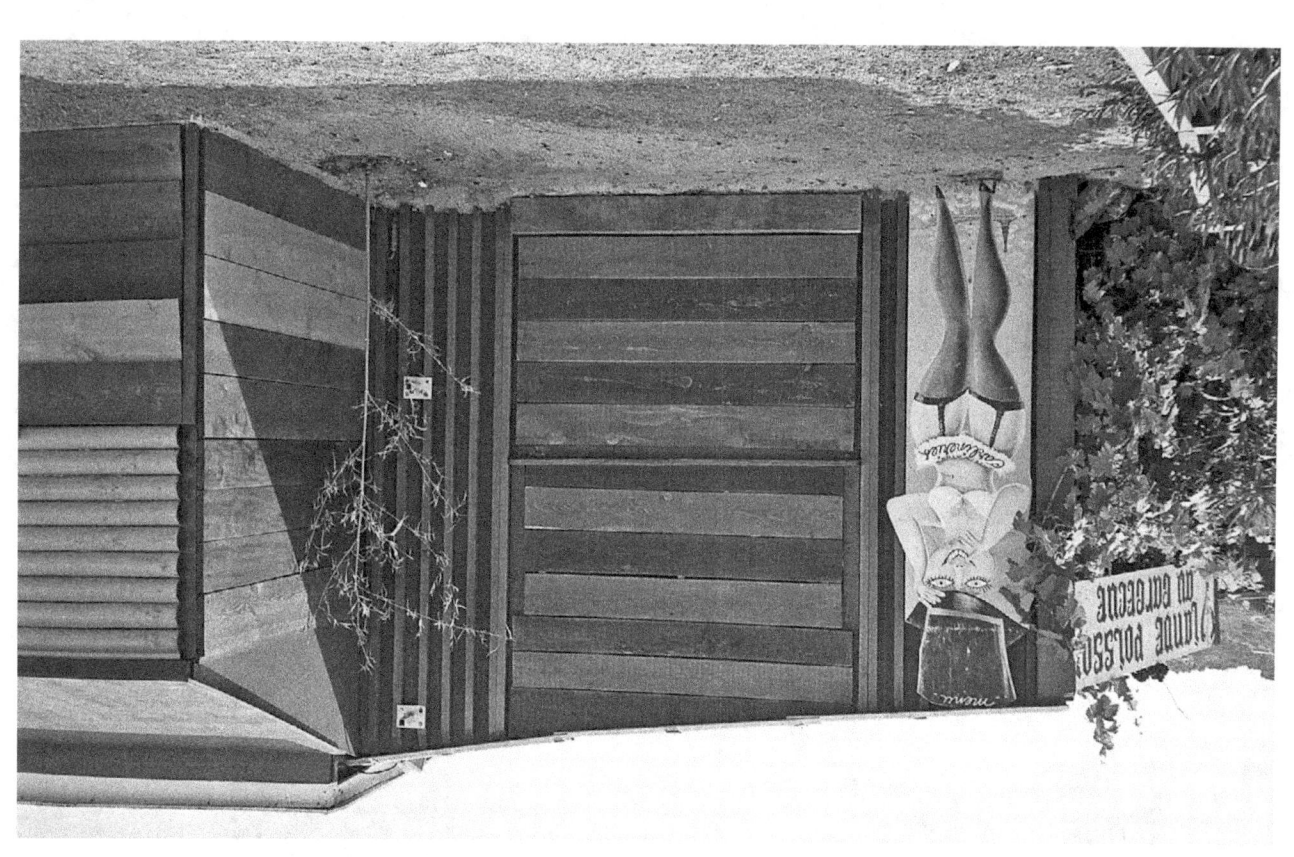

Plage de Pero, Corsica, 2000

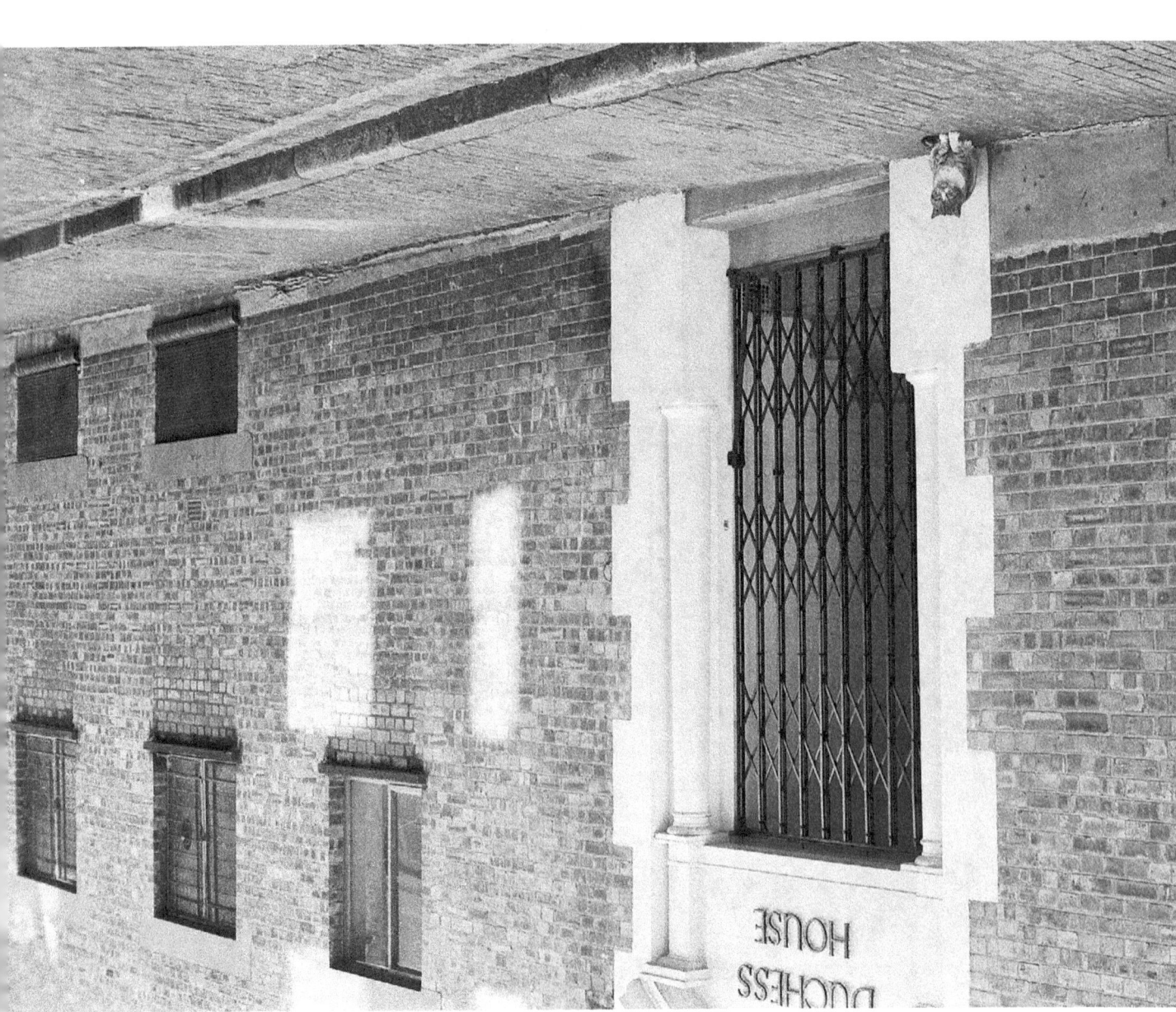

London, 1988

Berlin, 1990

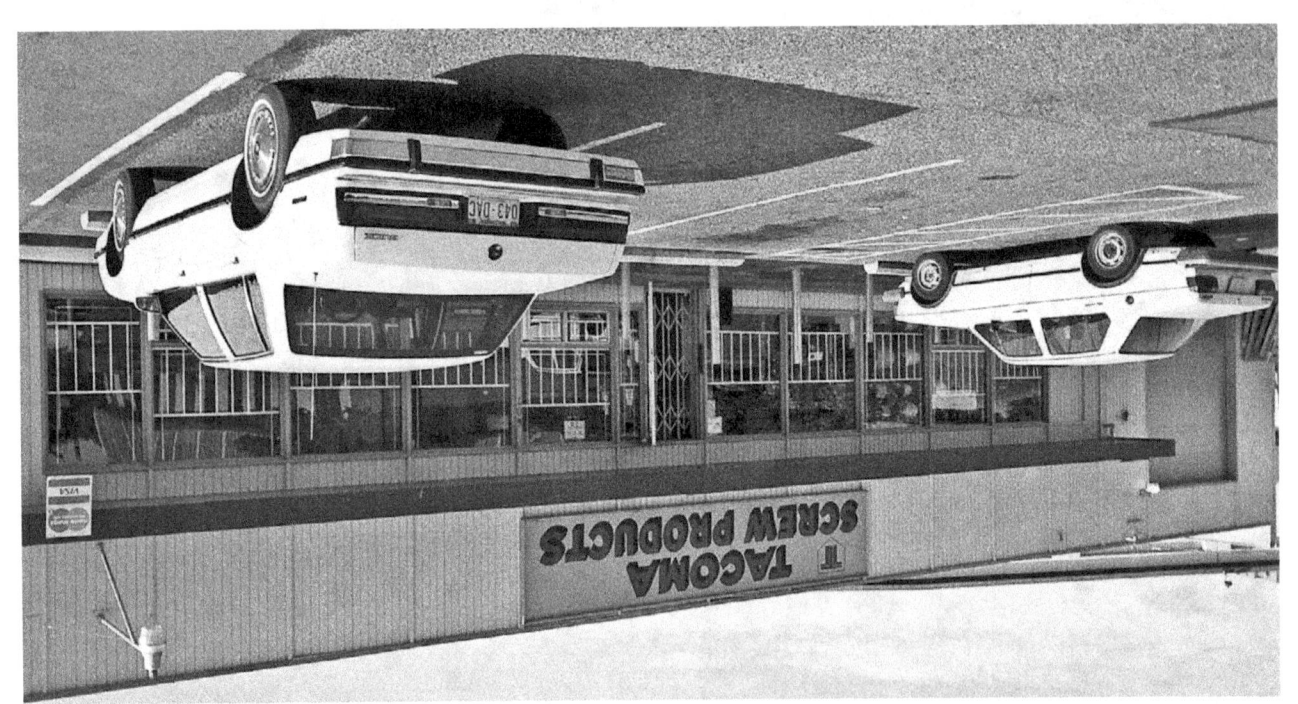

Seattle, 1990

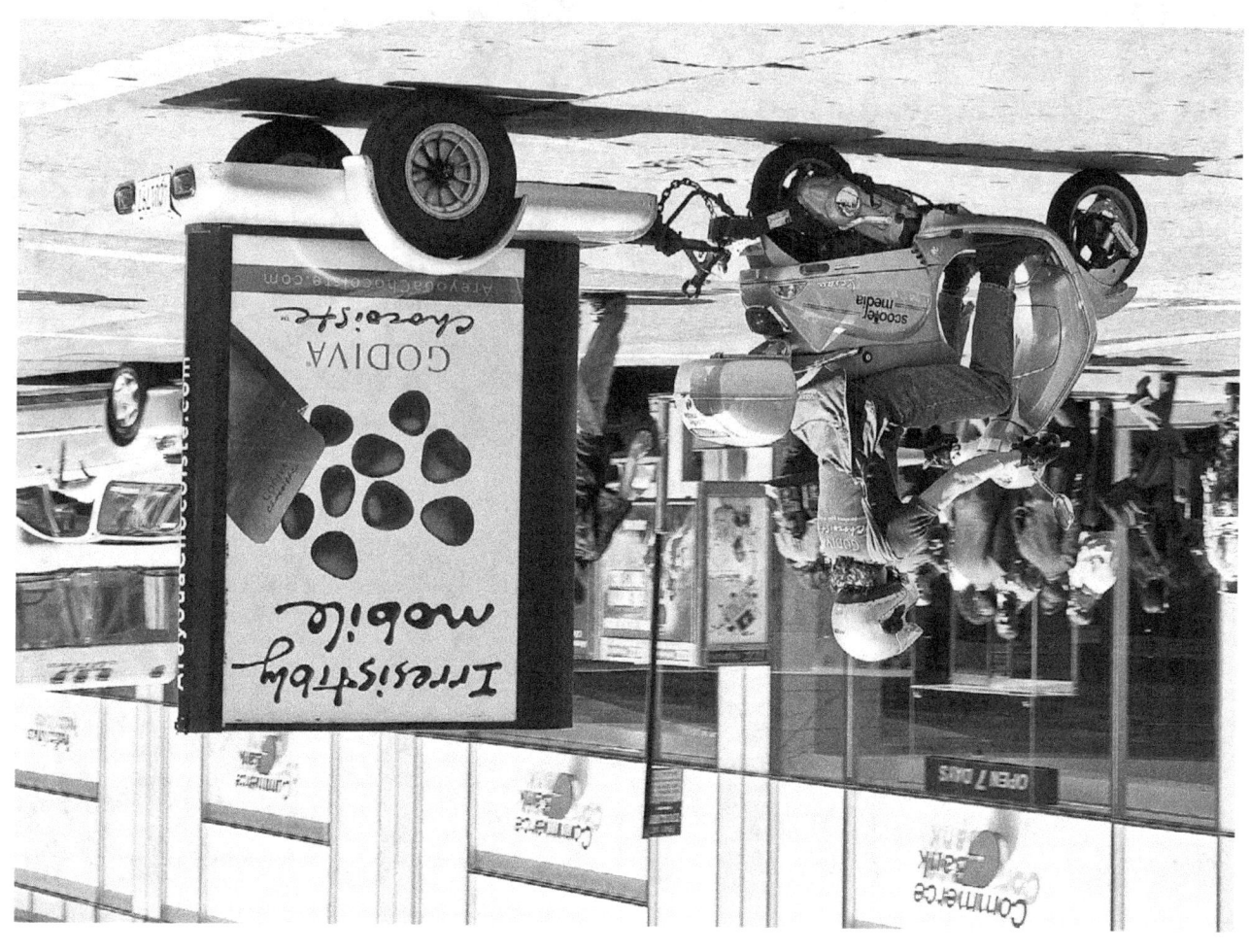

New York, 2007

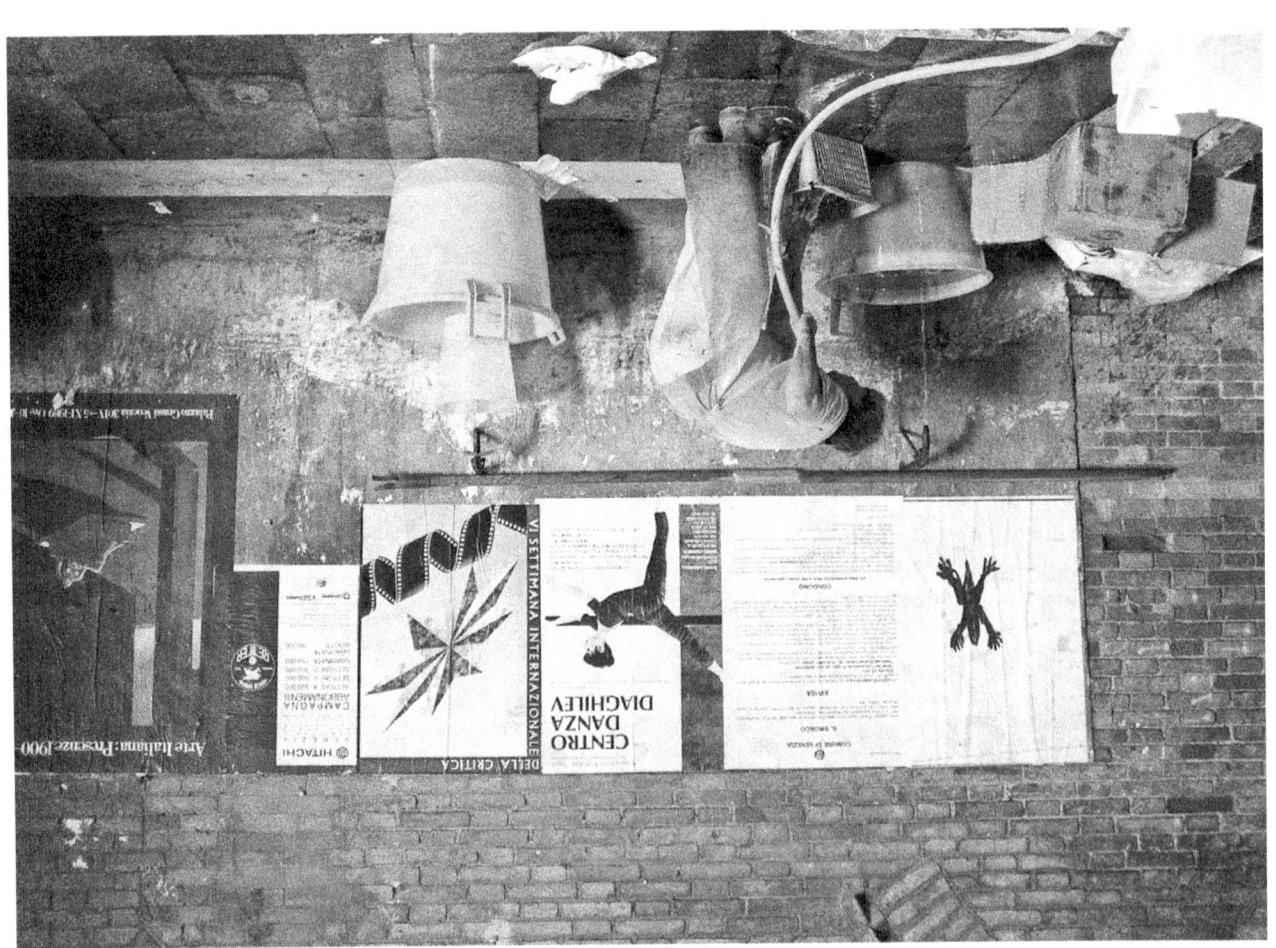

Venice, Italy, 1989

Phoenix, Arizona, 1986

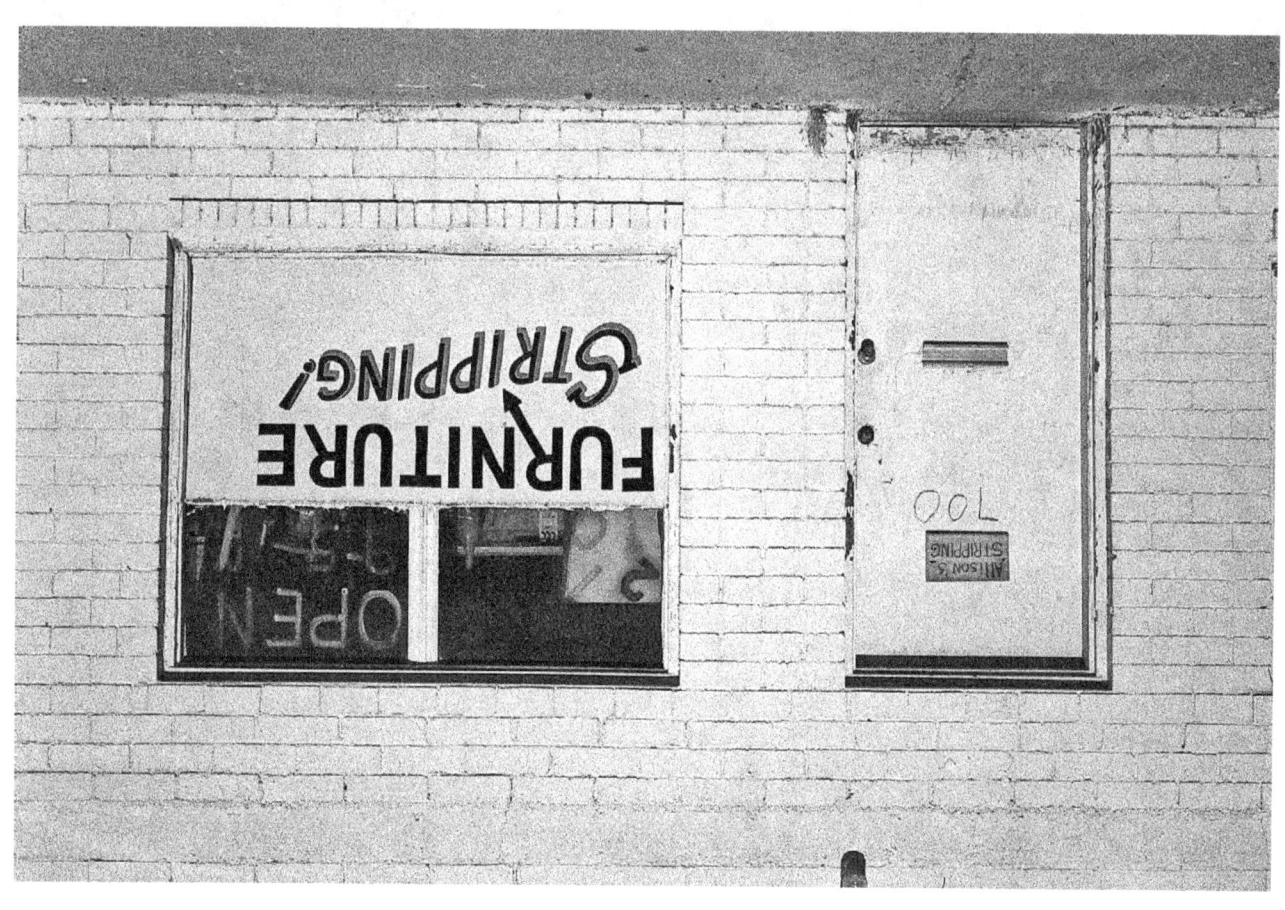

Stockholm, Sweden, 2006

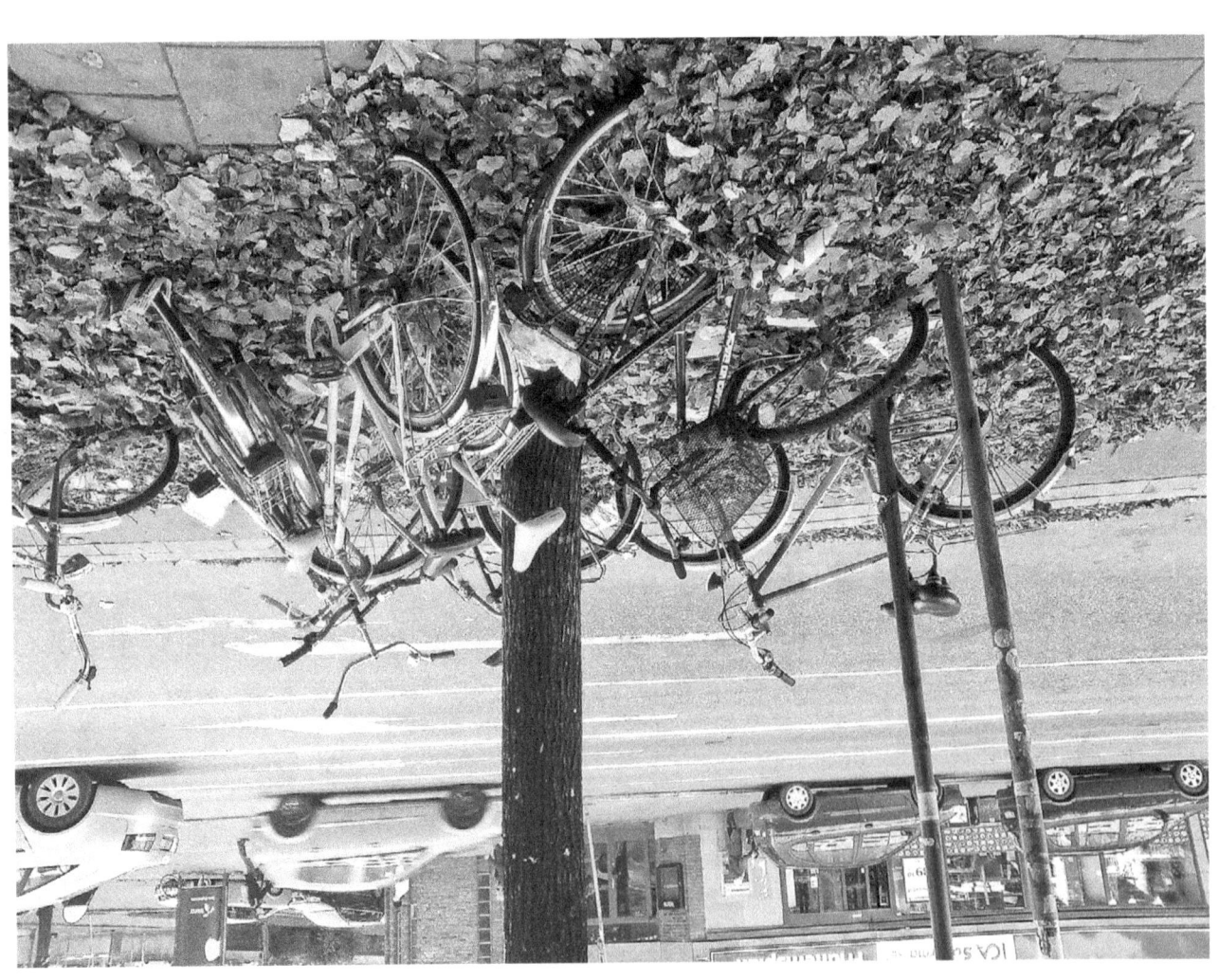

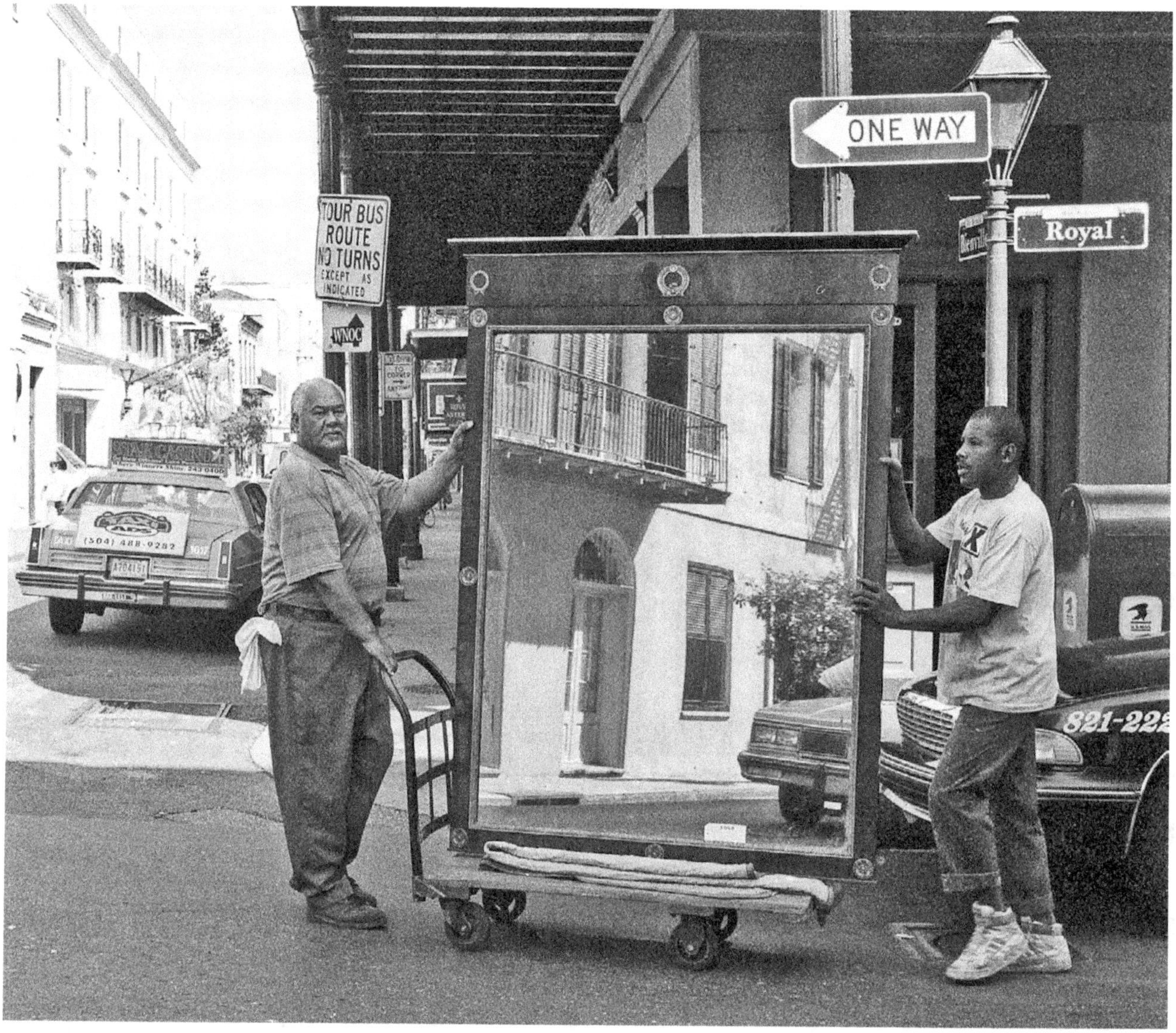

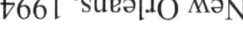

New Orleans, 1994

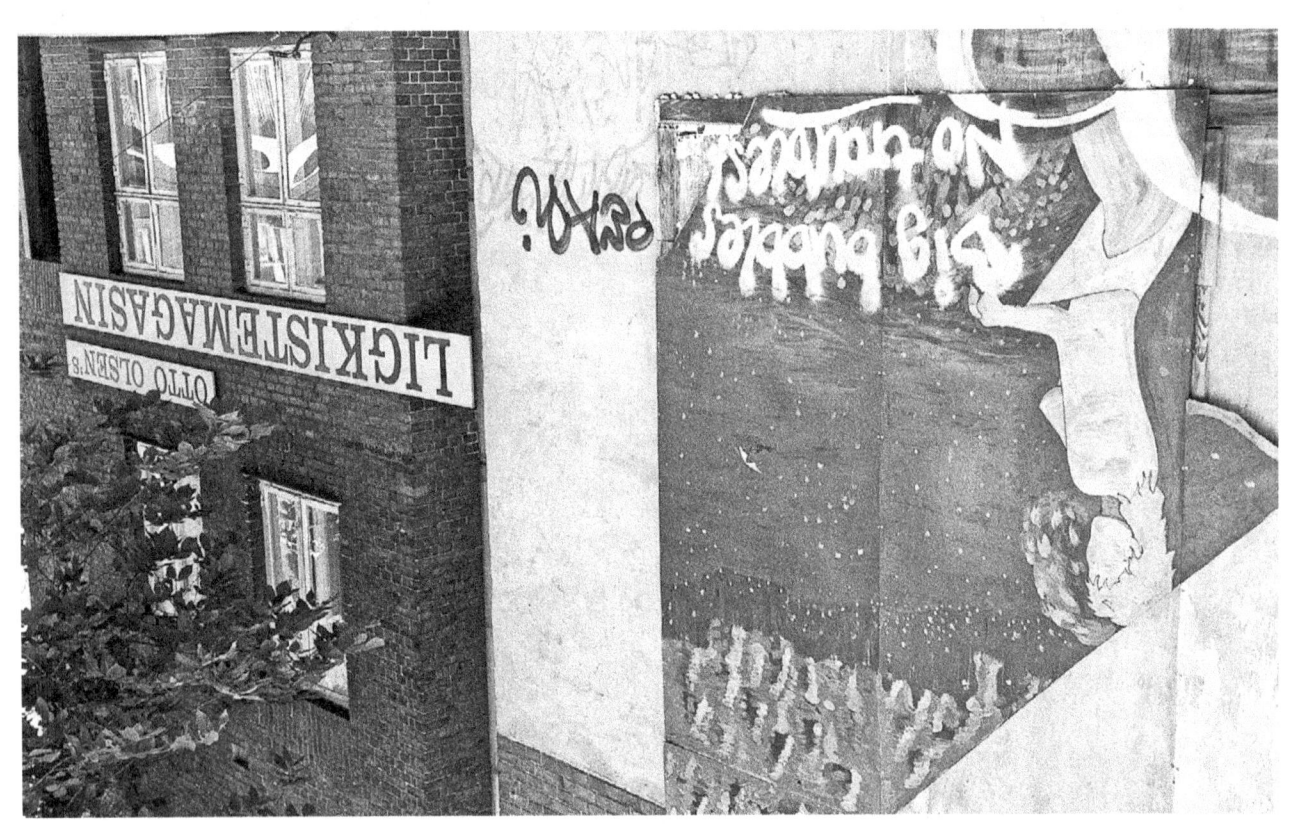

Copenhagen, 1996

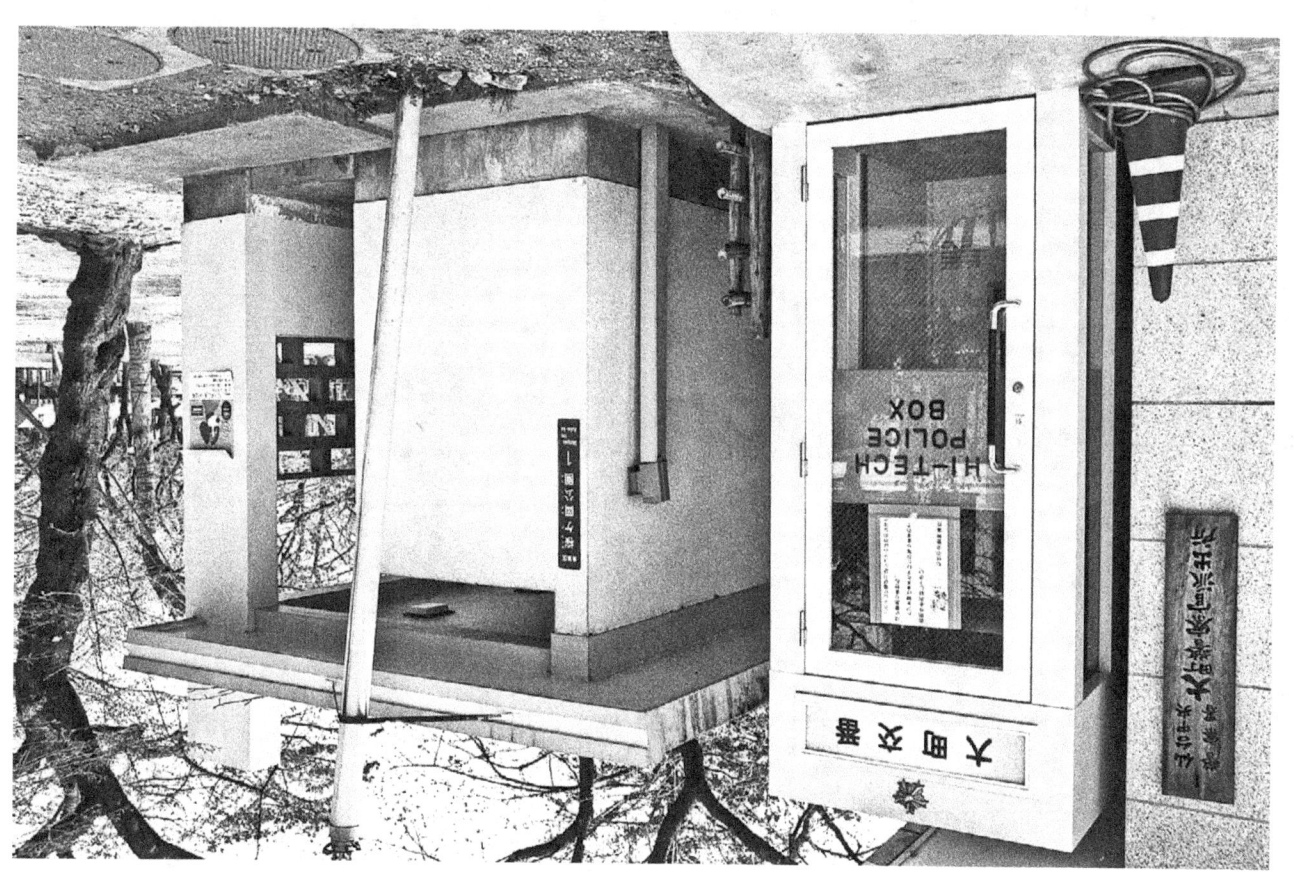

Sendai, Japan 1994

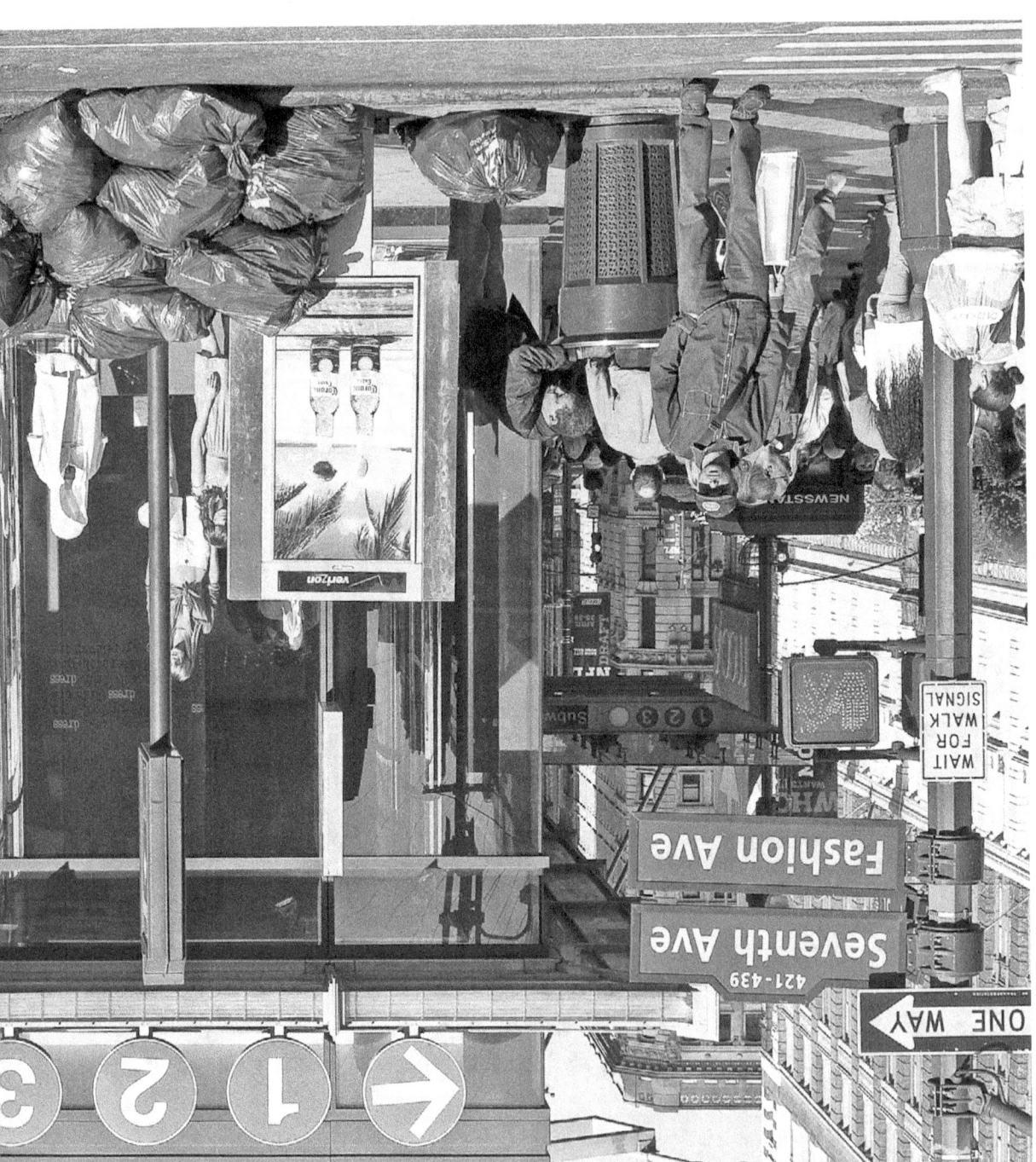

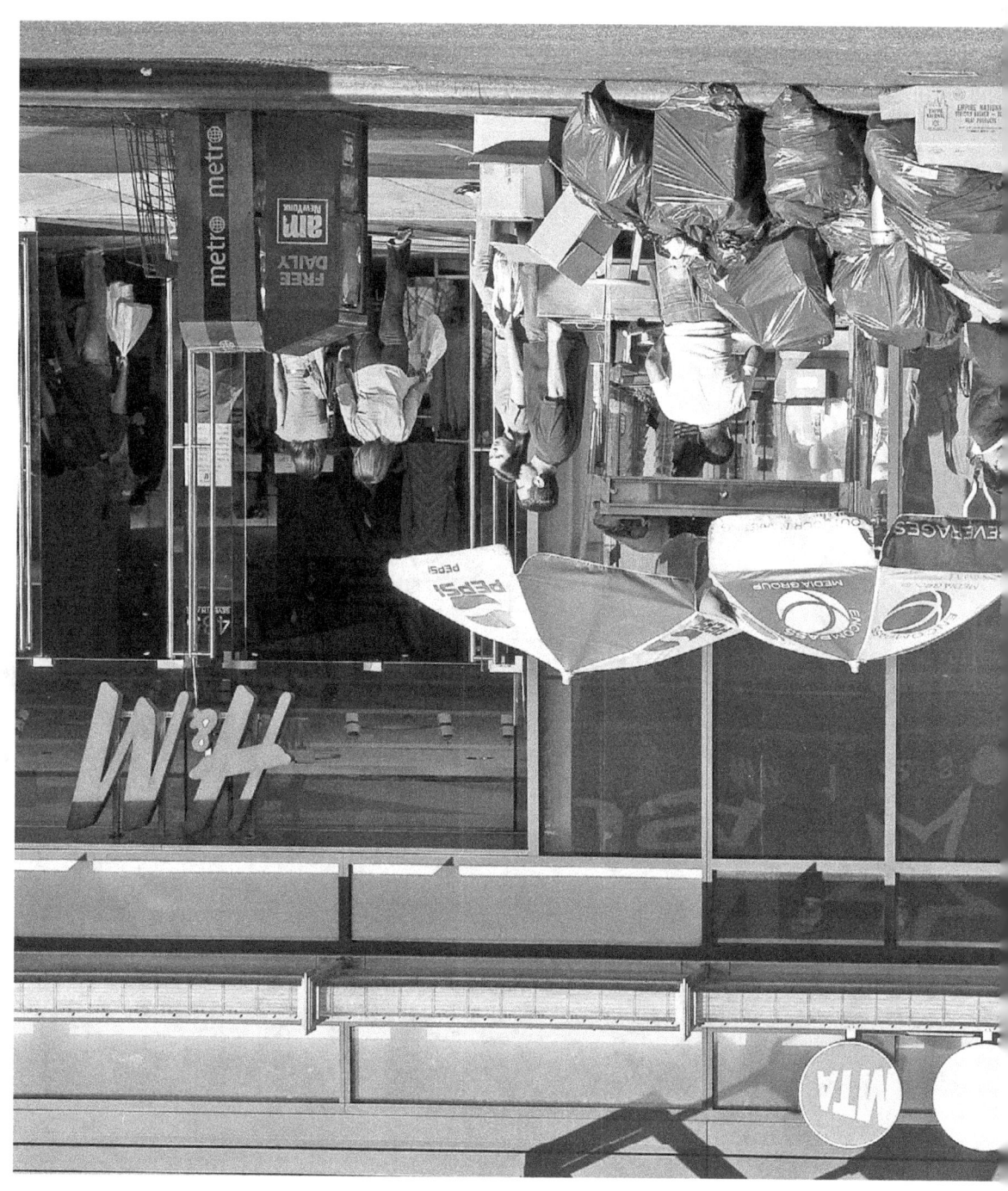

New York, 2007

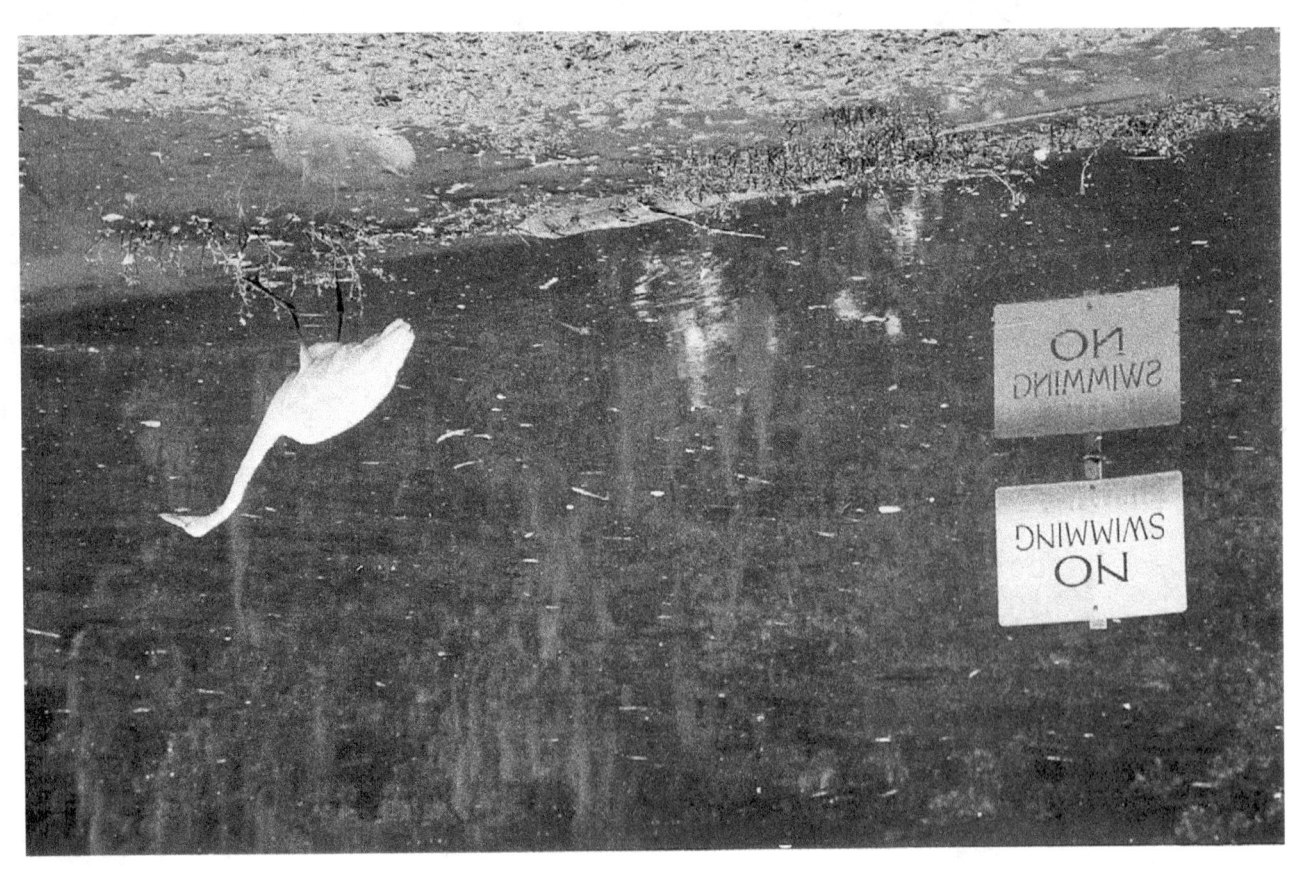

New Orleans, 1994

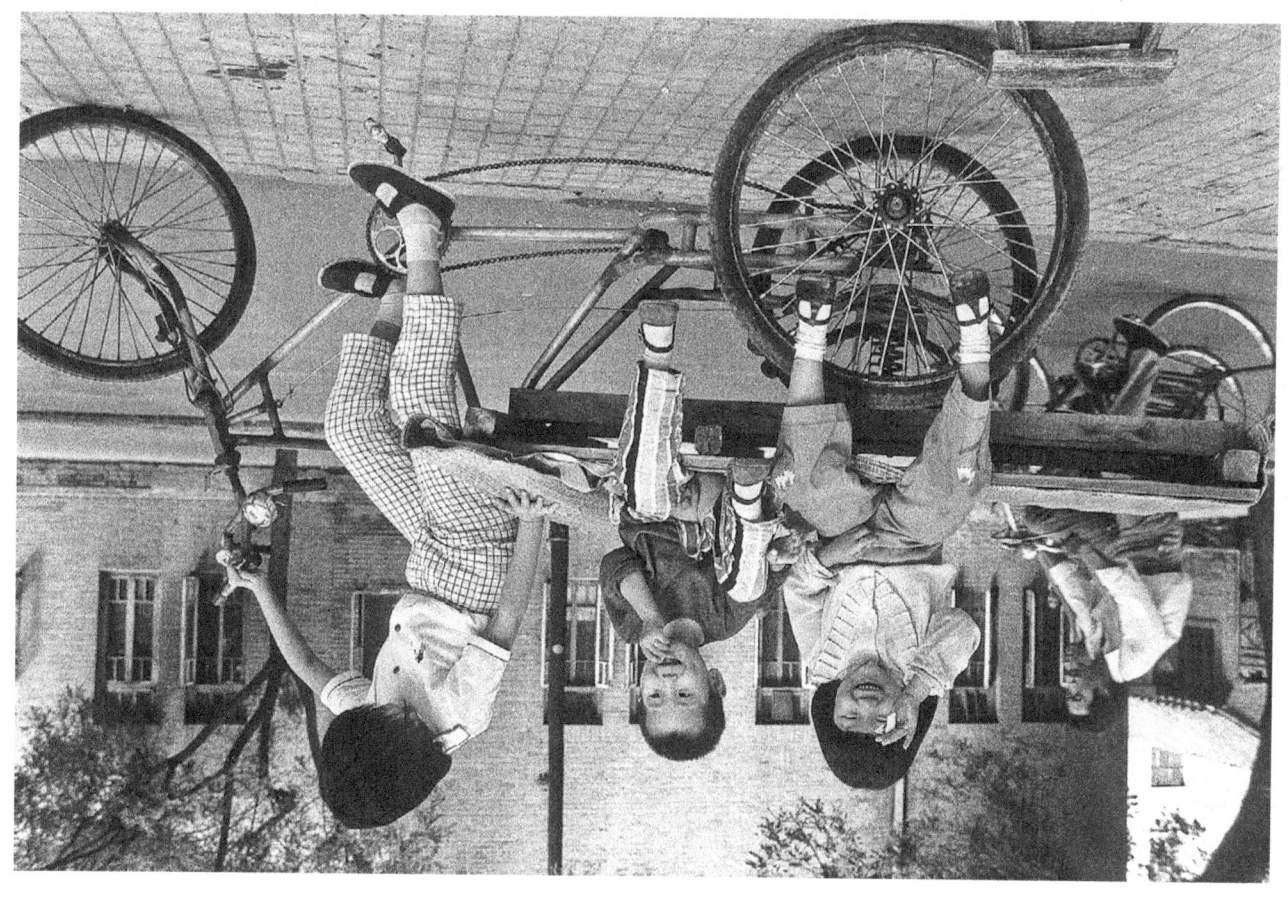

Beijing, 1986

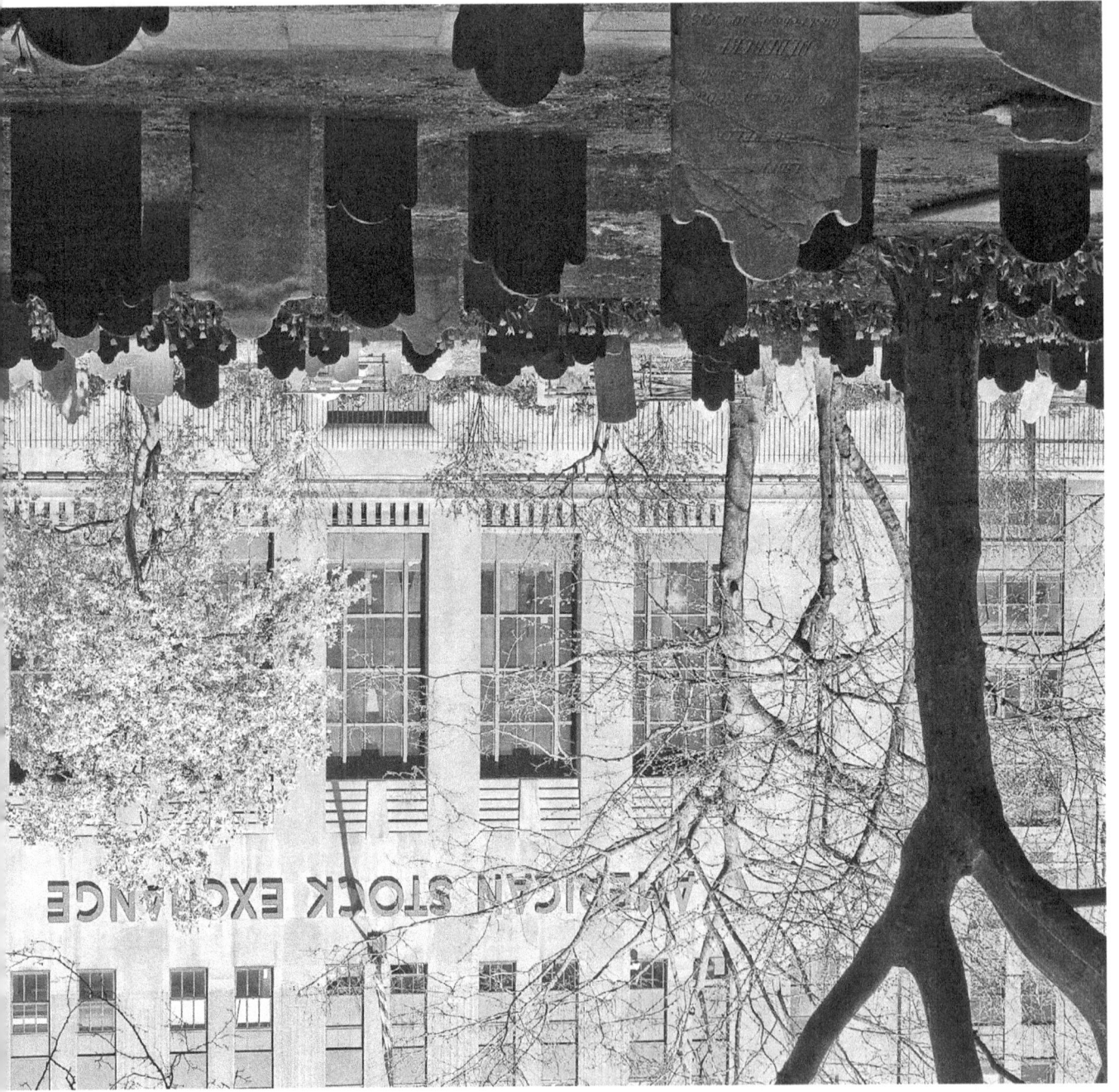

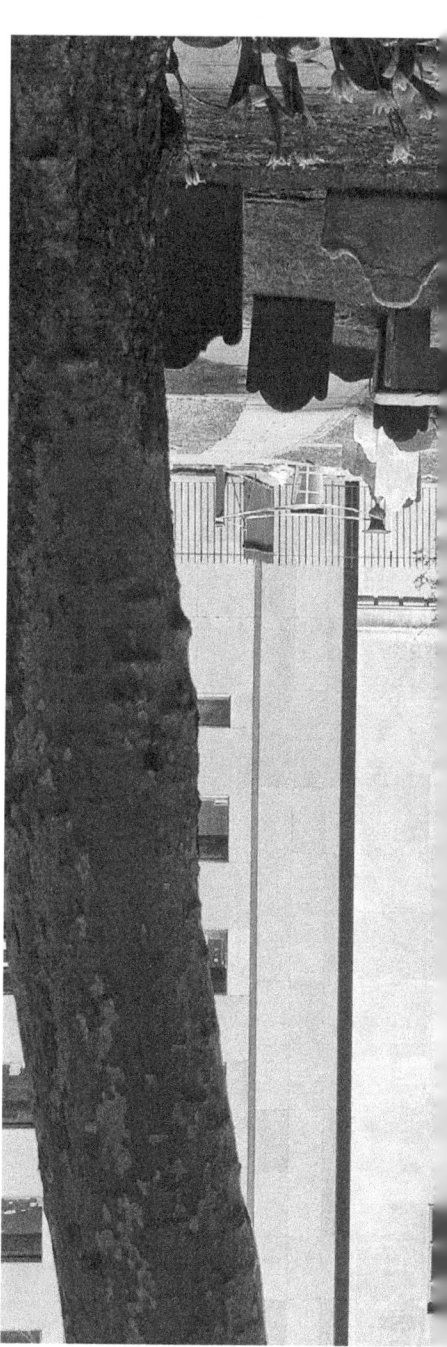

New York, 2007

www.ingramcontent.com/pod-product-compliance
Lightning Source LLC
Chambersburg PA
CBHW083342205026
4547OCB00008B/2505